The Way We All Became The BRADy Bunch

The Way We All Became The BRADY Bunch

HOW THE CANCELED SITCOM BECAME
THE BELOVED POP CULTURE ICON WE
ARE STILL TALKING ABOUT TODAY

KIMBERLY POTTS

GRAND CENTRAL
PUBLISHING

New York   Boston

Grand Central Publishing
Hachette Book Group
1290 Avenue of the Americas, New York, NY 10104
grandcentralpublishing.com
twitter.com/grandcentralpub

First Edition: December 2019

Grand Central Publishing is a division of Hachette Book Group, Inc. The Grand Central Publishing name and logo is a trademark of Hachette Book Group, Inc.

The publisher is not responsible for websites (or their content) that are not owned by the publisher.

The Hachette Speakers Bureau provides a wide range of authors for speaking events. To find out more, go to www.hachettespeakersbureau.com or call (866) 376-6591.

Library of Congress Control Number: 2019948230

ISBN: 978-1-5387-1661-8 (hardcover), 978-1-5387-1659-5 (ebook)

Printed in the United States of America

LSC-C

10 9 8 7 6 5 4 3 2 1

For John,
with all my love

CONTENTS

INTRODUCTION

The House of *Brady*

When Vince Gilligan decided to set the penultimate episode of *The X-Files* inside the *Brady Bunch* house, his show's cast, crew, writers, and producers were excited. Given the storyteller's attention to detail, his cohorts knew the setting needed to look exactly like the real thing. When the real thing wasn't available—the owner of the Los Angeles split-level that was used for the exterior of the Brady home in the 1969–74 ABC comedy didn't want the hassle of accommodating the production—Gilligan did the next-best thing. The future Emmy-winning creator of New Golden Age of Television classics *Breaking Bad* and *Better Call Saul* reworked the episode, titled "Sunshine Days," to focus on the equally iconic interior of the Brady family homestead, and tasked the *X-Files* production team with re-creating it meticulously.

That weird horse statue that sat on a credenza near the living room staircase? Check. The vase Peter broke when he ignored Carol Brady's rule to not play ball in the house? Check, even though the props department had to grab some clay and fashion a knockoff guided by photo stills they captured while watching videotapes of the episode when an exact replica could not be found. The staircase itself, the living room doorway that led into Mike Brady's home office, the attic bedroom where Greg hung his groovy beaded curtain after sister Marcia magnanimously let him claim the space and be the only Brady kid to enjoy the privacy of a solo bedroom? Check, check, and check. Gilligan and company had pulled off this spectacular rebuild of the TV home, and they'd done it with an assist directly from the *Brady* universe.

"Sunshine Days" wouldn't have been possible without getting the permission of *Brady Bunch* creator and copyright owner Sherwood Schwartz, who also created *Gilligan's Island.* The coincidence of a man named Gilligan now readying to pay homage to his other classic sitcom both surprised and tickled Schwartz.

"I think Sherwood wanted to get on the phone with me and see if I sounded like a complete yahoo or if I sounded like I was going to be making fun of his show," Gilligan remembered. "I got on the phone with him, and I told him how much I enjoyed [*The Brady Bunch*] growing up.

"The really interesting thing about the conversation was the minute I got on the phone with him, his first words to me were, 'Is that seriously your last name?' I said to him, 'Mr. Schwartz… actually, yes, my real name is Gilligan, and I think you owe me some residual money for using my family's name.' He said, 'Haha, no, I don't think so.' We had a very nice conversation. He had a good sense of humor, and it was really cool that I got to talk to him. I wish I had met him in person."

Schwartz not only gave his thumbs-up to the *Brady*-themed story, but he lent the *X-Files* team the blueprints his production had used to create the original interior set for the Brady home. He, his son (and *Brady* producer) Lloyd, and his daughter (and *Brady* guest star) Hope also visited the *X-Files* set and posed for photos on Brady living room staircase 2.0.

Gilligan soon found out the Schwartzes were not the only ones excited about the retro TV home's reconstruction. News of the new set had traveled throughout Los Angeles's television community, and Gilligan and series star Gillian Anderson were among the *X-Files* staff who received calls from executives at Warner Bros., Fox, and Sony, as well as friends and family, all calling in favors to wrangle invitations to visit the set.

"They showed up from all over town. They came out of the woodwork, because they wanted the photo," Gilligan said. "It's not that they were big *X-Files* fans...they wanted their photo taken on the staircase of the *Brady Bunch* set, and this was, of course, before smartphones with cameras built in. People were showing up with their film cameras and snapping pictures of their loved ones on the *Brady Bunch* staircase, and that was, for a couple of weeks there, a really big deal. That was a hot ticket in Los Angeles."

What was it about getting the chance to see that living room, that weird horse statue, that bright orange kitchen, live and in person, that had everyone from actors and camera operators to executives who make daily multimillion-dollar decisions about their own TV shows—and even the *Brady Bunch* creator himself— giddy about a series that was, at that point, more than thirty years old?

Why, now fifty years later, do thousands of *Brady* devotees still travel to 11222 Dilling Street in Los Angeles each year just to get a look at that Studio City split-level, which, because it provided the exterior shots for the Brady hacienda for all five seasons of the show, is now the second most-photographed house in America (after the White House)?

To deconstruct the appeal of the *Brady Bunch* home, and every other iconic symbol of Sherwood Schwartz's seminal family comedy, is to deconstruct the enduring status of *The Brady Bunch* as a cultural touchstone.

In July 2018, newspapers and websites around the world rushed to report a big event in *Brady*world. If you happened to have a spare $1.9 million lying around and wanted to own the house on Dilling Street, you might be in luck. Boy band alum Lance Bass from 'N Sync, Disney star turned pop diva Miley Cyrus, and *Property Brothers* star Jonathan Scott were among the most famous names bidding for the privilege of owning the two-bedroom, three-bathroom, shag-carpeted domicile. "I'm obviously obsessed with *The Brady Bunch*. I mean, I grew up watching that show. Reruns!" Bass said. "I want to buy this house."

In August 2018, a surprise bidder emerged as the new owner of the Brady home: HGTV. The cable network paid more than $3 million for the property, and immediately began construction to expand the house, revamp the interior to match the look of the television-show interior set, and document the whole process for a TV series.

What happened inside the house of *Brady* happened elsewhere—on Paramount Studios Stage 5, eight miles away—but those Dilling digs remain the real-estate representation of TV's all-time happiest blended brood, which itself is the familial representation of the exact kind of childhood many TV watchers wished—still wish—they'd had.

* * *

To *The Brady Bunch* uninitiated, all this fuss about a house, both the real thing and the soundstage creation (and the Vince Gilligan–ordered re-creation), might sound like just more clickbait headlines for fans of a TV series that's long past its glory days. But, as even some *Brady* fans will be surprised to learn, the family comedy's best years all came after ABC canceled it in 1974.

The Brady Bunch has been spun off as a Saturday morning cartoon, a variety show, and an earnest dramedy called *The Bradys*.

It's been developed as a stage musical, two big-screen movies, and a 1990s theatrical production in which episodes of the original series were reenacted verbatim by future stars like Jane Lynch and Andy Richter.

It has been reverently spoofed by *The Simpsons*, *Family Guy*, and *Sesame Street*. Its iconic theme song and tic-tac-toe-board opening sequence have been copied by *Game of Thrones* and *The Avengers*. "Weird Al" Yankovic has sung about it. A casino company adapted it as a themed slot machine, complete with video clips and theme song. The porn industry has turned it into a XXX adult film (with four sequels).

Brady parents Carol (Florence Henderson) and Mike (Robert Reed) top lists of TV's all-time greatest moms and dads every year. *The Brady Bunch* was named the all-time favorite television series of Generation X, according to an MTV survey. Since the show launched in syndication in 1975, it has aired somewhere in the world every year.

For decades after its premiere—five decades, in fact, as *The Brady Bunch* marked its fiftieth anniversary on September 26, 2019—the show has only grown in popularity and in influence on popular culture. But its beginnings, and its entire original run on ABC, were modest. Critics ignored (in the best cases) and disparaged (in the worst cases) the series, dismissing it as nothing but a fluffy, unrealistic portrayal of blended-family life. Only kids were watching the Bradys, critics said, and they deserved better. *The Brady Bunch*'s Friday night ratings seemed to support those theories. In five seasons, *The Brady Bunch* was never a top 10 hit. Nor a top 20 hit. Nor did it ever crack the top 30. The best the Bradys could manage was in season three, when it finished as the 31st most-watched show on TV.

Which raises the questions: How did the Bradys become more popular than ever after being canceled? Why have fans demanded their return again and again, on TV, at the movies, in books, on stage, at casinos...in whatever venue viewers of those XXX films are getting their naughty *Brady* on? What about this show and its simple premise—a premise *so* simple that it's been the subject of derision almost as often as it's been the subject of fan love—has sparked tributes on today's most popular TV programs and influenced works by today's most respected TV auteurs? *Why do we still love* The Brady Bunch *so much?*

As a journalist covering television and pop culture for more than twenty-five years, I view *The Brady Bunch* now with a fresh perspective. Even with the hundreds of current TV series available to watch—so many that new, fantastic shows often get lost in the shuffle—*The Brady Bunch* is a classic I come back to again and again.

Any show that can not only stake out a place in TV history, but maintain and expand it into a permanent presence as a pop culture icon, is worthy of respect. And it's worthy of examination, of a chronicle on how and why it endures, of answers to that question: *Why do we still love* The Brady Bunch *so much?*

The answers, as we'll explore in the pages ahead, are legion, but they all tie back to one fact: Simplicity can be powerful. If you didn't have a family like the Bradys, you wanted one. If you did have a family like the Bradys, you identified with the show. If you were a big brother, the forgotten youngest one, a middle child who always felt the need to do something outlandish to draw more attention, a little sister who loved to tattle on her siblings, or the older sister who seemed impossibly perfect to her junior brethren, there was a Brady kid and dozens of their comedies and dramas with which to relate.

Not to mention a mom and dad (and don't forget Alice!) whose every waking moment was devoted to nothing so much as the happiness of all six children.

The Way We
All Became
The BRADY Bunch

CHAPTER ONE

A Hunch About *The Bunch*

As he perused the *Los Angeles Times* during a routine weekday breakfast in 1966, a surprising statistic caught Sherwood Schwartz's eye: More than 29 percent of all marriages now included at least one child from a previous marriage.

Schwartz was in the middle of producing the third season of his high-concept CBS sitcom *Gilligan's Island,* but his next big series seemed to be leaping off the newspaper page at him. If this was suddenly such a prevalent family configuration, wouldn't TV viewers be drawn to a weekly depiction of one of these new, modern families?

He felt so confident in the concept and all the new storyline possibilities it opened up that he left his eggs and coffee behind and immediately started to draft a general outline of the show, along with a handful of episode ideas. Time was of the utmost essence, he felt. He needed to put down his marker on the idea before any of his fellow TV scribes got there first. So with just those few pages in his hands, Schwartz set off to the Writers Guild of America West offices on Sunset Boulevard, where his plan for a series about a blended family, titled *Yours and Mine*, was officially registered as a Sherwood Schwartz joint.

Now he was free to develop this new family comedy further. And then he was free to wait...and wait, and wait some more, through three years, with interest from all three major broadcast networks, for his future classic to finally make its small-screen debut.

* * *

Sherwood Charles Schwartz had stumbled into the television-making business by way of medical school. Born in Passaic, New Jersey, in 1916 and raised in Brooklyn, the middle son of Herman and Rose Schwartz graduated from the famous DeWitt Clinton High School in the Bronx (where his fellow alumni included Neil Simon, Paddy Chayefsky, James Baldwin, Stan Lee, and Garry Marshall) before entering New York University as a premed student. "I grew up loving a book called *Microbe Hunters*," Schwartz said. "That's really what influenced my life. It was about the great humanitarian doctors who were guys like Dr. [Frederick] Banting, who discovered [insulin]. He was the one who discovered [its] relationship to diabetes and the effect it has on your body. I wanted to become an endocrinologist."

But despite top grades at NYU, Schwartz was told he'd never get into a med school program because of an unofficial medical school quota system meant to limit how many Jewish students would be admitted. His NYU counselors even advised him to change his last name to "Black" and lie about his religion on his application. He refused to do either.

Schwartz had also been advised that additional credentials, like a graduate degree, might help him break past the anti-Semitic barrier of the quota and into med school. So he followed his older brother Al, a comedy writer for Bob Hope's radio show, to Los Angeles, and in 1938 earned a master's in biological sciences from the University of Southern California. While living with Al and waiting for news about his med school application, Sherwood asked his sibling if he might make a few bucks writing some jokes for Hope. "It never seemed that difficult to me to write jokes," he said. So he typed up four pages of monologue bits for the comedian and submitted them.

Sherwood's jokes landed, earning big laughs for Hope. And the comedian offered him a surprise in return: Instead of throwing some cash his way for the material Sherwood had already written, Hope had his agent, Jimmy Saphier, propose that the younger Schwartz sign a seven-year contract to become a writer for *The Pepsodent Show*, Hope's radio classic.

Sherwood was flattered. He hadn't considered a career as a writer. That was Al's thing. Al had completed a law degree and passed the bar exam solely because their parents had insisted. He then gifted his diploma to his mother and told her, "Here, now I can write."

Not that Sherwood's writing talents hadn't earned him praise before.

One of his NYU professors had returned a test essay to him with the message, "Get out of premed and become a writer" scrawled at the top in red...but what about medical school? He'd moved across the country and put forth the effort to earn a second degree, on just the chance that he'd get a shot at his dream of becoming a doctor.

So while he appreciated Hope's generous offer, he told Saphier, and certainly didn't want to offend him by turning down the job, he had to see this med school journey through.

When Saphier relayed the news to Hope, he countered. Schwartz would find out shortly whether or not he had landed a spot in a medical school program, right? Hope was about to leave Hollywood to spend his show's summer hiatus in England. Before he went, Hope signed that seven-year contract. If Sherwood was admitted to medical school, Hope would wish the future Dr. Schwartz good luck. But if he wasn't, all he had to do was countersign, and he would have a job as the newest writer for *The Pepsodent Show.*

With the contract in his pocket, Sherwood returned to New York City, where he'd scheduled a meeting with an assistant dean at the medical school of Flower Hospital. Knowing what a long shot his admittance was, the future legend of TV comedy had a dramatic gesture planned for the interview. He knew the dean would ask how badly he wanted to be a doctor. And when the question came, Sherwood pulled out his seven-year contract, signed by Hope, and explained what it was. The dean was impressed. Sherwood explained he was so committed to a career in medicine that he'd be willing to rip up that contract then and there.

The dean, impressed even further, decided he had to be honest with Schwartz. He confirmed what Sherwood had already been told about the quota for Jewish doctors, a quota the AMA would never acknowledge, Schwartz later said, and one that would no longer be enforced after World War II. But in 1938, the quota would work against him, he was told.

The Flower Hospital dean offered to allow the very academically qualified Schwartz to fill out his own evaluation form—which the dean would then sign—assuring him the quota would prevent him from getting into the med school no matter what he wrote. Sherwood refused. The dean wrote a glowing recommendation himself, which he showed to Schwartz. Upon Sherwood's return to Los Angeles, he received a telegram.

He didn't get into the Flower Hospital program. He was the number one alternate, and the telegram advised him to stand by for a second telegram, should anyone drop out.

* * *

That second telegram never arrived. It was a good thing the dean hadn't insisted Schwartz follow through with tearing Bob Hope's contract to shreds.

It broke his heart to leave his plans to be a doctor behind, and for the rest of his life he would think about the good works he might have done, the patients he could have helped, the diseases he might have cured. *Brady Bunch* star Ann B. Davis said she was once brought to tears by Schwartz's wistful tale about how much he had wanted to be a doctor. His daughter, Hope Juber, said he kept a black medical bag beside his desk throughout his life. He even made one of his most-loved TV characters, eldest *Brady Bunch* son Greg, a physician.

He saved a copy of the wait-and-see telegram for decades, Juber said, and finally demanded a decision as only a comedy writer would. "When Dad was in his late eighties, he sent a letter to that particular medical school [now renamed New York Medical College], saying, 'I'm a patient man, but I have to get on with my life.'"

Sherwood signed his name on Hope's contract and officially joined brother Al in what would become the Schwartz brothers' family business (youngest brother Elroy would soon follow his siblings to Los Angeles and work as a Hollywood writer).

Sherwood spent more than four years penning jokes for Hope on *The Pepsodent Show*, then was assigned to write for the Armed Forces Radio Service (serving his time at an Army desk in Hollywood) when he was drafted during World War II. He jumped right back into the comedy world after the war, declining the chance to return to his job at *The Pepsodent Show* so he could try his hand at situation comedy.

A stint as a writer for *The Adventures of Ozzie and Harriet*, the radio version of the future TV show, led Schwartz to a writing gig on *I Married Joan*. The 1952–55 *I Love Lucy*-ish NBC comedy starred Joan Davis as Joan Stevens, a Lucy Ricardo–like character with similar gifts for physical comedy and turning misunderstandings into screwball gems. The series was not only Schwartz's first foray into TV, but Joan's husband, Judge Bradley Stevens, was played by Jim Backus, an actor who would later play a key role in Sherwood creating his own series for the first time.

But before that, he shared an Emmy with his brother Al and two other writers in 1961 for their work on *The Red Skelton Show*. The volatile Skelton had been unhappy with the output of a previous head writer, Schwartz's former *I Married Joan* colleague Artie Stander, so he shot a loaded gun at the man's feet to encourage him to turn out more creative scripts. Sherwood had helped steer the program out of the bottom of the ratings heap to success as the series' head writer, a job he took only after CBS guaranteed he wouldn't lose any appendages.

"I have ten toes, and I want to keep them all," Sherwood told CBS executives, who desired Schwartz's services so badly that they promised he'd never have to meet with the star of the show. He would write the scripts, and they'd be delivered to Skelton. For seven years, star and head writer never had an in-person meeting.

Schwartz also spent a year as the script supervisor for *My Favorite Martian*, one of the many '60s series—like Screen Gems' *I Dream of Jeannie*, *Bewitched*, and *The Flying Nun*—that tried to freshen up the stagnating situation comedy with fantastical elements.

By this point, though, he'd had enough of writing other people's stories. He had important ideas he wanted to tackle, points he wanted to make with his writing. And, as he was about to illustrate, he certainly wasn't above using a grand, outside-the-box concept himself to share his philosophies with sitcom viewers. Like stranding seven people on a deserted island, as a social microcosm showing what can result when disparate people are forced to live together and find a way to coexist peacefully, and maybe even happily.

That was the lofty premise of Schwartz's pitch for *Gilligan's Island*, in which SS *Minnow* charter-boat captain Jonas "The Skipper" Grumby, his first mate Gilligan, wealthy marrieds Thurston and Lovey Howell, movie star Ginger Grant, Roy "Professor" Hinkley, and farm girl Mary Ann Summers are shipwrecked on a deserted island in the Pacific Ocean after their three-hour tour meets a tropical storm head-on.

But before he could get the idea in front of TV executives, he first had to convince his longtime agent, George Rosenberg, that this Robinsonade vehicle wouldn't get him laughed out of the pitch meeting.

"Are you outta your fuckin' mind?" Rosenberg asked Schwartz. "Who the hell is gonna tune in week after week to watch those same goddamn people on that same goddamn island?"

Sherwood was undeterred. When "Rosey," who was not only his agent but also a personal friend and godfather to Sherwood's son Ross, couldn't be sold on the pitch, Schwartz, with his friend's blessing, took the idea to another agent, Perry Leff. Leff, too, thought the series was pretty out there, but agreed to make a call. CBS, Schwartz's network employer for *The Red Skelton Show* and *My Favorite Martian*, was interested.

Knowing the skepticism he would face about how he could turn this idea into a new episode week in and week out, Sherwood started jotting down episode ideas. He took a long sheet of white butcher paper and tacked it to the walls of his office, wrapping it all the way around the room. In just a week, he'd filled the paper with dozens of plots, and he removed the sheet—all thirty-one feet of paper—rolled it up, and secured it with a rubber band. He was ready to hand it over to anyone who questioned if he could sustain this "social microcosm" for thirty-some episodes a year.

None of the CBS executives ever unspooled that tube of paper. CBS programming president Jim Aubrey had only one major concern about the *Gilligan* premise: Valuable time would have to be spent at the beginning of every episode to explain how the Skipper, Gilligan, Mr. and Mrs. Howell, the Professor, Ginger, and Mary Ann ended up marooned on the island. It would grow tiresome, Aubrey insisted, and viewers wouldn't tune in. He was so insistent this was a hurdle that couldn't be overcome that he spent one entire meeting between Schwartz and CBS honchos showing his obvious lack of confidence in the series by fashioning memo sheets into paper airplanes and launching them around the room while Schwartz pitched.

Schwartz remained resolute: *Gilligan's Island* was a solid idea, and he knew a snappy opening theme song could double as weekly exposition. The night before a pivotal meeting with the network, he spent a few hours hastily writing a tune about "the tale of a fateful trip"...a three-hour tour (a three-hour tour!) "aboard this tiny ship" that ended with a crash landing on an "uncharted desert isle" after some rough weather. Schwartz went to the next morning's meeting with lyric sheets he passed around the room. Aubrey didn't want to read the theme song, though; he wanted to hear it.

Sherwood obliged. Aubrey's only response was to suggest the middle part of the song needed a little work, which served as his confirmation that Schwartz had ensured *Gilligan's Island*'s place in the network's lineup, and eventually, in TV history.

Schwartz was just relieved Aubrey hadn't turned the theme song lyric sheets into paper airplanes.

* * *

Gilligan's Island was a ratings winner for CBS and Schwartz, finishing its first season as a top 20 hit. Season three, however, would end with a surprise cancellation, not because of poor ratings but as collateral damage from CBS president William Paley's insistence that *Gunsmoke* retain a spot on the network's schedule. To keep the long-running Western in play, Gilligan and the rest of the marooned travelers of the SS *Minnow* were tossed overboard from their primetime spot.

That left Schwartz free to focus on his idea for a new sitcom that would, just like *Gilligan's Island*, allow him to prove his theory that broad, sometimes silly comedy was the most palatable way to share bigger, more substantial ideas with viewers.

"I was unsatisfied until I developed my own shows and I created *Gilligan's Island*," Schwartz told L. Wayne Hicks at TVparty.com. "That was what I wanted to do. I wanted to say something important, but in very comic terms. And I think that show did it."

The Brady Bunch—a series he was, at the time, calling *Yours and Mine*—would say important things, too. But because he knew he would be judged by the last thing he did (the critically drubbed *Gilligan's Island*), Schwartz felt he needed to try a new approach to pitching *Yours and Mine*.

As with *Gilligan's Island*, the family-focused *Yours and Mine* would be a parable about the ways any group of people can learn to live well together, a personal philosophy of Schwartz's that he saw as key to a more peaceful world. But this time the group didn't have to cooperate to survive together on an uncharted island. In this case, the biologically unrelated group must somehow form a family.

To make certain network executives would understand that slapstick comedy would give way to more heartfelt moments on the new series (lest they assume, as star Robert Reed would later on, that *Brady* would be "*Gilligan's Island* with kids"), Schwartz decided to write an entire pilot script. It would set up the series premise— that a widow with three kids would marry a widower with three kids, and they'd merge their families together for better and (sometimes, to comic effect) for worse—introduce all the characters, and provide an important taste of the plots, pacing, and tone he was proposing.

The script immediately resonated with executives from all three TV networks. They understood Schwartz's vision that this scenario provided inherent but fresh ideas for telling family stories. "Everybody can relate to a family trying to get along, because they have to," he said, and he used examples from his own children's lives to convince network executives how fertile a storytelling patch the blended *Yours and Mine* family would be.

Schwartz's young daughter, Hope, had recently come home from school upset about a classmate's dilemma. A school pageant was being performed in a small space, which meant students were limited to just one ticket each. Hope's friend was torn: Should he invite his mother to the show? If he did, his new stepfather might feel left out. But if he invited his new family member in an effort to help bond the new household, he might hurt his mom's feelings.

It might seem like an incredibly insignificant worry to adults, but Schwartz knew his daughter's schoolmate's problem loomed large for the boy, and for his daughter, who felt bad for her friend. This was the kind of issue *Yours and Mine* would tackle (and *The Brady Bunch* did, in season one's "Eenie, Meenie, Mommy, Daddy"). The show would reverently present the concerns of the *Yours and Mine* children, no matter how small they might seem in the larger scheme of things. And not just because that is what children really experienced in their lives, but also because, Schwartz felt, it was these little things that build the connections and forge the emotional bonds that create the fabric of a family.

But while CBS, NBC, and ABC executives loved Sherwood's script, they all wanted tweaks.

CBS, the first place Schwartz pitched the idea, didn't want to do a "pilot pilot" episode. The *Yours and Mine* script told the story of how the couple with the individual families got married and moved into their new home as a new combined crew. CBS wanted Schwartz to instead save that story for the seventh or eighth episode of the first season. Paul King, the head of CBS's comedy development, wanted to jump right into the action with the new family already in progress, reasoning that viewers would happily figure out the backstory.

"I said, 'Why do you have to figure out what happens?'" Schwartz recalled. "'I think it's pretty good the way it is. We show them what happened.'"

CBS stuck to its no "pilot pilot" rule, however, and Schwartz stuck to his pilot pilot script. *Yours and Mine* would not make its debut on the same network that hosted its Schwartz sitcom sibling, *Gilligan's Island.*

Next up, NBC's comedy development executive, Peter Robinson. He also loved the script and had just one request for a change that would affect only the last few pages. Those pages were the final scenes of the pilot, though. Robinson was asking for an entirely new ending. In Schwartz's script, the newlyweds left their newly blended brood behind to go off on their honeymoon. But when attempts to enjoy themselves left them miserable, they realized why: They missed their children. So, still in their bathrobes, they drove home, packed up the kids (and housekeeper Alice), and returned with the whole family—Fluffy the cat and Tiger the dog also included—to enjoy their lodge vacation.

"Viewers will never buy it," Robinson said. No one would ever believe that newlyweds would take children on a honeymoon… especially not six children. And a housekeeper!

"I think people will love people who love their children that much," Sherwood responded. But he'd reached another impasse. Neither side would budge on the ending, so it was time to go to ABC.

Finally, in his Goldilocks-like quest for just the right network home for *Yours and Mine*, Schwartz met with development honchos at Paramount Television, which produced series for ABC. Happily, those executives—future Hollywood moguls Barry Diller and Michael Eisner—liked Schwartz's pilot script the way it was. They liked how it would introduce the series to viewers. They liked the ending. They liked the entire script so much, in fact, that their only demand was that Sherwood make it longer.

Diller had recently developed the two-hour, original-TV movie concept for ABC, and would go on to score major successes with *Duel*, the November 1971 thriller that was Steven Spielberg's first feature-length film, and, later that same month, *Brian's Song*, the Emmy and Peabody Award–winning sports classic about the friendship between Chicago Bears legend Gale Sayers and his cancer-stricken teammate, Brian Piccolo. Diller and Eisner thought the half-hour *Yours and Mine* script would be a fantastic fit with the new format. But they needed the script to be three times as long (leaving room for commercials, of course). If Sherwood would agree to it, he had a deal, and a *Yours and Mine* TV movie would launch a *Yours and Mine* TV sitcom on ABC.

No problem, Sherwood said. He would add a half hour to the front of the script, telling the story of how the couple met. For the second half hour of the movie, he'd explore the issues the couple face with getting their children on board with their relationship. Then the original script, featuring the wedding and honeymoon, would end the movie.

But Eisner and Diller didn't want him to add anything to the script. They wanted him to stretch the half-hour tale he'd written into a ninety-minute story.

"Stretching it into ninety minutes with no additional story will make it dull," Schwartz argued. "If it's dull, no one will watch. If no one watches, you won't get ratings. And if you don't get ratings, you're not going to want this show on your network."

Schwartz was hoping for a guaranteed home for his new show. But he'd been in the television business a long time, certainly long enough to understand there were ways around guarantees if a project landed with a thud. As far back as that signed contract from Bob Hope he carried with him to the meeting with the Flower Hospital dean... The dean was impressed Schwartz had been offered a seven-year commitment from the superstar comedian, but what he didn't know was that the contract also came with the option for Hope to pick up the contract for thirteen-week periods or cancel it altogether at the end of each thirteen-week run.

Eisner and Diller would simply exercise similar exit options if *Yours and Mine* flopped, as Schwartz was certain it would under the format and parameters they were suggesting. Again, the network loved his series idea. Eisner and Diller loved his script. And again, Sherwood was being asked to make a compromise that he felt would ruin the very thing he was trying to create.

So, with the "fuck-you money" of *Gilligan's Island* in his bank account, he said no to ABC's movie/series offer, and put *Yours and Mine* on hold.

Until April 1968. On April 24, United Artists released a family comedy movie called *Yours, Mine and Ours*. Based loosely on the real-life story of Frank and Helen Beardsley, the movie unfolds the marriage of naval officer and widower Frank (Henry Fonda) and nurse/widow Helen (Lucille Ball), who fall in love, marry, and merge their children—all eighteen of them!—into one chaotic household.

The movie was the eleventh top box-office earner of the year, and ABC, remembering Schwartz's similar series pitch—with a similar title—from a couple of years earlier, came calling. Network execs have always loved nothing as much as the idea of a "new" project based on already proven material.

It didn't escape Schwartz's appreciation for the often-ridiculous vagaries of his profession that ABC was now approaching him to do the exact series he had wanted to do two years earlier, the exact way he had wanted to do it. And the network's catalyst for reconsidering the project: the big-screen movie that had been successful in telling the story Schwartz had proposed—to follow a couple from a meet-cute to their complicated courtship and through to their wedding and household merger—the exact way he had proposed it be told when ABC asked him to lengthen his original pilot script.

The important thing was that he'd stood his ground in the face of interest and attempts to meddle with his vision from all three networks. Now *The Brady Bunch* (known under the working title *The Bradley Brood* at this point) had received a thirteen-episode order to premiere on ABC.

The comedy series had been renamed to avoid confusion with the *Yours, Mine and Ours* movie, but the original title, and Sherwood's wise instinct back in 1966 to register his idea with the Writers Guild, turned out to be serendipitous when rumblings of a lawsuit threatened to dampen the show's September 1969 debut.

Yours, Mine and Ours producer Robert Blumofe contacted Paramount Television, noting there were a lot of similarities between the plot of his movie and the just-debuted show now known as *The Brady Bunch*. When Schwartz heard about the lawsuit Blumofe was hinting at, he assured Paramount's legal department they shouldn't be worried. He'd registered his idea for the series long before Blumofe's movie was released. In fact, he'd registered his show under the title *Yours and Mine*...maybe *he* should be suing Blumofe! The movie producer may not have found Schwartz's irreverence to be so funny, but it did put an end to any further discussion of a lawsuit.

So Schwartz would continue to tell stories in the comedy genre, but these would be tales of a happy, affectionate family. He had experienced a very happy childhood, with a father who loved him and respected his intellect, and a mother who had suffered two miscarriages before his birth; he theorized that the relief of his healthy arrival was why she didn't hide the fact that he was her favorite child.

Sherwood and wife Mildred created their own happy family, with four children and a marriage that would last for seventy years before his death in 2011.

Happy families were what Sherwood Schwartz knew, and that's what he insisted *The Brady Bunch* would be about. Critics would go on to have a field day mocking the show's simple humor and emotional tugs at the heartstrings as mawkish manipulations. Even *Brady Bunch* star Robert Reed would engage in a series-long war against Schwartz's scripts. But Sherwood Schwartz was in the happy-family business, and *The Brady Bunch* was going to be another example of what he believed was one of the most important ideas in life: that any group of people, no matter how different, no matter how little they might seem to have in common, could learn to live together.

He wanted the show to be groundbreaking and modern, to reflect this new and significant sociological change with the prevalence of blended families, and it did. He couldn't have planned for the decades-long impact his slice of Americana would have on television and every other avenue of pop culture, but it did indeed achieve that, too.

CHAPTER TWO

The Way *They* Became
The Brady Bunch

The Brady family began to take shape during the summer of 1968 after Sherwood Schwartz saw a girl about a horth. That's not a typo.

Seven-year-old Susan Olsen was among the hundreds of children—454, to be exact—Schwartz personally interviewed to cast the younger members of his new blended-family comedy. Olsen didn't need to dazzle him with a reading or a test screening. Instead, she became Cindy, the first official Brady and the only Brady kid who was hired after just one meeting with the series creator, after she told him about the guest role she'd recently filmed for *Gunsmoke*. Or "Gunthmoke," as Olsen pronounced it (for fans who still wonder, the lisp was real, not a creation for the series). Schwartz recalled in his memoir *Brady, Brady, Brady* that Olsen "told me about how she got to ride a 'horth,' and that there was a 'thnake.' She was adorable, and she got to be 'Thindy' based on that brief meeting."

Though selecting Olsen's on-screen siblings would occupy the rest of his summer, with many more interviews, readings, and test screenings (1,200 kids made up the initial pool of Brady candidates), Schwartz's vision for the series made his casting mission clear. Like few series had done since *Leave It to Beaver* premiered back in 1957, *The Brady Bunch* was going to unfold its stories from the children's points of view. Each episode would spotlight one of the Brady kids and his or her relatable issues, creating, Schwartz hoped, a series that would appeal to a wide variety of young TV fans and make for appointment viewing for the whole family. Adding to the portrayal of the Brady crew as a realistic bunch viewers would welcome into their homes every week, Schwartz also wanted the young actors and actresses depicting the characters to come across as down-to-earth, charming kids; he wanted no entitled child stars, no demanding stage parents to complicate the production. Instead of writing specific outlines of the characters ahead of time, the actors' personalities would shape the characters they were playing. He wanted the Brady six to be portrayed by dynamic young people with pleasant temperaments, capable of maintaining focus, working well together, and behaving professionally on the set.

Susan Olsen, he was certain, was the perfect little girl to fill that role as Cindy, the youngest one (in curls), even though she was the one junior cast member who differed in some significant ways from her character. Olsen's vivacious nature—and, yes, her lisp—became Cindy Brady hallmarks, though Olsen wanted fans, and later her school classmates, to know that Cindy's habit of snooping and tattling was pure writers' fiction. She also, unlike Cindy, was not fond of frilly dresses. She was not afraid of spiders and snakes. As she told a reporter who visited the *Brady* set, "Cindy's too sweet! She looks like candy canes and gumdrops. I'm a lot rougher. And she's afraid of bugs and mice. I love 'em." Susan also preferred pants to dresses and lacy ankle socks. "I don't have to worry about getting them dirty or my knees skinned," she reasoned. Florence Henderson recalled her TV daughter as "such an independent little cuss," and the "toughest little kid you ever ran into."

The other Brady kid performers inspired their characters' signature traits, right down to specific episodes and scenes throughout the series. Barry Williams was the youngest of three boys in his family, and all the time he'd spent with his big brothers and their friends afforded him a certain maturity that impressed upon Schwartz that he'd be a terrific Greg, the oldest of the Brady sibs. He would also be the oldest of the young cast, and Schwartz knew that would be important on-screen and off, when Williams would serve as a leader and good example for his TV relatives. Christopher Knight said of his TV big bro, "He was definitely the big man on our campus." And Williams' youngest TV sibling, Olsen, said, "Barry, to me, was like way older, so he was almost in the realm of being an adult." Williams, whose acting ambitions were sparked, at least in part, by his admiration for his next-door neighbor, *Mission: Impossible* star Peter Graves, had already made guest appearances on series like *Dragnet 1967*, *It Takes a Thief*, *The F.B.I.*, *Gomer Pyle: USMC*, and *That Girl*. Fashioning his stage moniker from his middle name, Barry William Blenkhorn made the most of those early roles. His appearances on *Gomer Pyle* and *That Girl* were helmed by well-respected director John Rich, who went on to direct the first seven episodes of *The Brady Bunch*. Rich was a Williams proponent during the arduous audition process with Sherwood Schwartz. Williams also wrung extra mileage out of his time on the *It Takes a Thief* set with star Robert Wagner. When the young actor arrived at casting calls and faced a large group of competition, he liked to casually, but loudly, talk about how he "was talking to RJ the other day...and he gave me some really great character-building tips. I think I'll try them out today."

When the Pacific Palisades resident wasn't spending his after-school hours on the audition circuit or hanging out with TV stars like Wagner and Jim Nabors, he was a self-proclaimed sports nut who was especially fond of baseball and surfing. Coincidence that Greg Brady was ready to quit school to become a professional pitcher in "The Dropout," or that he showed some groovy moves on his surfboard during those season-four *Brady* episodes in Hawaii? It is not.

Like Williams, Eve Plumb was the youngest member of her family (consisting of four siblings), but in TV land (and TV Land), she became the icon of Middle Child Syndrome, Jan Brady. Six-year-old Eve began her acting career when a children's talent agent moved next door to her family in Burbank. The agent encouraged Eve's parents to send her out on auditions, and Eve nabbed the job of pitching Final Touch fabric softener in her first tryout. More commercials followed—including a 1968 Mattel spot for the new Talking Barbie, who uttered phrases like "I love being a fashion model!" and "What shall I wear to the prom?"—before she segued to series work and guest appearances on *Lassie, Mannix, Gunsmoke, It Takes a Thief,* and *The Big Valley.*

Most of Plumb's pre-*Brady* TV work had been in dramas, and both Sherwood Schwartz and *Brady Bunch* co-star Ann B. Davis later called her the finest performer of the young cast, especially when it came to handling Jan's angst-filled storylines. Her most notable pre-*Brady* sitcom appearance, a 1968 episode of CBS's *Family Affair* called "Christmas Came a Little Early," showcased Plumb's dramatic acting chops. In a true tearjerker of a story, she played Eve, a very sick, bedridden classmate of twins Buffy (Anissa Jones) and Jody (Johnny Whitaker). Buffy's vision of her Uncle Bill (Brian Keith) as a hero capable of fixing any problem led her to promise Eve he'd be able to find a way to make her well. Spoiler alert: The title of the episode—written by Sherwood Schwartz's brother Elroy—refers to the pre-Christmas party Uncle

Bill arranged so his kids could celebrate the holiday with Eve . . . because Eve wouldn't be able to celebrate with them later. The nature of Eve's illness went unspecified, as did confirmation of her fate (though the episode ends with Buffy sobbing in her bed). Plumb's charming, earnest performance made it easy to see why Sherwood Schwartz cast her to play Jan after just a couple of interviews—no screen test or reading required. *Brady* producer Lloyd Schwartz called Plumb the most like her character, recalling in his entry of the *Brady, Brady, Brady* book the "standoffish attitude" that sparked many of the show's storylines in which Jan saw herself as a misfit among her siblings.

Another part of Sherwood Schwartz's plan to make the Brady kids as appealing as possible was to match up the three girls and the three boys by age. Starting with Cindy and Bobby as the youngest boy and girl, continuing with Jan and Peter as the sister and brother a few years older, and with junior high students Marcia and Greg as the oldest sibs, Schwartz felt younger audiences would always have a Brady kid they identified with, even as they themselves grew up. Today's elementary school students who worried about missing Kitty Karry-All dolls and kazoos would grow into preteens fretting over their more accomplished sister and their lack of an engaging personality, only to hit their high school years and be faced with real heavy drama like being a responsible employee at your first job and deciding where to hide a goat after you've stolen a rival school's mascot (or maybe something a little more universally and timelessly relatable, like a sibling tussle over who gets to ditch roommates and move into a solo bedroom). This prescient decision by the series creator is as key to the enduring popularity of *The Brady Bunch* as the fine casting choices Schwartz made and the scripts' trademark happy endings. For the entire five-season original run of the series and the subsequent decades of syndication airings, the Brady kids' adventures covered a broad spectrum of topics that would keep kids tuning in, and draw new generations of kids to find the show, even when new episodes were no longer being produced.

With Cindy, Greg, and Jan cast, Schwartz still had to find the perfect young talents to portray their same-age, opposite-sex counterparts, Bobby, Marcia, and Peter.

Seven-year-old Mike Lookinland would prove to be the exception to another of Schwartz's rules for casting the Brady kids. Because the younger characters were hired before the performers who'd lead the Brady household, Schwartz decided to choose two teams of six kids each. One set would have three girls with brown hair and three boys with blond hair, and the other would have three girls with blond hair and three boys with brunette hair. Which ones ended up on-screen when the show hit ABC airwaves depended on the hair color of the actress and actor chosen to play Carol and Mike Brady, a fact that Barry Williams puts in proper perspective in his memoir *Growing Up Brady: I Was a Teenage Greg*: "Even after surviving the interviews, the callbacks, and the screen tests, my big break still hinged upon a fictional character's hair color." Fictional-character-hair-color fate wasn't as kind to a dark-haired actress named Debi Storm, for example, who was going to play Jan Brady if Carol had been played by an actress with brunette hair. Debi still spent some time with the Bradys, guest-starring as Molly Webber, the wallflower whose ego spins out of control after schoolmate Marcia gives her a makeover, in the season-three installment "My Fair Opponent."

Though it was the brunette-haired boys and blond-haired girls who made up the Brady six, Schwartz had been so impressed with the inquisitive, energetic, and sandy-haired Lookinland that he hired him to play youngest Brady boy Bobby. Lookinland, a Utah native whose parents moved their family to Los Angeles after an agent saw a photo of Mike on his father's desk and suggested he'd have a successful acting career, would be making his TV series debut with the role, provided he and his parents agreed to one condition: He'd have to dye his hair brown to match up with his TV dad and brothers. The Lookinlands agreed, though it was a decision Mike would have to deal with every day, as the hot lights of the set at Paramount's Stage 5 often caused him to sweat and the dark dye to trickle down his head.

All in all, the family was happy with their decisions. They'd given Mike the opportunity to experience a career as a young actor with their move to Los Angeles, and he quickly built a résumé that featured more than two dozen commercial appearances, including ads for Band-Aids, paper towels, and Cheerios. And despite no series experience, Mike's commercial work and natural enthusiasm had earned him not only the role of Bobby Brady but an offer to play the role of the titular son on *The Courtship of Eddie's Father*, the ABC sitcom starring Bill Bixby as a widowed father raising his six-year-old. The Lookinlands never doubted they'd made the right decision when they chose the blended family of the Bradys for Mike's first series, versus the single-father TV life of *Courtship*. That series ultimately ran for three seasons and made Eddie portrayer Brandon Cruz a star. But as part of the *Brady* ensemble, Mike had five other kids to hang out with at work, and a trio of adults who were impressed by and protective of their young television kin.

For middle brother Peter, Schwartz chose ten-year-old Christopher Knight, the only Brady kid who didn't actually want the job. When he'd come home from school and find his mother all dressed up, his heart would sink, knowing it meant he had an audition. Chris would rather have been outside playing baseball and football with his siblings and the other children in his neighborhood.

But Chris's father, Edward, was an actor, and had moved his

family—including Chris's two brothers and sister—from New York to Los Angeles in hopes of finding more work. The elder Knight made guest appearances on series like *The Rockford Files*, *Mission: Impossible*, *Hogan's Heroes*, *My Three Sons*, and *Bonanza*, but failed to find the steady work that would allow him to support his household. Chris recalls his father advising Mrs. Knight to feed the kids every other day to stretch their budget, but the solution to the family's money woes instead came from the commercials and TV guest work Chris began to rack up. Ads for Toyota, Tide, and Marx Toys led to small roles on *Mannix* and *Gunsmoke*, and when Schwartz met the friendly, fun-seeking sports fan and animal lover, he knew he'd found the boy who'd go on to make pork chops and applesauce a classic TV dinner.

Completing the lineup of young talent that would soon anchor ABC's Friday night schedule and fill the pages of teen magazines with color pinups was twelve-year-old Maureen McCormick. After winning the Baby Miss San Fernando Valley beauty pageant when she was seven, Maureen attracted the attention of an agent who helped her land a series of TV commercials for Mattel's Baby Pattaburp and Chatty Cathy dolls. Commercials for Pillsbury cookies, Kool-Aid, Barbie, and bubble bath followed, as did guest appearances on *I Dream of Jeannie*, *My Three Sons*, and *Bewitched* (where she played Samantha and Darrin's daughter in a Darrin fantasy sequence, and later, a magically transformed child version of Samantha's mom, Endora). She also co-starred in a La Jolla Playhouse production of *Wind It Up and It Breaks* with future *Mannix* star Mike Connors, the actor Marcia Brady referred to as a "far-out" guy in the *Brady Bunch* episode "Mail Order Hero."

And then came *The Brady Bunch*, which began for Maureen with a series of interviews with Sherwood Schwartz. In her 2008 memoir *Here's the Story*, McCormick described herself as a drama queen who noticed right away how "supercute" her three male kid co-stars were . . . so very Marcia-like. She was originally chosen to play Carol's middle daughter—Marcia Brady was almost Jan Brady!—but when Sherwood Schwartz decided to tinker with the ages of the kids to represent a narrower span of childhood, Maureen became the oldest girl, paired in a group with Eve Plumb and Susan Olsen. The three had met before during previous auditions for other projects, including Maureen's and Susan's tryouts for parts in the 1969 Elvis Presley movie *The Trouble with Girls*, which Susan landed. Their instant chemistry won over Schwartz and director John Rich, who spent the summer of '68 helping Schwartz cast the series. When Florence Henderson was hired as Carol and the crucial hair-color question had been answered, Maureen got the call that she and Eve and Susan were going to be TV sisters.

Finally, with two-thirds of the cast set, it was time to add some grown-ups to the mix, and that, surprisingly, would involve a lot more drama than rounding up half a dozen potential child stars.

Despite the fuss about the hair color of the Brady parents, the detail that largely determined the casting of the girls, all three candidates to play Mom Carol were blondes. First, there was Shirley Jones; Mama Partridge was almost Mama Brady! The Oscar-winning actress was looking for an opportunity to star in a television series, and she initially considered an offer to take up residence in the Brady house. "I turned it down because I didn't want to be the mother taking the roast out of the oven and not doing much else," she said, obviously unaware that it was almost always Alice who was responsible for the family's baked entrees.

Schwartz continued to interview potential leads, and though some actresses pursued by the Paramount casting department wanted no part of potentially being typecast by playing a mother of six on TV, others played hardball to try to win the part. He didn't name names, but in *Brady, Brady, Brady*, Schwartz revealed that one actress presented him with a portfolio of totally nude photos. Another suggested she would give a better reading if they could go to his house or meet at hers to go over the script. When he tried to shake the hand of another Carol wannabe, she stuck out her hand a few inches lower and shook something else. Spoiler alert: None of these performers was Florence Henderson, i.e., none of them got the job.

Schwartz and John Rich offered the part of Carol to Joyce Bulifant, a theater actress and frequent TV guest star who had appeared on *Gunsmoke*, *My Three Sons*, and *Perry Mason*. She was also one of the titular stars of the 1964–65 sitcom *Tom, Dick and Mary*, part of a short-lived NBC block of comedies called *90 Bristol Court* in which three separate series (including *Karen* and the Jack Klugman starrer *Harris Against the World*) were linked together by the main characters of each show, who lived in the same Southern California apartment building.

Bulifant had tested well with Robert Reed, the top candidate to play Mike Brady, and was so excited about her new gig that she threw herself into preparations without complaint, even when she was asked to lose five pounds in a week. Her round face might appear even rounder on TV screens, network suits thought, so she employed the services of massage therapist Louise Long. Long's Sherman Oaks studio was a hot spot for actresses about to begin a new project, as her aggressive body poundings would leave the stars bruised and several pounds lighter. The cellulite-banishing treatments that had been suffered by everyone from Marlene Dietrich and Lana Turner to Sally Field and Jane Fonda did the trick for Bulifant, though the all-eggs-and-tomatoes diet Long prescribed deserved some of the credit, too.

When Bulifant wasn't being massaged black and blue, not eating, and not sleeping because of her grumbling stomach, she spent the rest of the week helping the show's costume supervisor select outfits for the pilot episode. There was a pretty yellow dress she'd helped choose for the big backyard wedding of Carol Ann Tyler Martin to Michael Paul Brady, and a smart blue suit for Carol's postnuptial outfit. She was pleased, after the grueling effort she had put forth to do what her producers had asked of her in such a short time, to show off Carol's beautiful wardrobe. But when Schwartz and Rich visited her in the wardrobe department a couple of days before filming was to begin, they didn't look happy. She knew something was wrong.

"Joyce, sit down, honey," Schwartz said. "We have a problem."

Bulifant had fully committed to the show, but the show, or rather the network people behind it, hadn't fully committed to her. Network executives thought Bulifant was too young to play Carol; Broadway star and frequent TV guest star and hostess Florence Henderson was the perfect Carol, Bulifant was told, and Schwartz did not disagree. Bulifant, even after her week of eggs, tomatoes, and being pummeled at Louise Long's studio, accepted the decision gracefully, and was given one of the Carol Brady outfits she'd helped shop for as a parting gift.

As for the new Carol, Schwartz and company had tried to get Henderson to meet with them earlier in the process, but she was doing her nightclub act in Houston and didn't want to make the trip to Los Angeles. She also wasn't sure she wanted to star in a television series. She had four children, a marriage that was not on altogether solid ground, and a thriving music career that afforded her the flexibility to take on a new project like filming the movie *Song of Norway* (in Norway) or performing in Las Vegas. Her family's home base was New York City, and signing on for a TV series in Los Angeles not only meant a time obligation that would limit her career choices but also uprooting her family to the other side of the country for a significant portion of the year.

Still, her manager pushed her to at least meet with Schwartz and the network. A TV show was a major time commitment, yes, but TV stardom could significantly expand Henderson's fanbase and her career options. Being in people's homes every week, especially as the mom in a happy-family sitcom, would mean millions of new viewers who might never have seen Henderson on Broadway or in a nightclub but who would now be interested in her musical releases or buying any products she could be paid to promote in commercials (she would later, after all, prove to have Wessonality).

Henderson finally agreed to talk to Schwartz, as long as she could fly into LA, take the meeting, hop on another plane, and be back in Texas for the rehearsal of her show at the Shamrock Hotel the next day.

Arriving at the Paramount Studio lot, she chatted briefly with Schwartz, Rich, and Paramount executive Douglas Cramer, who would oversee the series for the studio. They clicked, and the *Brady* team asked her if she would be willing to do a quick screen test. After reminding them of the plane she needed to catch later that day, Henderson was sent off to a nearby studio lot makeup trailer to spruce up for the camera. She immediately met one of her future Paramount co-workers, as William Shatner began to complain—completely within her earshot—about her stepping into his *Star Trek* makeup trailer. A few minutes later, she was back in Schwartz's office, and after filming a screen test with a potential Mike Brady (not Robert Reed), she bid the group adieu and scooted off to that flight to Houston.

Within two days, Henderson got a call with the offer to star as Carol Brady, and Joyce Bulifant was out of a job. Bulifant soon began a recurring role as Marie, the wife of Gavin MacLeod's Murray on *The Mary Tyler Moore Show*, and would also become a regular panelist on game shows *Match Game* and *Password Plus*. After delivering the bad news about *The Brady Bunch*, Schwartz promised her they'd work together again, and he kept his word. Bulifant co-starred in the Schwartz-produced 1976 NBC comedy *Big John, Little John*, about a forty-year-old teacher (Herb Edelman) who morphs into a twelve-year-old boy (*The Brady Bunch* star Robbie Rist) after drinking from the Fountain of Youth. Bulifant was Mrs. Big John in a cast that also included child star and future reality-TV superproducer Mike Darnell (*American Idol*, *The Bachelor*, *The Voice*) and child star and future *The Young and the Restless* Daytime Emmy winner Kristoff St. John.

No one has questioned that Schwartz and ABC picked the perfect Carol, but the casting of Henderson did pose another dilemma in the effort to finalize the *Brady* bunch. Bulifant was considered a comic talent, whose Carol would carry most of the humor among the adult characters on the series. For live-in housekeeper Alice Nelson, who would be a more serious character, Schwartz had chosen Monty Margetts, a radio announcer and TV actress who was best known for hosting the first daily cooking show in the LA TV market and for being frank with her audience that she knew nothing about cooking. Her many TV guest appearances included *The Munsters*, *Hazel*, *Bewitched*, and *The Red Skelton Show*, during Schwartz's stint as that series' head writer. Margetts was a fine choice to play a sharp, no-nonsense version of Alice when Bulifant would be the more gregarious laugh getter. Florence Henderson, with decades of experience in Broadway and touring musicals and developing her own nightclub act, was no slouch in the humor department, either. But her Carol would be a more down-to-earth, realistic mother of six, and Schwartz thought that required an Alice actress who could help lighten the mood and Carol's busy household workload.

His first, and only, choice to play this Alice, a character whose importance to the success of *The Brady Bunch* is impossible to overstate: Ann B. Davis. Davis, like Schwartz, had started out with ambitions for a career in the medical profession, even majoring in premed at the University of Michigan (where *Brady Bunch* director John Rich was her classmate). Her twin sister, Harriet, was a drama major at the university, and after Ann saw her older brother, Evans, perform in a stage version of *Oklahoma!* she decided to make entertainment a true family business and pursue an acting career herself. She spent several years honing her skills in small theaters all across the country, and saved up enough cash from her modest earnings to move to Los Angeles. She was working in a Hollywood theater when she was spotted by a casting agent who'd already seen more than fifty actresses for the part of Charmaine Schultz, "Schultzy," in the NBC and CBS comedy *The Bob Cummings Show*. The next day, Davis was signed to play Schultzy, the secretary to Hollywood photographer and playboy Bob Collins (Robert Cummings). Schultzy had an unrequited love thing for her boss, and several of her many scene-stealing moments were spent trying to thwart his efforts to woo other women (Davis's portrayal of the character inspired the creation of Iron Man's secretary, Pepper Potts, who also had a crush on her boss, in the *Tales of Suspense* comic book in 1963). Davis earned four Emmy nominations, and two wins, for her performance, and among her many fans was Sherwood Schwartz. When he had the chance to hire the vivacious, happy-go-lucky actress for his own series, he made it clear to network and Paramount execs that she would be key to *Brady*'s success. They thought her Emmy cred would make her prohibitively expensive. He said he didn't care. They said she was already under contract to perform a nightclub act she'd developed in Seattle. He said, "Buy out the contract."

"I got this call on Friday, just before going on [stage]," Davis recalled. "They wanted me for the pilot, and they meant right away. So I flew down to Los Angeles Saturday for a [meeting], flew back to Seattle Sunday to get my car, and returned Monday to start shooting."

Six kids, one future iconic TV mom, and one beloved, blue-uniformed, ninth member of the family set; one quintessential TV dad still to be hired.

The legend about Gene Hackman almost becoming Mr. Brady is not true, or at least (actually, at most) is very exaggerated. Hackman was on Sherwood Schwartz's wish list for maybe Mikes, and he'd hoped to set up an interview with the actor to discuss the part. But once again, the suits had something to say about his idea, and the something they were saying was, no one knows who this guy is. It was 1968, and Hackman had made guest appearances on *I Spy*, *The F.B.I.*, and Robert Reed's legal drama *The Defenders*. He'd also earned his first Oscar nomination, a supporting-actor nod for *Bonnie and Clyde*. But his popularity among TV audiences, network execs said, was zilch, and they ultimately wouldn't sign off on Schwartz even scheduling an interview with Hackman. Things turned out okay for him, despite his lockout from the Brady universe. The year after *The Bunch* debuted, Hackman won his first Academy Award, for Best Actor in *The French Connection*.

As with the search to find the actress who would portray Carol, efforts to cast Mike were met with polite "no thanks" by some well-known actors who wanted neither the commitment a TV series required nor the risk that once they became known as a TV actor, movie work would elude them. But original *Star Trek* series star Jeffrey Hunter (he played Captain Christopher Pike in the first *Trek* pilot) was the pursuer for the job of playing Papa Brady. Hunter, who'd had some success on TV, and on the big screen with his performance as Jesus in 1961's *King of Kings*, interviewed multiple times with Schwartz, who told him he was simply too handsome (imagine *Comeback Special*–era Elvis Presley crossed with Golden Globe winner Matt Bomer) to be architect Mike. If Mike had been a shirt model, Hunter would be the man, Schwartz reasoned. But even after Hunter argued that he was aging, that the lines around his ice-blue eyes had given him character and a more mature look, the *Brady Bunch* creator couldn't picture the actor in the role. Hunter turned his attention back to movie roles, but in May 1969 he died after fracturing his skull in a fall at his home.

And then there was the actor who was just right for the role, no matter how much he hated that it was true. Robert Reed was a classically trained actor, a leading man in student productions as a drama major at Northwestern University, and a proud attendee of the Royal Academy of Dramatic Art in London. When he moved to New York City after his stint at RADA, he joined the Off-Broadway theater group the Shakespearewrights (playing the titular doomed hero in *Romeo and Juliet*), and then moved to Chicago to work with the company of the Studebaker Theater, where he co-starred with Geraldine Page and his future TV father, E. G. Marshall.

In *The Defenders*, Marshall and Reed co-starred as the Preston pair, father and son defense attorneys Lawrence and Kenneth, who handled the kinds of contentious topics that were not covered often, if ever, on TV at the time. The 1961–65 CBS drama saw the Prestons defend clients like a terminally ill comedian (Milton Berle) who wanted to be allowed to commit suicide, a teacher who lost his job after being accused of promoting atheism, an illegal immigrant facing deportation, and an allegedly corrupt politician who claimed he was the victim of anti-Hispanic prejudice. Fourteen Emmy wins, including three as best drama series, across four seasons were the show's reward for groundbreaking storylines. One controversial episode, season one's "The Benefactor," found the Prestons defending a doctor who was arrested for performing abortions. The series' three regular advertisers refused to sponsor the installment (written by Oscar winner Peter Stone), and viewers saw the episode only after Speidel, makers of the Twist-O-Flex watchband, stepped in to buy the open ad time. The incident was the inspiration for a season-two episode of *Mad Men*, also called "The Benefactor."

Reed guest-starred in other series, but *The Defenders* was his quality standard for what TV could, and should, be. While shooting the series in New York City, he also took over for Robert Redford in Neil Simon's *Barefoot in the Park*, making his Broadway stage debut as buttoned-up attorney Paul Bratter, who's trying to maneuver newlywed life in a tiny, luxury-free New York City apartment with his more free-spirited wife, Corie. Redford returned to the character in the 1967 movie adaptation of *Barefoot* (opposite Jane Fonda), which opened a month before the Broadway production closed; Redford also guest-starred as an ex-prisoner who took Lawrence Preston hostage because he blamed the attorney for his incarceration in a December 1964 episode of *The Defenders*. But when Paramount and ABC wanted to adapt *Barefoot in the Park* as a comedy series, executives thought of Reed, who had signed a development deal with Paramount after his breakout role on *The Defenders*.

Barefoot in the Park was one of two Neil Simon plays ABC turned into a sitcom for the 1970–71 TV season. *The Odd Couple*, the future classic about disparate roommates starring Jack Klugman (another guest star on *The Defenders*) and Tony Randall, would follow *Barefoot* in the network's Thursday night lineup that fall, and with *Bewitched* as the lead-in for both Simon shows, ABC had big hopes for the pairing. Reed found out after he'd moved to Los Angeles for the show that ABC's plans for the romantic comedy no longer included him. The network had decided to hire an all-black cast for *Barefoot*, with comedian Scoey Mitchell playing Paul, *Love, American Style* regular Tracy Reed playing Corie, jazz singer and actress Thelma Carpenter as Corie's mom, Mabel, and comedian Nipsey Russell (Carpenter's future co-star in *The Wiz*) as Honey Robinson, a friend of Paul's with a love interest in Mabel.

Meanwhile, ABC was still down a role for one of its most promising, and well-paid, contract players in Reed.

Paramount vice president Doug Cramer told Reed about a new

series in the works, *The Bradley Brood*, from a producer named Sherwood Schwartz. To say Reed was less than thrilled about the project, especially when he learned Schwartz was the creator of *Gilligan's Island*, is an understatement of the word "understatement." Reed fancied himself a man of the theater, a Shakespearean fellow, or at least, an actor who was more suited to drama, the kind of topical, sociologically impactful narratives he'd been proud to play out on *The Defenders*. At Cramer's request—and mindful that he was only going to get paid if he signed on for a show—Reed met with Schwartz anyway, and Schwartz told him what had inspired the new series, the statistic about blended families. He told Reed he wanted to explore the issues those families faced, in a "general comic context" that would "represent American life to American people."

Reed was interested enough to agree to read the pilot script. That's when trouble, a years-long feud, began.

Reed hated the script. He didn't think it was funny or smart. And it contained none of the sociological explorations he felt he'd been promised during Schwartz's pitch.

Schwartz, impressed with a screen test Reed had done but already having doubts about the serious actor with leading-man aspirations signing on for a TV sitcom in which he'd be a father of six, said Reed just didn't get the comedy because he had no sense of humor.

But Paramount and ABC wouldn't allow Schwartz to cast Gene Hackman, his first choice for Mike Brady. Reed had no other starring role offers from the network with whom he very much wanted to earn his lucrative contract payment.

And that's the way Robert Reed became the head of *The Brady Bunch* (the Bradley surname had been dashed by that time).

Unexcited as Reed was about his new starring role, he also didn't believe it was a commitment he'd be tied to for very long. After shooting the pilot in September 1968, Reed assumed that was as far as the Bradys would go.

"I thought to myself, 'No one will ever see it again. They can't take this...we didn't do anything worth doing,'" he said in an *E! True Hollywood Story* episode on *The Brady Bunch*. "I wouldn't have given it a nickel's chance."

Doug Cramer, the Paramount executive responsible for flying to New York to sell the show to his corporate cohorts, was equally skeptical about the series' chances for showing up on ABC's schedule.

"The general feeling was that we hadn't quite caught it," Cramer said, "that there was a flatness to it, and, while some of the cast was terrific, that it was never going to work, that it was a little dated, a little old-fashioned. It played a little fifties-ish, in terms of *Leave It to Beaver* time."

As would become one of the recurring themes throughout the history of *The Brady Bunch*, the show defied expectations. It didn't hurt that ABC was in third place in the ratings war (back when CBS and NBC were the only other contenders), and that the network was on the hunt for fresh half hours to boost their chances of climbing out of the basement.

After years of trying to sell his blended-family show to all three networks, a whole summer spent casting the oh-so-important younger members of the family, two major, last-minute star switcheroos, and a leading-man casting search that had ended with a choice that almost certainly was going to be fraught with drama for the lighthearted comedy production, all eight members of the Brady family—plus Alice!—were set.

CHAPTER THREE

Here's How to Tell the Story

Sherwood Schwartz now had nine faces to spotlight every week, and a series backstory he didn't want to tell more than once.

As he'd done with the adventures of the SS *Minnow* and its passengers for the *Gilligan's Island* theme song, Schwartz decided to unfold the story of how the Brady family became a family via the opening theme song. He wrote the famous lyrics himself, just as he'd done with the *Gilligan* theme, and then turned to songwriter Frank De Vol to help him morph his words into the TV earworm we all know as well as we know "Happy Birthday" and probably better than we know the lyrics to "The Star-Spangled Banner." Only 40 percent of US citizens know the national anthem. Even people who've never watched an episode of *The Brady Bunch* can sing about a "lovely lady who was bringing up three very lovely girls."

Save the *Gilligan* theme and some violin lessons his brother-in-law had given him when he was a kid, Schwartz had little musical experience. De Vol, however, grew up around music, as the son of

Herman Frank De Vol, the bandleader at the Grand Opera House in Canton, Ohio. He was already composing music at age twelve, and by sixteen was helping his dad arrange the musical accompaniments for the movies that were shown at the Opera House. Frank was particularly skilled at hitting just the right notes for the big-screen dramas, but comedy—both in the films and from the live performers who entertained at the theater—was what really interested him. His parents paid for music lessons and urged him to study law in college, but funny business was his first love. He made everyone happy, and himself infinitely employable, by combining his musical abilities with comedy as the writer of theme songs for TV sitcoms *My Three Sons* and *Family Affair*, in addition to *The Brady Bunch* (where he also appeared on-screen as a saxophone-playing father at the Westdale High Family Night Frolics in season four's "The Show Must Go On??").

At the movies, De Vol's scores for *Guess Who's Coming to Dinner* and *Pillow Talk* earned him two of his five Oscar nominations. He had number one hits as the arranger of Nat King Cole's "Nature Boy" in 1948 and a co-producer of the Supremes' theme song from the 1967 comedy film *The Happening*. His exhaustively impressive résumé also included scoring *What Ever Happened to Baby Jane?* and *The Dirty Dozen*, guest-starring in series like *The Jeffersons*, *I Dream of Jeannie*, and *Bonanza*, playing the head of the boys' camp in *The Parent Trap* (the Hayley Mills original), and stealing many a scene as the bandleader, humorless Happy Kyne, in the short-lived, Norman Lear–created, talk show–spoofing *Mary Hartman, Mary Hartman* spin-offs *Fernwood 2 Night* and *America 2 Night*.

De Vol was a music and comedy all-star, but his catchy contribution to *The Brady Bunch*'s branch of pop culture was a happy happenstance. George Wyle, co-writer on "The Ballad of Gilligan's Island," was contractually obligated to *The Andy Williams Show* when Schwartz asked him to collaborate on the

Brady theme. Schwartz's second call was to De Vol, and the rest is, truly, television history. The composer crafted the sound for that twenty-one-line theme song in just one day, and, Oscar nods aside, it was his signature work. Later in his career, De Vol often entertained on cruise ships, where he'd share stories about his seven decades in Hollywood. "When I mention *Brady Bunch*," he said, "that's when the audience really applauds."

For the first season of *The Brady Bunch*, the theme was performed by the Peppermint Trolley Company. A California pop band that featured brothers Danny and Jimmy Faragher, the group had a hit single, "Baby You Come Rollin' Across My Mind," that peaked at number 59 on the *Billboard* Hot 100 in the summer of 1968, the same year PTC appeared on an episode of *Mannix* and sang its follow-up release, "Trust."

Though their music was getting positive reviews, the Faraghers and their bandmates still weren't breaking through the way they wanted to. Even with a hit record, Danny Faragher said he and his friends were on such a tight budget that they'd share a single cup of coffee at famous 24/7 Los Angeles diner Norms and live on nothing but a giant box of cheap pancake mix for a month at a time.

So at the beginning of 1969, when their producer at Acta Records, Dan Dalton, called them to his office above a Chinese restaurant on Sunset Boulevard with an offer to record the theme song for an upcoming television series, they happily accepted the chance to make some cash.

PTC guitarist Greg Tornquist recalled that the band received the *Brady* theme lyrics but added chords to the music and arranged the tune themselves. After recording it, for lucrative union wages, they didn't have high hopes for the TV series they had sung about to become a hit. "I remember thinking, 'This is the dumbest idea in the world for a TV show. Nobody will buy this!'" Tornquist said. "Little did I know; *The Brady Bunch* is still in syndication!"

The Bunch, in fact, outlived PTC, by a lot. Shortly after recording the *Brady* theme, the group members had a falling-out with Dalton and left Acta. Dalton hired a trio of studio singers—John Beland, Lois Fletcher (Dalton's wife), and Paul Parrish—to perform the *Brady* theme vocals over the music PTC had recorded. PTC's original version was used for the pilot presentation; the redo with the session singers opened the rest of *The Brady Bunch*'s first-season episodes.

It wasn't until season two that the *Brady* kids took over as singers of the series theme song, and they'd record a new version each season thereafter (YouTube clips offer the chance to compare them all). Each rerecording was proof that, like the Silver Platters sang, when it's time to change, you've got to rearrange (sha na na na na). In this case, that meant new recordings that reflected the young cast's evolving voices.

* * *

Schwartz's next big project was pairing the finished theme song with an opening sequence that would, harkening again back to *Gilligan's Island*, make *The Brady Bunch* a must-visit primetime destination for viewers from the first seconds to the closing tag scene that punctuated nearly every happy ending.

One of Schwartz's philosophies of TV production was that "close-ups are what television is all about." Trying to regularly get close-ups of nine different characters into the episodes would be challenging enough, but trying to get them all into a sixty-second opening would have flummoxed a less creative producer. While sitting in his office doodling ideas one afternoon, Schwartz drew a checkerboard, and immediately recognized it as his solution. Nine squares, nine openings, nine smiling Brady family faces (including Alice!) to fill them. Simple enough.

Except that nothing else about getting *The Brady Bunch* to the airwaves had been that easy, and this opening sequence, too, would provide a few extra challenges. For one, yes, there were nine smiling faces, but the order in which they appeared in those nine boxes was very important. The six kids were mostly newcomers, but the three adult stars of the show were veterans, with agents to whom details like the exact wording of the introduction for each weekly episode mattered greatly. It was in Ann B. Davis's contract, for example, that she would get a unique intro, so she appears last in the opening sequence, in the middle square, with the words "And Ann B. Davis as Alice" providing a shout-out to her status as an Emmy-winning comedy veteran.

For the Brady parents, Florence Henderson's face is the first one that pops up in the checkerboard (or tic-tac-toe board, grid, *Brady* box, and many other terms people have used to describe that three-by-three square that we all agree reminds us immediately of *The Brady Bunch*). The girls appear to her left on the screen, followed by Robert Reed and the Brady boys, to his right on-screen. But when it comes to textual billing of the stars' names, Reed's name appears first, then Henderson's. Davis's special credit is the last name in the sequence; the kiddos' names aren't displayed at all, and those precise details are all a result of contractual obligations.

With those general decisions made about the overall layout of the grid, Schwartz knew he wanted something more than a static image to greet viewers at their TV sets when "Here's the story..." started to play. Visual effects artist Howard Anderson would sprinkle something extra on the tic-tac-toe idea to make it the oft-copied icon of graphic design and ensemble roundup videos the *Brady* opening became.

It wasn't Anderson's first time at the TV title sequence rodeo.

His father, Howard Sr., was a Hollywood special effects whiz who created the storm effects for Cecil B. DeMille's *The King of Kings*, the 1927 middle movie of the filmmaker's trilogy of biblical stories. As a preteen, Anderson Jr. worked at the special effects company his dad launched, and after stints at UCLA, as a camera operator, and in the Navy, he joined the family business in 1946 with his brother and helped run it for nearly five decades.

Among the younger Anderson's most famous projects: the title sequences for *I Love Lucy* and *The Addams Family*, and later, *Cheers*, *Charlie's Angels*, *Happy Days*, and *Little House on the Prairie*. Lucy's satin heart, the snapping fingers in the *Addams* opener, and the spinning record and neon title of *Happy Days* were all handiwork of Anderson and his company.

As well as *Star Trek*. Anderson and his brother Darrell created the opening credits for Gene Roddenberry's hit (one of the only TV series to enjoy an enduring pop culture presence that rivals *The Brady Bunch*), and just as importantly, they were responsible for the transporter effects. Scotty's ability to beam Captain Kirk and anyone else onto the starship *Enterprise* was made possible by the fine work of the Anderson brothers.

It was Howard Anderson's idea to film individual videos of each of the nine *Brady Bunch* cast members looking up, down, to the left, to the right, to the upper left and right corners, to the lower left and right corners, and straight ahead. Howard personally shot the videos, directing the actors to hit all the directional looks and hold each one for five seconds, as he had meticulously planned the timing of the looks to match up with specific lyrics in the theme song. The looks on their faces in those moments? Actor's choice (Anderson confessed he was partial to Florence Henderson's facial expressions in the opening credits). Speaking of confessions, the Andersons did additional effects work for *The Bunch* throughout the series, including Peter being haunted by the ball that breaks his mom's favorite vase in the dream sequence of season two's "Confessions, Confessions."

For the opening credits, the key to making Schwartz's idea and Anderson's vision a reality was the multi-dynamic image technique, a creation by Canadian filmmaker Christopher Chapman. All nine videos could be merged into one, with each separate section showing one of the Bradys looking all around the grid to his or her siblings and parents in their own individual squares.

Chapman invented the process for his film *A Place to Stand*, produced for the World's Fair event Expo 67, a celebration of Canada's centennial year, in Montreal. The movie was a dialogueless, eighteen-minute ode to life in Ontario, and before it won the Oscar for best live action short, more than two million people, some waiting in line for hours, saw it in the Ontario Pavilion at Expo 67. Chapman, hired by the Canadian government to make the film, spent a year shooting footage of Ontarians at work and play. He shot the province's most beautiful locations, from city to farms, sunny waterfronts to snowy ponds where a father, his son, and a dog were ice-fishing with a tree branch. He zoomed in on a little boy and a sports fan noshing on hot dogs, alongside video of frankfurter buns baking inside a factory. Using his original technique, he was able to show as many as fifteen images at a time on-screen, and fill those eighteen minutes of documentary running time with nearly ninety minutes of footage.

An estimated 100 million people across the world saw Chapman's film when it was released into theaters, but that's just a fraction of those who've seen the split-screen innovation in action since. Steve McQueen was such a fan of the work after seeing it in a private screening that he recommended Norman Jewison, his director on *The Thomas Crown Affair*, see *A Place to Stand*. Jewison did, and decided to use the multi-image process in that 1968 Oscar-winning film's memorable opening sequence. But most viewers will recognize the technique from television, where it's been used in the credit sequences for *Mannix*, *Barnaby Jones*, *Dallas*, *The Bob Newhart Show*, and *24*.

And, of course, *The Brady Bunch*. In the *Hollywood Reporter* headline on Christopher Chapman's 2015 obituary, he was credited as the "Oscar-Winning Creator of 'The Brady Bunch' Effect."

* * *

Casting: check. Theme song: check. Opening credits sequence: check. All three elements of *The Brady Bunch* were ready to launch, and after a lot of hiccups here and there, Sherwood Schwartz was certain he'd made creative, clever choices for each. So were Paramount and ABC. Well, except for that series title…

Warner Bros. had a hit Western film in the summer of 1969, a few months before *The Brady Bunch* was set to premiere. *The Wild Bunch*, directed by Sam Peckinpah and starring William Holden, was a tale about a group, or bunch, of aging outlaws. One of the top 20 movie releases of the year, *The Wild Bunch* was also widely criticized for its violence, and Paramount worried: Would viewers associate *The Brady Bunch* with *The Wild Bunch*? If so, would they think this new family sitcom was actually a violent, not-suitable-for-family-viewing drama? Would *The Brady Brood* be a better name?

Schwartz toyed with alternative titles, hoping to land on one that would continue to honor his appreciation for alliteration. "Bunch," "brood," they both did that. Though only one of them rhymed with "hunch."

Finally, as Ann B. Davis recalled in her pseudo memoir/recipe book *Alice's Brady Bunch Cookbook*, the series creator took a poll on the set. Did the people playing the Bradys prefer to be known as *The Bunch* or *The Brood*?

"I certainly thought 'bunch' was a funnier word," Davis wrote. "I guess others agreed with me."

And that's the way they all *didn't* become *The Brady* (or *Bradley*) *Brood*.

CHAPTER FOUR

Here's the Story

Hi, honey...they're home!

But before Carol, Mike, Marcia, Greg, Jan, Peter, Cindy, Bobby, Alice (and Tiger the dog) could take up residence in their blended-family home at 4222 Clinton Way, Mike Brady and Carol Martin would have to get hitched.

The Brady Bunch began its five-season run in ABC's Friday night lineup on September 26, 1969, in an episode titled "The Honeymoon." Carol and a very nervous Mike (who wouldn't be terrified about responsibility for the care and feeding of an instantaneous family of eight—and Alice?) had met and matched up off camera before the series began.

In "The Honeymoon," an elegant backyard wedding at the home of Carol's parents made "television's first conglomerate family," as Sherwood Schwartz called the Bradys, official. The tone of what viewers could expect from the comic stylings of the family was established, as the Brady boys' dog, Tiger, tore around the yard after the Martin girls' cat, Fluffy, in a wild chase that covered many a wedding guest's lap and ended with Mike wearing a mask of wedding cake. The kids got an earful about their pets crashing the ceremony, which left them feeling guilty about the cake brouhaha, and Carol and Mike feeling guilty about yelling at the children and then going off for some decidedly adult fun time.

So they left their honeymoon suite—still in their pajamas—and drove home, packed up the kids, and returned to the resort, with all six kids and their luggage, Cindy's doll, Fluffy, and Tiger in tow. Oh, and Alice, because as she wisely pointed out, someone was going to have to mind the kiddos while Mike and Carol were, ahem, busy. That all that was going to take place in one very crowded suite wasn't something to be questioned; this was the exact kind of *Brady* happy ending, easily and quickly arrived at, that would become the series' trademark.

TV critics took issue with such shenanigans right away.

"They return to the hotel and Robert Reed marches the whole family upstairs to some sort of Army cadence. One wishes that they would keep right on marching," Bill Martin wrote in the *Los Angeles Herald Examiner*.

"*The Brady Bunch* is produced by Sherwood Schwartz, who brought you *Gilligan's Island*, which helps explain why...the dog and cat make a shambles of the wedding, and the bridegroom ends up with cake all over his face," concluded *TV Guide* in its annual Fall Preview issue.

The magazine did not intend that to be a complimentary judgment of the new series. The majority of other reviewers agreed after their first taste of life with the Bradys.

"Where has creativity and imagination gone in television?" asked syndicated Hollywood columnist Dick Kleiner. "*The Brady Bunch* has all the elements of trite-and-true television—a bunch of children (cute) and two parents (appealing) and a dog (lovable) and a maid (witty). It all sounds as new and different as this year's model of soap."

"It would be easy to dismiss ABC's new offering, *The Brady Bunch*, as a 'typical situation comedy.' But that would be inaccurate. The show isn't good enough to be typical and isn't funny enough to be a comedy," Martin continued in the *Herald Examiner*.

Viewers weren't especially drawn to the premiere, either. The show's Nielsen ratings competition in that 8:00 p.m. time slot was NBC's *The High Chaparral*, a Western from the creator of *Bonanza*, and *The Good Guys*, a CBS comedy that starred Schwartz's old *Gilligan's Island* pals Bob Denver and Alan Hale Jr. Both shows, *Chaparral* in its third season and *Good Guys* in its second, beat *The Brady Bunch*'s series premiere. By week two of the season, *The Bunch* bounced back to best *The Good Guys*, but by the fourth episode of ABC's new comedy, the Bradys were surfing the bottom third of the Nielsen ratings.

Early episodes focused on the new family unit's efforts to bond, but some critics charged that Schwartz's examinations of the specific problems faced by blended families were painfully unrealistic.

Cleveland Amory, chief critic for *TV Guide* (which, at its peak in the 1970s, was an influential magazine that reached nearly twenty million households), wrote in a February 1970 review of the series, "There's nothing really wrong with *The Brady Bunch*. But nothing is really right, either. Everything is so contrived that you don't believe what goes on any more than you believe sketches in a variety show. If the show has a point—except to be a show, which doesn't seem enough—it escapes us. There are millions of stepchildren nowadays and surely their problems, and those of their parents, deserve, even in a comedy series, something more than this mish-mush."

Amory and company, though, failed to see that these storylines they, as adult viewers, as professional critics, deemed overly simplistic and uncomplicated were exactly what younger viewers responded to.

In "Dear Libby," the second episode of the series to air, the whole family read a letter in a newspaper advice column and thought it was written by Carol or Mike. "Harried and Hopeless" was desperate for Libby's input on his or her new marriage and stepfamily, which included the joining of three kids with three new kids. "Harried" was only pretending to love the stepchildren, and worried that would ultimately doom the new household. Marcia and Greg read the Libby letter and assumed one of their parents had written it, setting off a plan by them and their siblings to be the perfect Stepford stepchildren to keep their mom and dad together. Even Carol and Mike (and Alice!) wondered if the missive originated from inside their home, but an honest discussion between the newlyweds and a visit to the Brady house from Libby herself assured everyone that things were, so far, going swimmingly. In their own resolve-everything-in-a-half-hour way, the Bradys gave us our first lesson in how we shouldn't make assumptions, and how we should always talk to each other about our problems.

In "Eenie, Meenie, Mommy, Daddy," Cindy was crushed to find out a limit on tickets meant she could only invite one of her parents to see her in the school play. Does she disappoint her mom, or does she make her new dad feel like he's not important to her? The happy ending to the fourth episode came courtesy of Cindy's teachers; they got her co-stars in *The Frog Prince* to agree to put on a private dress rehearsal of the play for an audience of eight: Carol, Mike, and the other five Brady kids (and Alice!). As Mrs. Engstrom said, "I guess children don't understand sometimes it's possible to bend the rules a bit."

The most overt nod to the Bradys as a stepfamily came in episode ten, "Every Boy Does It Once." Bobby watched *Cinderella* on TV, and after Carol asked him to clean the fireplace and his brothers and sisters left the house without saying goodbye to him, he decided Carol was a wicked stepmother and no one in the house cared about him. It was a plot that was admittedly dizzying in the kid logic it took to get from Cinderella to Bobby's decision to run away from home, but the crisis was averted when Carol proved her love for the youngest Brady boy by packing a suitcase and offering to run away with him. And lest he ruminate on the whole stepmother thing, Carol assured him, the only "steps" in the Brady abode were the ones leading upstairs to his room.

Cleveland Amory failed to see the charm in the writers' stab at bursting the fairy-tale bubble of stepmothers as necessarily evil and stepchildren as the less-loved members of the family. Bobby "decides to run away," he wrote. "Our theory is that he didn't really want to run away from home—just from the show."

By this time, plenty of critics weighed in with anti-*Brady* quips of their own. "So dull and superficial," Donald Kirkley wrote in the *Baltimore Sun*. "Florence Henderson as the mother and Robert Reed as the paterfamilias are pleasant people, but they have been thwarted by poor scripts and commonplace direction. The six children remain unidentifiable after all these weeks, which should have been obvious when ABC-TV first considered the series. They simply clutter up the set, uttering childish nothings."

Cecil Smith added in the *Los Angeles Times*, "As to the worst show offered [for the new TV season], there's no competition. It's *Brady Bunch*. It is so cloyingly, nauseatingly sweet, so insufferably cute, so embarrassingly bad that discussing it becomes an ordeal."

From Harry Harris in the *Philadelphia Inquirer*: "[It's] a bunch alright. Of baloney."

Sherwood Schwartz planned for audiences to see the show as a groundbreaking spotlight on this hipper, burgeoning demographic of blended families. He was also committed to telling the Bradys' stories with all the humor and heart he thought such a topic and such an audience deserved, and that caused some of the disconnect between his intentions and how the series was received. Critics were convinced it was far too light on the comedy, far too heavy on the earnest sentiments. *Seinfeld's* motto twenty years later was "No hugging, no learning," but Schwartz insisted *The Brady Bunch* be "a show without explosions…it's a show without drugs, it's a show without rapes. It's a show about nice, decent, normal people." In other words, lots of hugging, plenty of learning; the "normal" people Schwartz sought to impress were the viewers he remained certain would come to view the Bradys, to use another more modern term, as Must See TV.

"You really had to accept his philosophy, and then try to tweak it wherever you could," Paramount executive Douglas Cramer said. "And find ways of having [the series] not be so molasses and cotton candy."

Not that Schwartz didn't try to put some modern touches on the show, only to have the network nix them. In his vision, Mike was a widower and Carol was a divorcée. In "The Honeymoon," Carol's parents, the Tylers, host her wedding to Mike. Martin, then, is her married name…but what became of Mr. Martin? Death? Divorce? The answer was left purposefully ambiguous, because the network insisted Schwartz make reference to the *late* Mr. Martin. He compromised by writing a pilot scene where Mike assures Bobby he doesn't have to hide a photo of his late mother to avoid hurting Carol's feelings; Mike, it's clear, was a widower. But Mr. Martin's status is one of those officially unanswered questions, like what happened to Fluffy after "The Honeymoon."

Florence Henderson, whose own sense of humor was much bawdier than Carol Brady's corny quips would have us believe, joked in 2015, forty years after *The Brady Bunch* ended, that she could finally reveal the truth about Mr. Martin. "I killed my husband," she said. "I was the original Black Widow. Nobody ever said, but I always say I just got rid of him."

What Cramer and ABC executives would come to understand was that some critics and adult audiences found *The Brady Bunch* too sweet, too unrealistic, but younger viewers were tuning in faithfully on Friday nights. They liked the characters and the actors playing them. By the third season, Barry Williams alone received 6,000 fan letters a week (no small feat in the pre–social media era when teen magazines were the main way to promote the younger cast to younger viewers). Young viewers, as Schwartz predicted, also identified with the characters and their dilemmas, especially when the plots started to focus less on the issues specific to blended-family life and more on the general trials and tribulations of being a kid. Getting a crush on your teacher or a favorite celebrity, worrying that you look "ugly, ugly, ugly!" wearing your new braces, and the angst of feeling ordinary and unrecognized as the middle child were first-season storylines that resonated (and still do) with children.

While most critics had nothing but barbs for the series, there were reviewers who saw the appeal of *The Brady Bunch*'s brand of throwback warm and fuzzy humor, focusing less on the sillier aspects of the plot and more on the sincerity and kid-friendly tone.

"*The Brady Bunch* is cute, and that's just what a lot of people are looking for," Sherry Woods wrote in the *Palm Beach Post*. Echoed Margot Reis-El Bara in *Florida Today*, "We wouldn't call *The Brady Bunch* a great series, but it isn't bad either... it's a refreshing change of pace. Certainly the small fry will enjoy it."

It was that audience, ultimately, that kept the show on the air for five seasons, even though *The Brady Bunch* never finished a season among the top 30 programs on television. During the first year, the cast didn't know if the show would be greenlit for even an entire season, let alone a sophomore year. After filming the first half of the season, Florence Henderson returned to her home in New York and focused on her nightclub act and interviews promoting *The Brady Bunch* while awaiting news on whether she'd be returning to Los Angeles to film another batch of episodes that would expand the debut season. When she saw how much her own children enjoyed the series, she had an inkling young viewers would propel the series forward for additional episodes, and even another season.

Children and their parents often wrote letters to their local newspapers, expressing their opinions about *The Brady Bunch* and asking if the show would continue on ABC. The letters from younger readers were almost always positive and hopeful that the Bradys would continue to be a part of their Friday nights. The letters from adults were more evenly split between those who wondered why this show was taking up a primetime slot and those who were happy to have a program they could watch with their families.

CHAPTER FIVE

This Group Must Somehow Form a Family

Like any group of people who've grown up together and been a part of each other's lives for five decades, the *Brady* cast has had its squabbles (more on that later). But they *have* remained a part of each other's lives for fifty years, by choice. That's a testament to them, of course, and to Sherwood Schwartz's production and his overall goals for the series.

"His approach is pure. He's a wonderful innocent in that sense, because he feels this way about family values," *Brady* director John Rich said. "And I think it touches a nerve."

Despite tough slagging from critics, and in the face of constant volleys of insults and tantrums from his leading man, Schwartz was confident in the content and tone of *The Brady Bunch*, committed to making it a show that told stories about and for its youngest viewers. If the critics didn't understand that, if the network executives didn't understand that, if Robert Reed threatened to quit the series after filming just a handful of episodes, it wouldn't shake

Schwartz's core beliefs. He'd waited years to get a network to green-light his idea. This was the show he was going to make. This was the only way he was interested in making this show.

Years later, after *The Brady Bunch* had been in syndication, after all the spin-offs and movies, Schwartz would continue to get letters from young fans, and fans from all across the globe. He would get fan mail from clergy, asking for ideas for their sermons. He'd get letters from prisoners, asking for photos of the cast. Kindly, he'd make sure they received the pictures they asked for, without judgment, and with appreciation when they'd tell him the show brought back memories of happier times for them, before they'd ended up on the wrong side of the law.

During *The Brady Bunch*, as early as the first season, Schwartz also started to receive letters from young viewers who loved and admired the Bradys so much they wanted to become one. Literally. They would write to the series creator and tell him they planned to leave their homes, as far away as Ohio and Florida, and come to sunny California. Never mind that there simply weren't any available squares in that opening sequence, and definitely no more space in the kids' rooms for another bed, or another toothbrush in that toiletless bathroom shared by the Brady six.

Schwartz took those letters seriously, worried that the viewers who seemed sincere in their desire for a better homelife were also sincere about their intentions to run away from their families to find one. He responded to the first few personally, sending a letter to the wannabe Bradys' parents, at the return addresses on the envelopes. Once these missives started to arrive more frequently, he made a form letter that could be mailed off right away, in the hopes of preventing unhappy teens from taking actions that might have them facing dramatic consequences.

These letters, this connection young people were making with this fictional family, didn't surprise Schwartz, and he did feel a responsibility for the stories he was telling, the image his series was projecting. As happy as his childhood had been, and as idyllic a childhood as he and wife Mildred were providing to their kids, he was aware that wasn't always the case in the rest of the world. But no matter what critics—and Robert Reed—would charge about the unreality of the Bradys' family life, there wasn't a doubt in Schwartz's mind that providing this example of what a happy family could look like was something television viewers wanted, and maybe even needed.

Outside Paramount Studios' Stage 5 (where, coincidentally, *Yours, Mine and Ours*, the movie that had helped convince ABC execs to greenlight *The Brady Bunch*, was also filmed) viewers were confronted with a lot more change and turmoil every day.

The war in Vietnam raged, as did protests of it. Richard Nixon was sworn in as president. Hurricane Camille killed more than 250 people in 1969 and caused nearly $1.5 billion in damage (roughly $10 billion in 2019 dollars) along the Gulf Coast. Jimi Hendrix and Janis Joplin played the Woodstock festival in August 1969, then died within weeks of each other the next year. The Beatles broke up. The Stonewall riots in New York City began the modern gay rights movement. Neil Armstrong walked on the moon. The Manson Family murdered pregnant actress Sharon Tate and four of her friends.

Archie Bunker and Fred Sanford were talking about race, and Maude Findlay had an abortion...just a taste of the social issues suddenly playing out on TV. More than 50 percent of American homes owned a color TV set (*The Brady Bunch* was the first family comedy to be broadcast in color) by 1971, and outside the Bradys' little slice of TV land, those realities were playing out all across the channels. Divorce rates started to rise in 1970 and would continue to climb all the way through the decade.

That last statistic is one often brought up in discussions about

The Brady Bunch and its popularity. Children being raised by single parents sometimes became latchkey kids, and those kids were a big demographic of viewers when the show made its very successful run in syndication beginning in 1975. Also, quite simply, for children who lived in unhappy homes for any reason, including divorce, watching *The Brady Bunch*'s family dynamic—chaotic, crowded, and contentious as it could be—was a utopian experience.

What kid wouldn't want to live in a household where your every basic need was met, where your problems could be solved in record time, and where you were surrounded by two loving parents (and Alice!), whose biggest job in life seemed to be tending to even the smallest problems facing you and your siblings?

In *Brady*world, angst about Marcia's unrequited crush on Harvey Klinger, a boy obsessed with bugs, was met with a level of parental concern usually reserved for failing grades or a broken bone in the real world (and in other less *Brady*fied TV households). Ditto season two's "Not-So-Ugly Duckling" and Jan's unrequited crush on Clark Tyson.

· When Jan lost her locket, the whole family (and Alice!) staged an elaborate middle-of-the-night reenactment to help her find it. Peter got a new job at Mr. Martinelli's bike shop (a job Peter would soon get fired from), and Carol and Mike decided to buy expensive new bicycles from the store to support him. Mike went to the trouble of locating a relative of Jesse James to show Bobby the outlaw wasn't the hero Bobby thought he was.

And let's not forget the celebrity mischief plots.

When Davy Jones fan club president Marcia promised she could get the singer to come to the school dance, and Bobby lied about knowing Joe Namath and told his friends they could meet him, Carol and Mike barely chastised them. Instead, they tried to help them keep their celebrity promises. Carol even prodded Mike to rack his brain for any acquaintance he might have who could help Bobby get Namath to their house.

It's also an incredibly silly but naively sweet moment when Carol assumed Mike was such a well-connected man-about-town that he *must* know someone who knows an NFL superstar from the other side of the country, and that this person would be able to get Namath to do such a big favor for the Bradys, complete strangers. As Christopher Knight once said, "You have to enter a specific kind of mental space when you watch the show."

The bottom line on the family's corniness and uncomplicated storylines is that *The Brady Bunch* was simply fun, relatable, wholesome entertainment for some viewers. For others, the show was an escape, a beacon of hope and a promise of an alternative life that came right into our living rooms and played out in full color, with family dinners; groovy wardrobes; a stable, clean, modern home; superattentive, supportive, and loving adults; and a houseful of siblings who would always ensure you had friends and playmates on call. "It's so sweet, so gentle, so innocent," Florence Henderson said. "We really believed what we were saying at the time...It seems to be the family that every child wants."

The impact on fans, whatever their motivation for parking themselves in front of the TV on Friday nights or, later, for the syndication airings on weekday afternoons, was universal.

In "celebrities, they're just like us" examples, future Oscar winner Tom Hanks was a son of divorce, remarriages, and stepsiblings. His unstable childhood included a lot of moving around (he'd lived in ten houses by the time he turned ten), a lot of uncertainty, and not always a lot of support. The version of the blended family he lived helped make him a lifelong fan of the fictional Bradys.

The show, eventually, even had a role in his future marriage to actress Rita Wilson, who earned her Screen Actors Guild card with a guest appearance on *The Brady Bunch*.

In season four's "Greg's Triangle," Greg was on the judging committee that was going to select the new head cheerleader for Westdale High, and that meant he was going to anger at least one of the contestants: his sister Marcia, or his new girlfriend, Jennifer. At the auditions, though, a new contender emerged, Wilson's Pat Conway, who performed the best tryout and got Greg's vote. (Marcia acknowledged that Pat was the best, but Jennifer dumped Greg for his decision.)

It would be almost a decade before Tom and Rita met in person, and sixteen years before they got married, but Hanks said he recalls that episode well, and specifically recalls agreeing very much with Greg's vote.

"I was actually at a friend of mine's house when it aired, and I remember thinking, 'That girl's cute.'"

Emmy and Golden Globe winner Jane Lynch, who would star as Carol Brady in the stage show *The Real Live Brady Bunch* in Chicago and New York, didn't have to do homework to familiarize herself with the character or the storylines. The *Glee* star is a lifelong television devotee whose fandom influenced her own career aspirations. Her all-time favorite show is *The Brady Bunch*, and she met Sherwood Schwartz, Florence Henderson, Robert Reed, Eve Plumb, Susan Olsen, and Christopher Knight when they were in the *Real Live Brady Bunch* audience. In her 2011 memoir, *Happy Accidents*, she even sums up one of her life's philosophies with a Carol Brady quote: "Find what it is you do best and do your best with it."

"Weird Al" Yankovic, whose parody songs are an infallible indication of a property's pop culture influence, is a childhood *Brady* fan who grew up and sang about the series in "The Brady Bunch," from his 1984 album *"Weird Al" Yankovic in 3-D*. Set to the music of "The Safety Dance," the top 5 *Billboard* hit (about pogo dancing) from Canadian band Men Without Hats, "The Brady Bunch" told the story of someone who definitely was not a happy *Brady* viewer. The singer lists any number of TV shows he'd be okay with the listener watching—*Three's Company*, *60 Minutes*, MTV. He's cool if you watch television until your eyeballs literally cease to remain inside their sockets. But please, he pleads, pass the remote control over to him if you're even thinking of turning on *The Brady Bunch*.

Doesn't sound like a fan, right?

Yankovic shared, "Almost without exception, whenever I write a song, it's not from my own viewpoint—it's from the viewpoint of whichever character that I'm assuming for that particular song. And for comic effect, the character in *this* song just happens to randomly hate *The Brady Bunch*. It's just a ridiculous thing to arbitrarily choose to loathe. Personally, I'm a fan, of course."

In fact, one of the reasons the five-time Grammy winner chose to parody the Bradys, and any other music, TV show, movie, performer, or foodstuff, is also one of the reasons for the enduring popularity of the Sherwood Schwartz series: We know it well, and it is comforting and entertaining to revisit it again and again.

"Obviously, when you parody something, it behooves you to choose something that people are extremely familiar with—and back in the monoculture days of the early seventies, *everybody* knew *The Brady Bunch*. And every character on that show was relatable and left an indelible impression. It's always better to lampoon or caricature something that has very distinct and recognizable characteristics, because then when you exaggerate or draw outside the lines, it's immediately funny."

Yankovic met Hope Juber at a party once. She told him the whole Schwartz family "got a big kick" out of "The Brady Bunch." And that's not his only connection to the series.

"I had the pleasure of working with Mrs. Brady herself when I cast Florence Henderson to be in my 'Amish Paradise' video. She was beyond amazing, and we remained friends for the rest of her life."

"Amish Paradise" was probably a hit with the Schwartz family, too. Not only did the video feature Henderson, but the song quotes lyrics from that other Schwartz-verse TV and theme-song classic, "Gilligan's Island."

Though *The Brady Bunch* was a homogenous series in terms of main characters and even guest cast—not unlike many of its TV brethren at the time—there is some diversity among the show's famous fans. The appeal, of course, is universal: As Sherwood Schwartz intended, *Brady Bunch* fans love the family's closeness and see their happiness as aspirational, whether the viewers come from happy homes themselves or from a more dysfunctional family.

Spike Lee told the late Roger Ebert the Bradys were a must-see in his household when he was growing up in Brooklyn. His family owned one TV, and he and his siblings weren't allowed to watch it on school nights. On Fridays, in front of the TV set was the place to be.

"The Knicks were usually on Channel 9. They were on against *The Partridge Family* and *The Brady Bunch*, and what was on the TV was decided by a vote. So I tried to lobby with my brothers and sister: 'I'll give you a piece of candy. I'll give you a dollar. Just let me watch the game!' I always got outvoted, and we had to watch those shows," Lee said. The Oscar, Emmy, and Peabody Award–winning filmmaker paid homage to those Friday night TV fights in his 1994 movie *Crooklyn* (to be fair, it's the Partridges who get a clip in the movie, so score one for them if you believe in a *Brady/Partridge* rivalry).

Another Brooklyn filmmaker, Matty Rich, released his first film, *Straight Out of Brooklyn*, when he was nineteen. The 1991 movie, which featured the debut of Lawrence Gilliard Jr., future star of *The Wire*, *The Walking Dead*, and *The Deuce*, won Sundance Film Festival and Independent Spirit Awards recognition. Based on Rich's experiences growing up in the Red Hook housing projects, the movie revolves around the Brown family, and a desperate, dangerous plan by son Dennis (Gilliard) to rob a local drug dealer and use the money to move his family out of Brooklyn and onto a more hopeful path. Things end badly for all involved, including Dennis's mother and his alcoholic, abusive father.

The Brady Bunch, Rich said, was his inspiration for making the movie.

"I used to watch that show and then turn to my mother and say, 'I'm going to create a family just like that someday, only in black life' ... [the Brady family] was happy and my family was in rage, and even though I knew what was on TV wasn't real, I wanted what they had. I wanted to go on camping trips like them. I wanted that kind of family atmosphere."

When Michelle Obama's big brother, Craig Robinson, talked about her during his speech at the Democratic National Convention in 2008, he noted her fandom for the Bradys. "This is the person who—even though we were allowed only one hour of television a night—somehow managed to commit to memory every single episode of *The Brady Bunch*," he said. In Peter Slevin's 2015 biography, *Michelle Obama: A Life*, he wrote that Obama has an "encyclopedic knowledge" of the series. She showcased it on *The Jay Leno Show* in 2009, when the host challenged her to name all the Brady kids. She did, in less than ten seconds, and earned bonus points for adding Cousin Oliver to the list.

Piyush Jindal may be the most committed *Brady Bunch* fan of all time. You know him better as Bobby Jindal, the former governor of Louisiana. Piyush, whose parents moved to Baton Rouge from India while his mother was pregnant with him, had an after-school routine that centered around watching syndicated episodes of *The Brady Bunch* every day. He particularly identified with youngest brother Bobby, because they were roughly the same age and both were far more interested in football than girls.

"So one day my mom was picking me up from school, and the teacher said, 'Well, your son has got a new name.' And she said, 'What are you talking about?' And apparently I just showed up one day without asking [my mom] for permission and told all my friends to call me Bobby from that day on, and they did."

* * *

For everyone who's ever loved *The Brady Bunch*, and even those who don't, family is at the center of everything the show is about. That was certainly the atmosphere Sherwood Schwartz (and several members of his family) set for the production.

With a full two-thirds of the main cast legally required to be in a classroom three hours a day, the production schedule revolved around the kids. They were also limited to working just four hours a day, so workdays for everyone began early, and the children's scheduled times on set were staggered so some could be available to film while others were in Frances Whitfield's classroom.

Most of the kid actors' mothers were constantly on the set, but Mrs. Whitfield was their schoolteacher and set social worker; she was one more adult present to make sure their best interests were always being considered. Whitfield had been a teacher previously. After earning a master's degree in theater arts, she became a member of the theater faculty at the University of Mississippi. Frances had aspirations to become a performer, but when her daughter Annie turned seven, she turned her focus to jump-starting Annie's career as an actress. Annie would go on to star in *White Christmas* with Bing Crosby, and appeared in a long string of TV series that included *I Married Joan* (on which Sherwood Schwartz was a writer), *Father Knows Best*, *The Donna Reed Show*, and *Bonanza*. Annie went on to graduate from Hollywood High School, but she also spent plenty of time in classrooms on movie and TV sets. When she turned sixteen and decided to take a more independent approach to her career, her mom/acting coach/manager suddenly had a lot of time on her hands.

"She didn't quite know what to do with herself," Annie said. "But she'd been on [sets] a lot with me and enjoyed it...so she became a teacher again on *The Brady Bunch*, and she just loved the kids [on the show]."

Whitfield had only a converted dressing room to work with as a classroom, but she turned the tight space into a colorful, comfortable place for the Brady six to learn. She decorated the walls inside the classroom and throughout the soundstage with their artwork, and one wall was covered with school photos fans sent to the young stars.

Later, when the kids would form a singing group and travel around the country performing in concert, Mrs. Whitfield was part of the entourage accompanying them, and part of the audience that would cheer them on. Three other teachers worked with her throughout the show's run, but she was the only one with the series for all five seasons. And she was the only one invited along for the fantastic ride to New York City and London when Robert Reed took his TV children on a vacation aboard the *Queen Elizabeth 2* cruise ship. Mrs. Whitfield was so beloved to the children and the entire production staff that she was cast in season five's "Snow White and the Seven Bradys" episode. She played—what else?— a schoolteacher, named Mrs. Whitfield. The "character" had been every Brady's favorite teacher, even Carol's, and her impending retirement led Cindy to volunteer the whole family to put on a play to raise money for a fancy set of books to gift Mrs. Whitfield. Even Alice's boyfriend, Sam the butcher, was called into showbiz duty to play a dwarf, along with the kids, while Carol was Snow White,

Mike was Prince Charming, and Alice really chewed the scenery as the wicked queen. Because of a boneheaded move by Cindy, the play was performed in the Brady backyard, and another boneheaded move by Alice (she ate all the apples, leaving none for the queen's poisoned prop) left Carol scrambling to distract the audience while Mike and Sam went off to the market (in full prince and Dopey costumes) for more.

Finally, the show did go on, and though the especially corny episode almost certainly won't top anyone's list of favorites, it is obvious the cast wasn't acting when they led Mrs. Whitfield up on the stage and covered her with kisses. Knowing the backstory of her relationship with the kids, and just how important she was in keeping them happy, nurtured, well schooled, and ready to perform, makes "Snow White and the Seven Bradys" fit right in with the heartfelt, positive family vibe Sherwood was committed to perpetuating with the series. Years later, Mrs. Whitfield, who passed away in 2005, would keep in touch with the Brady cast, and attended Reed's memorial service in 1992.

Though we think of the Brady kids running around as a six-pack most of the time, they were in fact together as a whole bunch just a couple of times each episode. Schwartz's plan had always been that one Brady kid would be the focus of each episode. They'd all get a turn in the spotlight, and the cycle would start anew, with each kid again becoming the star of his or her own episode. So, though they all faced the same schedule limits, not all the kids were busy with the same thing at the same time. And when they weren't filming or doing schoolwork, there was no lack of fun and interesting places for them to explore around the Paramount lot. Barry Williams and Maureen McCormick loved to watch Jack Klugman and Tony Randall at work on the *Odd Couple* set, and McCormick confessed she had a crush on Klugman. *Mission: Impossible*, *Bonanza*, and *Happy Days*—the hit family sitcom that was getting started just as *The*

Brady Bunch was winding down—filmed on the lot, and had fans in the *Brady* cast, who liked to ride their bikes around Paramount and pop in to see what their TV-land brethren were up to. The studio commissary was another hangout for the young and adult Bradys. One of Florence Henderson's favorite memories on the Paramount lot was the first time she met John Wayne. "He stood up to greet me, which I just thought was kind of wonderful," she said. "And I just remember thinking how incredibly tall he was" (the Duke stood six foot four; Henderson was five foot three). When the cast wanted to spend their forty-minute lunch break away from the set, they would go right outside the studio for a quick lunch at Oblath's or Nickodell, two star-packed, and now sadly defunct, eateries that were frequented by Paramount employees who liked their hearty food and the servers who were pros at getting them in and out and back on set for their next scene.

With the busy schedule that usually included filming two episodes per week, and balancing the kids' schoolwork/recreation time/work limit requirements, the whole cast spent a lot of time inside Stage 5. It was essentially a giant rectangular box, 247 feet (and four inches) wide, and 76 feet (and four inches) in length and, in addition to *Yours, Mine and Ours*, had also hosted the filming of *Vertigo*, *Rosemary's Baby*, and *The Graduate* (and would later be the filming location for TV series *Angel* and *Monk*, and the very un-*Brady*-ish *Mommie Dearest* movie).

The kids might be together answering their fan mail, which had become so plentiful that the network started an official fan club for viewers to join. For two dollars (plus twenty-five cents for postage and handling; three dollars total for international fans), fan club members would receive a kit that featured a record, on which each member of *The Brady Bunch* had recorded "a personal message just for you"; autographed portraits of each star "for your wall, locker, or scrapbook"; *Brady* stickers; a membership card; autographed wallet-size photos; and a book, exclusive to club members, where you could "find out what each Brady is like." Such revelations included: Barry had a horse named Ya-Ta-Hey; Maureen's first car, when she turned sixteen, was a new Mercedes; Chris wanted to meet Henry Kissinger (who did visit the *Brady* set with his son and daughter, fans of the show); Eve kept the mouse who played Myron in the *Brady* episode "The Impractical Joker"; Mike was a team captain for his school playground group; and one of Susan's favorite pets was a German shepherd puppy gifted to her by TV dad Reed.

The fan club kit wasn't the only option *Brady Bunch* fans had for spending their allowances to show their love for the series. A 1970 Thermos-brand metal lunchbox, with depictions of Carol and Mike's wedding on one side and the family camping on the other, was a popular way for *Brady* devotees to ferry their peanut butter and jelly sandwiches and Twinkies to school. Today, the lunchbox is still a sought-after collectible that can fetch hundreds of dollars on eBay. It's also part of the collection in the Smithsonian's National Museum of American History.

Fans could also collect *Brady* trading cards, coloring books, paperback novels, View-Master reels, paper dolls, Halloween costumes, stickers, puzzles, bracelets, jumping ropes, toy tea sets, dominoes, checker sets, and Cindy's Kitty Karry-All dolls.

All the youngest Bradys were teen magazine stars, with Maureen even writing an advice column for *16* magazine. She shared her thoughts on boys, beauty, and relationships with friends and family and, in one special Dear Maureen column, quizzed her castmates to come up with dating tips, or, as the headline read, "The Bradys—60 Sex-y Secrets." Included: "Be yourself! Be sincere! Be impulsive!" (Maureen); "Keep your hair long, simple, and clean— and please don't tease it. No guy wants to run his fingers through teased hair. Yuck!" (Barry); "Carry around a sketch pad or some other prop of your choice. Guys are curious and lots of them will ask you about it." (Eve); "Start a stamp collection—then you can trade stamps with the boys in your school." (Susan); "Be concerned about making this world a better place, cos that matters a lot to me." (Chris); and "Walk your dog (or cat) around town. Boys always stop to pet a cute dog—especially when he's tied to a girl!" (Mike).

Eve started her own publication, *The Brady Bugle* (note the love of alliteration that apparently ran through the Brady universe). She printed the weekly, two-page newspaper by hand. In it, *Brady* set insiders could read such riveting news as which cast members were taking their lunch breaks together.

Sometimes the kids brought their outside interests into work. Chris Knight had a collection of pets at home that included a kit of pigeons. In "How to Succeed in Business?" a season-four episode directed by Robert Reed, after Peter got fired from his job as Mr. Martinelli's bicycle repairman, he went to a park and sat by himself feeding pigeons. He even talked to them, with one of them perching on his hand as he related how tough it would be to tell his parents he's a "failure at fourteen." If that pigeon seemed particularly interested in Peter's tale of woe, it's because he wasn't just some random bird, or even a trained Hollywood actor pigeon. The pigeons in the park were played by Knight's own pets.

When there was the rare bit of sitting-around time on Stage 5, one of the cast's favorite ways to pass it was with—wait for it— needlepoint.

Ann B. Davis dabbled in craftwork in her downtime, and eventually she would get the entire rest of the cast involved, including all six kids and Henderson and Reed. Henderson wasn't faking her way through all those needlework projects Carol worked on while sitting in the living room or family room with Mike; she became so enamored of the hobby that she would carry projects with her on her many plane rides back and forth between Los Angeles and her home in New York, and gift loved ones with her needlepoint work, including a Raggedy Ann design for her daughter.

Davis liked to display her handiwork in her trailer, and once collaborated with Sherwood Schwartz's daughter Hope Juber on a needlepoint project that turned into a design on Davis's director's chair on the *Brady* set. The December 1972 issue of *Aunt Suzy's Needlecraft Journal* magazine even made a visit to the Stage 5 production for a cover story all about how *The Brady Bunch* was "hooked on needlework." The cast found needlepoint, as well as hooking rugs and embroidery, to be a good way to work out their nervous energy—"group therapy," as Henderson called it.

Mike Lookinland created his own hook rug design, all three girls created needlework displays of bugs and animals, Chris Knight was especially fond of embroidery, and Reed, the last one to be convinced to join in the fun with his TV family, fashioned a small butterfly for his first needlework project, which he said he was going to sew onto his jeans. "I don't think I'd crochet or knit, but I won't be embarrassed to needlepoint," he said. "This does seem to be very relaxing."

* * *

The theme of family unity the Bradys projected on camera and on set didn't end with the cast. Hope Juber, Henderson's daughter Barbara, and Reed's daughter Karen were among the many relatives of cast members who appeared in *Brady Bunch* episodes. McCormick had grown especially close with Barbara, and helped convince the adults they should be co-stars. In season two's "The Slumber Caper," Marcia hosted a slumber party at Casa Brady, with Barbara playing her friend Ruthie and Karen playing a pal named Karen. Sleepover guest Jenny (Juber) had been uninvited to the festivities when Marcia thought Jenny had gotten her in trouble at school.

The misunderstanding was cleared up when another friend confessed to being the real cause of Marcia's trip to the principal's office, and everything ended well (because, *Brady Bunch*), with Jenny reinvited to join the soiree.

Two more family ties with "The Slumber Caper": E. G. Marshall, who played Reed's father on *The Defenders*, guest-starred as Mr. Randolph, Marcia's principal, and the episode's director, Oscar Rudolph, would make directing Bradys a family affair in season three when his son, Alan Rudolph, joined the show as an assistant director.

Meanwhile, Henderson's son Robert played a tree in Cindy's class play in "Eenie, Meenie, Mommy, Daddy"; Mike Lookinland's little brother Todd played an adopted boy named Matt in "Kelly's Kids," the season-five episode that was meant to be the first *Brady Bunch* spin-off; and Chris Knight's dad, Edward, played Monty Marshall, the host of the *Question the Kids* quiz show Cindy froze on in season four's "You Can't Win 'Em All."

And in the series finale, "The Hair-Brained Scheme," both Hope Juber and Henderson's daughter Barbara returned as guest stars, this time playing classmates of Greg's who ran into him at the hair salon. Also at the salon, underneath one of those retro giant hair dryers: Mildred Schwartz, Sherwood's wife. Juber's appearance (then as Hope Sherwood) was her fourth guest spot on the show; she had also played Greg's date Rachel in "The Big Bet" and "Greg Gets Grounded."

Behind the scenes, the family connections were just as strong. Sherwood's brothers, Al and Elroy Schwartz, were writers on the series beginning with the first season. Husband-and-wife team Lois and Arnold Peyser, who also wrote episodes of *Gilligan's Island*, *The Dick Van Dyke Show*, *My Three Sons*, and the Elvis Presley movie *The Trouble with Girls*, wrote season one's "Every Boy Does It Once."

"Tom and Helen August" was the pseudonym used by husband-and-wife writing duo Alfred and Helen Levitt. The Levitts had been unable to find writing gigs for five years after being blacklisted by the House Un-American Activities Committee in 1951, but they eventually returned to TV and movie work with scripts for *Bewitched*, *That Girl*, *The Bionic Woman*, a Writers Guild Award–nominated episode of *All in the Family*, and season two's "The Drummer Boy" and "Coming Out Party" and "Click" in season three for *The Brady Bunch*.

Emmy-nominated writers on *The Carol Burnett Show*, marrieds Adele and Burt Styler wrote season four's "Career Fever," while Burt wrote solo on the season-one gem "54-40 and Fight" (a.k.a. the trading stamp episode) and season two's "The Impractical Joker."

Even the original band that performed the series theme song, the Peppermint Trolley Company, included a pair of brothers, Danny and Jimmy Faragher (who later formed another band, the Faragher Brothers, that included four more Faragher siblings).

And then there was Lloyd Schwartz, Sherwood's son, who was coaxed by his father into joining *The Brady Bunch* as the dialogue coach for the kid cast and ended up becoming a producer, director, showrunner, manager of Robert Reed temper tantrums, and inter-rupter of randy teenage actors.

Lloyd J. Schwartz (not to be confused with Lloyd Schwartz, poet and Pulitzer Prize–winner for his classical music reviews at the *Boston Phoenix*) was fresh out of graduate school at UCLA when he joined the Brady universe. The pilot had already been shot, but Sherwood wanted him on board as the first season got under way. Lloyd had run a Malibu summer camp for kids and had worked as a dialogue coach; he had not run a TV show. He did not particularly want the job. He had his own plans. He'd done some acting, had been part of a black-and-white comedy duo named Carruthers and Blood, wrote his own plays. And, since he was in his early twenties and unmarried, the *Brady Bunch* subject matter wasn't exactly his scene. He'd been an active anti-war protestor at UCLA. Carruthers and Blood (he was "Carruthers"; "Blood" was a Black Panther) had been kicked out of most LA clubs, he explained, for being too controversial. Now his dad was asking him to come wrangle half a dozen children and coach them through saying their lines correctly for the camera?

But Lloyd had worked with his dad before, as a dialogue coach on *Gilligan's Island* and an Imogene Coca comedy called *It's About Time*, about a prehistoric married couple (even in that high-concept scenario, it was all about family). Father and son both felt he could do the job, so, despite worries that he would give up his independence taking this position with his dad, he signed on.

Most of his time during season one was spent with the Brady six, making sure they knew their lines and how to deliver them, making sure they were where they needed to be when they needed to be there, bonding with their parents, and unlike on some productions, keeping the stage mommies and daddies nearby and involved in anything related to their particular Brady kid.

He also helped develop the characters' personalities, or rather, make it comfortable for the young actors to let their own personalities shine through on camera, thereby forming who their Brady counterparts became. Sherwood Schwartz had cast them for their real-world qualities; none of the Brady girls or boys had lengthy character descriptions when filming began. Lloyd had the freedom and responsibility, then, to get Barry, Maureen, Chris, Eve, Mike, and Susan to shape who Greg, Marcia, Peter, Jan, Bobby, and Cindy would become.

His primary motivation tool: fun. Not only were Brady-kid parents welcomed on set, so were their real-life siblings. They became friends with each other, as did the moms, who would carpool with their kids to the studio oftentimes, and who watched out for each other's children when they had to be away from the action on Stage 5. Lloyd fought to make sure the kids were free to explore the backyard set, the soundstage, the rest of the Paramount lot. Mike and Chris liked to hurry through their commissary cheeseburgers to head off to the *Bonanza* set and play gunfighters or hide and seek. The kids also discovered some giant iceboxes they liked to play in inside an abandoned commissary on the lot, but that fun came to an abrupt halt once their parents found out about the dangerous games they'd been up to. Studio executives weren't charmed by these rambunctious, curious kids running around their lot. The noise, the chaos, the potential liabilities! But every time Lloyd, who had become known as the person in charge of making things run smoothly with the kids, was told to calm them down and keep them inside Stage 5, he pushed back, pointing out that children needed to be allowed to act like children, not just actors saying lines as TV show characters.

This genuine care and concern for the children helped him bond with them, which made his job as their dialogue coach and unofficial acting teacher all the more fruitful. *The Brady Bunch* was filmed as a single-camera show, like a movie, which not only made it look better but meant the children didn't have to maintain long stretches of focus without breaks. There were lots of setups for short scenes, lots of close-ups of the actors and actresses, which allowed Lloyd to coach them through dialogue and how to deliver it, how to understand the meaning of the scene and convey it on camera. The lack of a live audience (which is a staple of multi-camera productions) also meant those laughs we heard every time Sam the butcher dropped one of his meat-related puns on Alice or every time Alice was nearly run over by a running group of Brady kids were courtesy of the dreaded laugh track (that laughter that comes not courtesy of a live, in-studio audience, but via prerecorded giggles that are intended to signal to viewers when something is funny—something, as the laugh track's detractors point out, that should be fairly obvious in a sitcom, and which also displays a lack of faith in the viewing audience's comedy recognition skills).

The close relationships Lloyd had with the kids would help in other ways throughout the series, as he became an associate producer (the youngest one in network TV at the time), and, for the final season, a producer. First, his constant presence on the set, in each of his roles, meant he could handle most issues that would pop up regarding the cast. That left his dad free to focus on the scripts, the writers, and the editing.

Also, because Lloyd was, throughout the entire five-season run of the show, the adult in the production who was closest to the kids, he was privy to many of those romances *Brady* fans have been obsessed with for years. He knew about Bobby and Cindy's—rather, Mike and Susan's—innocent "makeout" (read: hugging) sessions in Tiger's doghouse. He also knew when Mike and Susan got married, then unmarried (by repeating their Maureen McCormick–officiated original ceremony in reverse) when Mike started noticing the more quickly developing girls on set. And he certainly noticed the ongoing mutual crushes McCormick and Barry Williams had on each other.

These very unsibling-like feelings for each other were even becoming noticeable on camera, especially by the time they were ready to film the season-four finale, "A Room at the Top." Another *Brady* classic, the episode finds Greg and Marcia both trying to lay claim to the Brady attic, which they each want to turn into their own private teenage refuge. After much fighting over the space, Marcia finally decides to let Greg have the room, reasoning that he's older and she'll be next in line for the space once he goes off to college (the same reason she conceded the school election to him in season one). But before she delivers this magnanimous decision to him, they're sitting together on Jan's bed, alone, and when she starts crying, he decides to give her the room. She's so touched that she hugs him and puts her hand on his shoulder. When you see the episode as a kid, it just strikes you as a very nice thing for a brother to be doing for his sister, and a sister being sincerely appreciative of her brother's act of generosity. But watching the episode as an adult, as Lloyd Schwartz was back then, you notice something more. You notice Greg and Marcia seem to be looking at each other in a goofy, romantic way, speaking to each other softly, that Marcia's hand on his shoulder doesn't seem very sisterly at all. And you would be reading the situation correctly.

Lloyd was directing "A Room at the Top" and noticed the very same thing unfolding as he watched the two teens through the lens. He thought he'd better do something about it, at least for long enough to keep things looking nice and family-friendly on-screen. So he took Barry aside and had a man-to-man talk with him. They both agreed, Maureen was really cute. She was a very special girl. She also had a lot of really cute, nice friends. Wouldn't it be in Barry's best interest, Lloyd suggested to Barry, to remain friends with Mo and leave himself available to spend time with all those pretty friends of hers?

All in a day's work for the producer. His subtle psychological trickery—along with the on-again, off-again fickleness of teen romance—managed to keep hormones under control to the point of being able to finish the series without any major behind-the-scenes drama (among the kids, anyway).

Some of the adults proved harder to handle. As the series moved along, Lloyd quickly proved himself more than capable of not only managing the kids but also running things on the set. "It was like a big electric train," he said of juggling all his responsibilities. Sherwood spent most of his time in an office at Stage 5, steering preproduction and postproduction on the series. Being the one on the floor meant Lloyd was working with directors and the crew, many of whom had worked with his dad previously. Many of them had known Lloyd since he was a kid, back when they referred to him as "Lloydy" and attended his bar mitzvah. Now he was their producer.

That was fine most of the time. Lloyd perfected a work style in which he projected competence and confidence in his duties, but which also left him open to suggestions from those who'd been working on TV shows a lot longer than he had. His respect for those around him prevented his position and his relationship to the boss from becoming an issue on the set. Most of the time. And then there was Bob Reed, who didn't seem to give a damn about Sherwood, Lloyd, or their relationship to each other.

Reed's unhappiness about being the star of *The Brady Bunch* and with the series' writing and subject matter was no secret. Neither were his frequent, loud, and often cruel expressions of these feelings. He usually saved his worst diatribes for after the kids had gone home for the day (because of the kids' requirements and time restrictions, the adult cast filmed a good portion of their scenes when the kids weren't around). Lloyd was an adult, but it still hurt to hear Reed rant—to the rest of the cast and crew—about his father's lack of talent, how his father was a hack, how he had no sense of what good, funny writing was, no idea how to make the show realistic. Reed often made the comments while the camera was rolling, meaning the footage shot would be seen by network and studio executives who looked at the footage each day. Lloyd would want to respond, to defend his father, explain to Reed that Sherwood knew exactly what he was doing, had been an award-winning comedy writer for decades. He wanted to demand that this man show his father respect, and appreciation for a job that, though no one knew it at the time, was going to make Reed a TV legend, one of the most iconic dads in TV history.

But he couldn't lash out, couldn't meet a Reed rant with one of his own. First, his father had told him not to. Sherwood didn't like Reed's behavior one bit more than Lloyd did, but he knew they both had to put the show first, keep things running smoothly. Second, Lloyd needed to keep his cool in front of the other adult actors and the crew. Florence Henderson wasn't sure how to deal with Reed's complaints and outbursts, either. The Schwartzes always advised her to let him talk, let him rant, never try to disagree with him or counter his bashing of the show. Allowing the actor to blow off steam usually led to them being able to get through the episodes, for the most part, in an otherwise happy, pleasant environment.

Sherwood and Lloyd also knew Reed would sometimes write letters (long, angry letters) to Paramount executives sharing his issues with the scripts. He already had made a habit of making nasty comments on film, and Lloyd didn't want executives to see him responding in kind on camera, so he forced himself to remain calm in the face of Reed's barrage of affronts to his father and the show.

It was best, Lloyd and everyone on set had realized, to try to focus on the happier aspects of the show, and there were plenty.

Henderson continued to do plays, perform her nightclub act, make guest appearances on other TV shows, and travel extensively while also raising her four children, and she was very happy to have her first starring series role. Between her own kids and growing up as one of ten children herself, she never had any issues being surrounded by so many Brady kids, who she praised as sweet, charming, kind, and professional co-stars. She talked about going to work when it was still dark in the morning and going home when it was dark out at night. She and Ann B. Davis were often the last cast members on set, as they would do scenes together without the kids if an episode needed a bridge or filler scene. When her children were in town, they often spent time with the Brady kids, with Henderson hosting barbecues and pool parties at her rented

Los Angeles home for her real and TV offspring. *The Brady Bunch* was a busy but happy time in her career.

Ditto Ann B. Davis, an old-school professional actress who appreciated the show Sherwood Schwartz was committed to making, and just as much appreciated the steady gig he'd brought into her life. Davis, single and childless her whole life, wasn't used to co-starring with a lot of children, and she didn't make any particular effort to spend a lot of time with kids outside of work, either. She loved her house and gardening and her pet poodle. She made several trips to Vietnam and Korea to entertain American troops. She loved her acting work and the aforementioned crafts she'd devote her downtime to on set. And she loved—*loved!*—fast, shiny sports cars, the faster and shinier, the better. During *The Brady Bunch*, she owned a Karmann Ghia convertible and a Porsche 914, and even in her later years, when she had retired from Hollywood and devoted herself to volunteer work for the Episcopal Church all around the country, her one personal indulgence was a bright red Mazda Miata she liked to tool around in.

As for the *Brady* kids, they were somewhat of an exception to her indifference about children. Alice could only pretend she had a tough outer shell around her young charges, and Ann B. (the *B* stood for Bradford, a family name) also had a pleasant relationship with her young castmates. For the rest of her life she would talk about what wonderful, professional actors they'd been, how much she'd enjoyed working with them, and how proud she was of the fine adults they'd grown into. She would tell stories of her and the kids sometimes calling each other by their character's name (which might also be chalked up to what Henderson called Davis's habit of forgetting the real names of everyone around her), and how the kids cared for each other so much that when Susan Olsen once fell asleep on Barry Williams' shoulder, he didn't budge for an hour, just to allow his TV sister some much-needed nap time. The kids—

young and adult versions—have always shared fond memories of Davis and how funny she was, and how she once surprised them by throwing a big Halloween party for them at her house in the Hollywood Hills.

She'd had a chance to bond with the kids even before they connected with their TV mother. In June 1969, Davis accompanied all six Brady kid stars and their mothers to the Domestic Relations Division of the Los Angeles County Superior Court as the actors visited Judge William E. MacFaden to have their work contracts approved. Davis and the kids posed for many a publicity photo—later sent to media with a press release that proclaimed "United They Stand" about the stars of the new series—and then stood before the judge as he decreed 20 percent of their earnings should be shuffled into US Savings Bonds before he would officially okay their work documents. Afterward, the gruff judge, the same one who granted Judy Garland's fourth divorce that same year, in that same courtroom, softened as he saw the smiling faces and told the kids they looked like a good group. "It's the Brady *Bunch*," Eve Plumb corrected him.

"What? Oh, yes," MacFaden said. "Good luck to the Brady Bunch."

When Florence Henderson replaced Joyce Bulifant as Carol, she'd already been cast in a major movie role, playing singer Nina Grieg in *Song of Norway*. The movie was filmed on location in the titular country, and although it was planned as an eight-week shoot, production stretched to five months. *The Brady Bunch* was delayed as long as possible, but time and money were of the essence on both projects, so Henderson returned to the land of fjords to complete the movie, and Robert Reed, Ann B., and the *Brady* kid actors got to work on Stage 5, with Sherwood Schwartz working out the schedule so Henderson could do her work on the episodes when she returned.

It was not an easy beginning. Reed was at his prickliest during this time, already unhappy with the scripts and grumpy about this unusual situation they all found themselves in, starting the family comedy without one of the most important members of the family.

When Henderson rejoined *The Brady Bunch*, the cast had to revisit the episodes they'd worked on in her absence. "It got confusing," Reed said. "They'd say, 'Get dressed for scene 43,' and we'd have to ask, 'For what show?' When we'd sit down to do a scene, we'd ask the director, 'Were we happy or sad in this one?'"

Where Reed was frustrated, and only became more so as the series went along, Ann B. remained a calming, happy presence, and a positive role model for the young actors who were not only looking to their older peers as examples of how to perform on camera, but also as models of how to behave like professionals on set.

Davis, like Alice to the Brady family, was an indispensable part of *The Brady Bunch*. She was the less glamorous glue that helped hold the show together with her stability, work ethic, and genuine contentment to be exactly where she was, doing exactly what she wanted to be doing for a living.

It was appropriate that when Sherwood Schwartz plotted out the tic-tac-toe board for the opening sequence on paper, Ann/Alice landed in the middle square. Nothing was truer; both the actress and the character were right square in the middle of everything good about the series.

CHAPTER SIX

What About Bob?

These are some of the things that made Robert Reed hate being Mike Brady.

Slippery eggs. In "The Grass Is Always Greener," a season-one *Brady Bunch* episode, Carol and Mike decided to swap activities for the day, so each would see how difficult the other parent's job was. That meant Carol had to help the boys prepare for Little League tryouts, and Mike would help Marcia earn a cooking badge. No surprise: Both jobs were tough. It *was* a surprise, at least to Reed, that both activities would lead to the Brady 'rents falling on the ground. Carol's wipeout came while showing the boys how to bunt. Mike's fall came, despite Reed's argument that it wasn't possible, after he slipped on some broken eggs in the kitchen. The episode aired as the penultimate of the season, but it was the eighth episode filmed. Reed had argued, as had already become his habit by this point, that the script was completely unrealistic, the handiwork of a hack, the kind of thing only someone who made a show like *Gilligan's Island* would think was actually humorous. No one would slip and fall simply from stepping on a broken egg, Reed maintained. But director George Cahan insisted he at least try it. He agreed.

And slipped on the egg he dropped on the floor.

Ann B. Davis, whose Alice was also in the kitchen scene, made sure he was okay, then asked him if he thought the gag might work after all.

"You know, Ann, all the way down," he said, "I was thinking, 'I deserve this!'"

He also hated the idea of talking to a mouse, and the appearance of fake ink stains. In "The Impractical Joker," the season-two episode that found Jan playing tricks on the household, the shenanigans turned serious (*Brady* serious, anyway) when Jan hid Greg's science experiment mouse and the mouse got loose in the house. Reed not only had a problem with the fact that Mike was supposed to talk to Myron the mouse while helping Greg train the vermin, he also wrote a multi-page memo about how the fake ink stain on Alice's uniform in the tag scene that ended the episode didn't look genuine enough. The memo, printed in Barry Williams' *Growing Up Brady* after Reed gave him a copy of it, waxed sarcastic about how the "magic stores" the props department scouted for realistic ink-stain spots didn't stock them. Reed also called the scene "unactable," and suggested it was so unfunny that "even a laugh machine would balk" at it. The mere discussion—tense and drawn out as it was—of the matter caused him physical upset, he wrote: "My metabolism takes two days to adjust."

Also, it angered him that Sherwood Schwartz believed strawberries had a scent when they were cooking. For season four's "Jan, the Only Child," Carol and Alice were having a friendly competition to see whose family recipe for strawberry preserves was the tastiest. With both women in the kitchen stirring big pots of strawberries on the stove, Mike was supposed to walk into the house and remark that it smelled like "strawberry heaven." But when Reed, who had a habit of scouring every script and fact-checking every little detail against his beloved *Encyclopedia Britannica*, read this, he freaked out on Schwartz. Didn't Sherwood know that strawberries don't have a scent while they're being cooked? It said so right there in the *Encyclopedia Britannica*! Schwartz went down to the set, where strawberries were cooking on the working stove, and pointed out that, in fact, the set did smell strongly of sweet, delicious strawberries. Reed didn't care. His encyclopedia said otherwise. Who was Schwartz going to believe, the book or his own nose?

Ridiculous though the argument had become (okay, was from the beginning), Schwartz was a patient man who tried always to keep the well-being of the show (and the cost of the production, which was being held up by such situations) in mind. He offered a compromise to his star, who simply was not going to say the line about the scent of strawberries.

Could you say, "It *looks* like strawberry heaven in here"? Schwartz asked.

That, Reed agreed to, though exactly what Mike ended up saying to Carol and Alice is, "I do believe I've died and gone to strawberry heaven." *Encyclopedia Britannica* couldn't argue with that.

The saddest fact about how *The Brady Bunch* wound down ties into another incident where Reed was unhappy with the reality of something in the script. This time, he refused to appear in the episode. It ended up being the *Brady Bunch* series finale. "The Hair-Brained Scheme" featured Greg preparing to graduate from high school, while Bobby was trying to make his fortune by selling hair tonic. Mike Brady, one of primetime's all-time greatest dads, didn't see his oldest son graduate, because he was "out of town." In reality, Reed had objected to the episode's titular storyline, in which Bobby's hair formula turned Greg's locks orange right before his graduation ceremony. Reed's chief complaint wasn't the general ridiculousness of the plot, about which few would disagree. He objected because Neat & Natural Hair Tonic, Bobby's (faux) get-rich-quick product, wasn't FDA approved.

The finale was the second episode Reed had refused to appear in. "Goodbye, Alice, Hello," from season four, revolved around Alice deciding to leave the Bradys' employ after the kids gave her the cold shoulder when they thought she'd shared their secrets and gotten them into trouble. It wasn't true, but Alice took a job waiting tables at a diner, and her friend Kay (Mary Treen) became the family's new housekeeper. Kay was fine, good at her job, but certainly not the warm, funny, devoted ninth member of the family that Alice was, so the kids tracked Alice down and begged her to come back home. Happy ending for them, certainly a happy ending for viewers, but for Reed, the whole story stunk from the beginning premise that had Alice fleeing because of a few misunderstandings with moody teenagers. Reed didn't believe the character would have taken such drastic action in the circumstance, and instead of dealing with his unhappiness with just a memo, or one of his many long, liquid lunches at Oblath's, he decided to sit this one out.

* * *

Robert Reed's problems with *The Brady Bunch* and with Sherwood Schwartz began with the beginning. He hadn't wanted the role of Mike Brady. He considered himself a much more serious actor, an actor who should be on Broadway, who should be performing the works of Shakespeare, not stuck on Stage 5 performing the works of Sherwood.

One of the many questions that persist about this complicated man's life after fans learned he'd hated the show that made him famous: Why did he sign *on* for *The Brady Bunch*? The answer to that one, simply, is that he liked to pay his bills. Having moved from New York to Los Angeles to star in a TV adaptation of *Barefoot in the Park*, only to have that rug pulled out from under him, Reed remained under contract at Paramount. Paramount executive Doug Cramer wanted him to play Mike Brady. Schwartz had wanted a different leading man but thought Reed could do the job. With *The Brady Bunch* as his best option to fulfill his contract, he became Mike Brady.

But why did he stick with the show when he became even more unhappy with the series almost immediately after it began? The simple answer, again, is money. If he had tried to get out of his contract, he would have been sued, and unemployed. Not long before he died in 1992, Reed shared with eldest TV son Barry Williams that he also initially thought the show had potential. He thought the kids were great, the best part of the series. He thought, with the right directors (first-season director John Rich was one of many people he butted heads with), he wanted to "stay around and watch it become something that we might not be ashamed of." (If that's as enthusiastic as he could be about the show nearly two decades after it had ended, it's not tough to see that his working relationship with producers, writers, and directors was doomed.)

At the core of the war between the actor and creator Schwartz was a difference of opinion on what the show could, and should, be. Schwartz wanted to tell stories about a blended family in a humorous, relatable way. Reed wanted less humor, more reality. Schwartz and company felt Reed just didn't appreciate, or know how to perform, humor. Reed said, in a years-long string of invectives that would include words like "ninny," "nincompoop," and "hack," that Schwartz and his writers weren't capable of turning out anything but slapstick, which he meant as an insult.

One of the many unfortunate aspects of the actor vs. producer feud is that they did want many of the same things, especially where the Mike character was concerned. Reed felt his character should steadfastly remain an authority figure—as should Florence Henderson's Carol. He didn't want Mike to become a buffoon, a father, like so many dads on TV, who was on the receiving end of fresh-mouthed comments by his children, basically presented as less intelligent than his sons and daughters. Schwartz said he very much wanted the same thing. "I have certain moral values which I try to inject [into] the show. One of the most important of these is the element of parental respect among the offspring. That is my principal obligation to the viewer."

The way they, especially Reed, went about working out their differences, however, all but ensured that even if a lot of fires might be temporarily extinguished, there would be no real, lasting resolution, or meeting of the minds, about how they could make a show they'd both be proud of, or, as per Reed's most optimistic outlook, not be ashamed of.

Reed, by his own admissions in later years—most notably and extensively in Williams' series memoir, *Growing Up Brady*, which was published just a couple of weeks before Reed's death in May 1992—decided to bypass working with Schwartz to try to get his point of view into the scripts. Instead, he'd send his extensive (again: multi-page memos) notes to the office of Paramount executive Doug Cramer, and Paramount would pass them to Schwartz as if the studio was responsible for the requested changes. When Cramer left Paramount in 1971 to start his own production company, Reed began sending his edits (which sometimes amounted to rewrites) directly to Schwartz. The producer acknowledged some and worked them into the scripts, but not usually to Reed's exacting satisfaction. "The system always seemed to me to work better when I'd say, 'You fucker! What the fuck is blah blah blah…?'" said

Reed, who proudly claimed he was responsible for the first migraine Schwartz ever suffered.

In an effort to alleviate the tension, Paramount hired a script editor for *The Brady Bunch*: Tam Spiva, a friend of Reed's since his college theater days at Northwestern. Spiva, who also wrote several scripts, including the season-four-opening Hawaii episodes, was talented and provided Reed with the feeling that he had an ally in the production. His hiring didn't make the set any more free from Reed's tantrums, however. Reed's critiques of the scripts and storylines, several of which he passed along to Williams to share in *Growing Up Brady*, were "written from the point of view of 'You stupid asshole, how could you possibly write anything this dumb?'" Reed said, adding in a bit of a mea culpa, "So there was crap on both sides of the fence, but certainly on mine."

Sometimes, Reed would deal with his frustrations with those cocktails during lunch at Oblath's. The "Impractical Joker" incident, in which he was incensed about being made to cheer on a mouse to get it to run through a maze, sent him straight to Oblath's, then straight back to the set—sloshed. He tried to film the offending scene in that state, prompting Lloyd Schwartz to create a diversion so production could be ended for the day, and network executives wouldn't see film of the actor in his inebriated state.

The Oblath's lunches, and libations, continued throughout the series, along with Reed's ever-present gripes about the writing. But to his credit, his drunken returns to the set almost always came after the kid actors had finished filming for the day. As impossible as he could be, there were aspects of the production he cared about, and the six he cared about most were Barry, Maureen, Chris, Eve, Mike, and Susan. They were aware of their co-star's feelings about the show, but his biggest blowups happened, for the most part, when they were not on the set.

Another of his most self-destructive behaviors where his self-appointed job as a *Brady Bunch* critic was concerned involved sharing his feelings—his real, unsanitized feelings—about the series with reporters. Newspaper writers covering television, and *The Brady Bunch* in particular, knew exactly how Reed felt about the show's quality, and how he felt about its chances of continuing.

The same season *The Brady Bunch* premiered, Reed started doing double duty on the Paramount lot, guest-starring as Lt. Adam Tobias on the detective series *Mannix*. He was happier with his job on that show, and the *Mannix* producers were so pleased with his performance and chemistry with star Mike Connors that he continued to pop up in the drama throughout the run of *The Brady Bunch*, despite the shows being on competing networks (*Mannix* aired on CBS). When a Hollywood columnist asked him before the *Brady* season-two premiere if he worried about appearing on two shows at once, Reed was dismissive of one of the shows. "Are you kidding? *Brady Bunch* isn't much of a challenge," he said, and then went on to explain his theory on why the sitcom had been renewed for a sophomore year. "I guess we caught on with the kids...if that's what people want..."

That same fall, he told the *Baltimore Evening Sun* critic Lou Cedrone Jr. the show had started to improve a bit at the end of the first season, because "they wrote out the cat, cut out the visual stuff...the visual stuff was awful. It simply wasn't funny." (At least that solves the long-running *Brady* mystery of what happened to Fluffy.)

In a 1970 cover story in *TV Guide*, Reed shared his unexpurgated thoughts on his workplace and his boss. "The pilot turned out to be *Gilligan's Island* with kids—full of gags and gimmicks. At first I went along and decided to do the best I could...Now I argue on the set, and I think the show is better. But Sherwood...as an old gag man, what he writes is gags. I can always tell what he has put into a script—it's like riding along a smooth concrete highway and then hitting a rough spot of asphalt."

Schwartz was given the opportunity to share his side—it was clear there were sides—of the story.

"Bob is so used to *Defenders* reality that he can't get used to situation-comedy reality. If we say that Denver has a population of so many thousand, he'll look it up and tell us how many thousand the population really is. He's always on the phone to the *Los Angeles Times* or the police department or looking in the encyclopedia to check some matter of fact. His attitude is one of pure logic."

Though it would be many years before Reed would acknowledge how difficult he had been in his relationship with Schwartz, the producer did share praise for Reed's performance with *TV Guide* writer Leslie Raddatz, saying his "qualities of sincerity and honesty come across on the screen and contribute to the character. That's why I think Bob does such a good job in the role."

Reed revealed one other thing in the *TV Guide* feature that put *Brady Bunch* dramas in a new perspective. He told Raddatz he'd once objected so strongly to a script during *The Defenders* that he'd skipped showing up on the set for a day. As a result, he'd had to pay for the day's production.

His story showdowns with Schwartz, his infamous memos, and his Oblath's un-happy hours were not just a reflection of an aversion to Sherwood Schwartz's approach to a family sitcom, then. He'd acted similarly on *The Defenders*, costing money, time, inconvenience, and a smirch on his professional reputation. And *The Defenders* was a show he loved being part of, a groundbreaking, award-winning, well-written, critically acclaimed drama that gave him the opportunity to perform in stories that were as realistic as any available on TV at the time.

Why, then, had Reed been difficult on *The Defenders*, too?

* * *

Robert Reed was a man who was particularly protective of his privacy. That wasn't, in fact, his real name. He was born John Robert Rietz Jr. and was persuaded to take his stage name when a producer told him John Rietz wouldn't look good on a movie poster.

As much as he liked being a part of Hollywood as a working actor, he did not necessarily want to be a part of the Hollywood lifestyle, and he definitely didn't want to live in Beverly Hills or Malibu or anywhere else where his neighbors would be the people he saw at work every day. That's why he chose "the stolid respectability of Pasadena" for his huge twenty-room, Mediterranean-style mansion instead of "the more gaudy environs of Hollywood," the *Los Angeles Times* reported in a 1970 profile. The Pasadena house was beautifully decorated and more than suitable for hosting dinner parties, though both Florence Henderson and Ann B. Davis said they'd never been invited to visit.

When he gave interviews during the *Brady Bunch* years, talk focused on his work, and he offered few details about his personal life. What little he shared amounted to this: He was divorced; he had a daughter, named Karen, who lived with her mother in Chicago; his parents, Helen and John Sr., who lived on a cattle ranch in Oklahoma, also spent a lot of their time with him at the house in Pasadena; he had a mutt named Stubby and a German shepherd named Sissy (the mother of a puppy he'd gifted to Susan Olsen); and he liked to run, not play tennis or golf like many California residents, to stay in shape.

There were other details he'd share, and sometimes they contradicted each other. He said often he had no intention of remarrying, yet he told a reporter for the *Evening Sun* in Baltimore he'd consider it: "I'd hate to spend the rest of my life alone." He was miserable playing Mike Brady, but he told *TV Guide* he "always look[ed] forward to going to the studio—even to arguing with Sherwood."

And there was the one thing he never, ever talked about with media, or most of the other people around him every day.

* * *

His wife, his TV wife, was the first one on *The Brady Bunch* set to know Robert Reed was gay. She found out during "The Honeymoon."

They were about to film a scene during the pilot episode where Carol and Mike were going to get "lovey-dovey," as Henderson recalled, with lots of kissing. They'd rehearsed the scene, and Reed was fine. But when cameras started to roll, "Bob started complaining about something, and all of a sudden that was the moment that I knew Bob was very nervous about the love scene." Henderson pulled Sherwood Schwartz aside. "I said, 'I really think you should back off, because Bob's gay, and he's having a problem with this scene.' I said, 'Let me handle it.' And they did, and we got the scene, and that's the way it was from then on."

Reed continued to be nervous during such moments, which he and Henderson would usually film at the end of the day, when the kid cast members had gone home. Henderson said she would often "see Bob's heart actually beating through his pajamas," and she had a lot of compassion for him.

Schwartz, too, said he was sympathetic to the difficult position Reed was in. "Here he was, the father of America, and he can't come out of the closet."

Doug Cramer, who knew Reed was gay but said he never talked to him about it, said it was "something everybody was a little nervous about, because it was the sixties."

Though major cultural shifts were happening in the real world, and elsewhere in TV land, sixties and early seventies television viewers probably weren't ready to find out the head of one of their favorite TV families was gay. Other members of the *Brady Bunch* production, as well as a few close friends, were aware of Reed's sexuality. Reed's friend and *Brady* script editor Tam Spiva said the actor had told him during their days at Northwestern that he was gay, although he continued to date women. Even the Brady kids knew.

"I was aware that he had a different lifestyle, but that wasn't something he brought into the set, and it wasn't something that he brought into the relationship," Barry Williams said. "It wasn't something he brought into his professional world."

Reed's personal life did become a much larger part of his professional world, or at least his public world, after his death in 1992.

In the spring of 1991, he was diagnosed as HIV-positive. Later the same year, he was diagnosed with colon cancer. Friend Anne Haney, an actress best known for her role as Greta, Jim Carrey's secretary in *Liar Liar*, and Mrs. Sellner the social worker in *Mrs. Doubtfire*, said Reed made an aggressive plan with his doctors to tackle both health issues. He had surgery for the cancer, and then began chemotherapy, but by the spring of 1992 it became clear he was not going to beat the cancer.

He checked himself into Huntington Memorial Hospital in Pasadena on May 1, 1992, with Haney and his daughter Karen the only visitors he allowed. He died on May 12. When his death certificate information was made public less than two weeks later, colon lymphoma was listed as the official cause of death, with HIV listed as a condition contributing to his death.

Tabloid magazines ran stories about his alleged secret life, and even mainstream media rushed to report the news that the *Brady Bunch* dad had been HIV-positive.

Haney, who would pick up Reed's medications for him to help protect his privacy, and who gave very few interviews about her friend, told *E! True Hollywood Story* producers, "It was not the way he would have liked to be remembered. He would have preferred to be remembered for his body of work rather than his personal life, but he also knew that would never happen."

Reed had maintained a secrecy around his sexuality partly because he truly did guard his private life in all matters that didn't pertain to work. But he was also realistic about how his career opportunities—especially for roles on TV and in movies—would have been impacted in the 1960s and '70s if the fact that he was gay had been common knowledge.

As recently as early 2019, Oscar, Emmy, and Golden Globe–nominated actress Ellen Page said in a Net-a-Porter.com interview that she had been discouraged from being open about being a gay woman, warned that it would be detrimental to her career in Hollywood. She was "pressured—forced, in many cases—to always wear dresses and heels for events and photo shoots."

Matt Dallas, an actor best known as the star of the ABC Family teen sci-fi drama *Kyle XY*, shared similar experiences during a YouTube chat with fans. "I was told to stay in the closet, not talk about my sexuality, to be on every red carpet with a girl on my [arm], because you could not be successful if you were openly gay in the entertainment industry, at least in front of the camera," Dallas said. "Because of the advice that was given to me to stay in the closet, I became very disconnected from who I was."

Given what a difference time *hasn't* made more than fifty years later, it's not difficult to understand why Reed remained in the closet, especially when, as his agent and friend Michael Hartig said, "His work was his life."

That doesn't mean, however, this was an area of Reed's life that was free from the complicated, often surprising choices he would make in other areas of his life. Especially with his post-*Brady* choice of roles.

One of Reed's most critically lauded performances came in a two-part episode of the CBS hospital drama *Medical Center*, which premiered the same year as *The Brady Bunch* and ran for seven seasons.

In the final season opener, "The Fourth Sex: Part 1" and "Part 2," Reed guest-starred as Dr. Pat Caddison, an internationally renowned vascular surgeon who had been working in South Africa. He returned to Los Angeles to share some major news with his good friend Dr. Joe Gannon (series star Chad Everett). Dr. Caddison arrived looking thinner—"softer," as he put it. It was the result of taking female hormones for the two years he'd been off working in South Africa. He completed the hormonal phase of sexual reassignment. Now he wanted "the surgical end of it performed at Medical Center." Specifically, he wanted Dr. Gannon to perform it.

Medical Center was the first television drama to tackle this topic. The storyline unfolded in 1975, more than twenty years after most Americans first became aware of sexual reassignment surgery when the December 1, 1952, issue of the *New York Daily News* ran a front-page story on George Jorgensen. The World War II veteran had traveled to Denmark to undergo one of the first sexual reassignment surgeries (*the* first reassignment that included the use of female hormones), and returned home to New York City in 1953 as Christine Jorgensen, a woman who would become a pioneer not just as a reassignment patient but also as an advocate for transgender people.

The two-part episode was a groundbreaking storyline then, not simply because of the subject matter but because of how thoughtfully the topic was treated. Caddison's case was complicated. He was married, unhappily, and upon hearing about his plans, his wife feared she was to blame, that she had failed to attract him sexually. He assured her she was not the issue. They never should have been married, he said, because he was a transsexual, "a male by the reason of my anatomy. But emotionally…I'm just like you are. Emotionally, I'm a woman," Pat told his wife.

Caddison's young adult son had a problem with his father's sudden announcement, too, as did his wife's sister, Jessica, who happened to be Dr. Gannon's girlfriend. Jessica was also a member of the Medical Center board, and without the board's approval, Gannon could not perform the operation at the hospital. What, not complicated enough? Throw in Caddison's minor heart condition, which gave the board the justification they needed to reject Caddison's request. And one more twist: Another patient at Medical Center, where Caddison once worked, was a macho race car driver, Skip, who might never walk again after a crash. When Caddison tried to assure him he was a man with what Caddison hoped was a temporary problem, the creep (who'd heard hospital gossip about Caddison's surgery) responded, "What would *you* know about being a man?"

Made distraught by loneliness, the negative reactions, and how much he knew he was hurting the people he loved, a drunk Caddison went for a drive and steered his car off a bridge. Gannon wondered if he'd been trying to kill himself. Caddison denied that, but said it was an "attractive idea."

Finally, after Gannon argued Caddison needed the surgery for his mental health, Jessica countered that Caddison's feelings were not the only ones that mattered. He had a family that was being torn apart by the situation, and she thought the committee should deny him the surgery at Medical Center. After another vote, Caddison got the okay, and Gannon successfully performed the reassignment.

While the episodes avoided delving into the medical specifics of the surgery, the end of part two included a reveal of Caddison, post-operation, in a dress and makeup, leaving the hospital to move to another country and practice medicine as a woman.

It's a sensitive portrayal that spent its double length of running time listening to the reactions of all the people Dr. Caddison's decision affected, without judging anyone or belittling anyone's point of view.

"[Writer] Rita Lakin's script is full of strong emotional scenes," Reed said when the episodes premiered. "We all agreed that playing it broadly would have made a mockery of this pioneer effort to examine the reasoning of a person who is convinced he truly belongs to the opposite sex, a woman trapped in a man's body... There's an undercurrent of desperation in this man in turmoil. It was a heavy experience."

"It was such a divergent role for him," *TV Guide* critic Mary Murphy later said. "And the irony of it, of course, is that in his own life, he was struggling with his sexuality. So for him to take this role was, I think, very important for him, a shock for the public."

Though groundbreaking, the episode wasn't entirely comfortable for Reed. He told a reporter for the *Tampa Tribune*, "Sure, I felt uncomfortable in women's clothing and a wig and makeup. That's why I smoked a cigar on location. There were so many jokes we didn't have time to get through them all. At the end, to lighten things, the rest of the cast and crew signed a brassiere and gave it to me."

But much media coverage of the episodes was positive, noting that Lakin's writing was evenhanded and that Reed and the cast gave outstanding performances. Reed earned an Emmy nomination for the role, making him a double nominee at the 1976 ceremony; he was also nominated for playing drama-stirring wealthy businessman Teddy Boylan (another anti–Mike Brady) in ABC's miniseries adaptation of the best-selling novel *Rich Man, Poor Man*.

There was one *Brady*-related moment during the *Medical Center* production.

Florence Henderson was guest-starring in "Torment," the third season-seven episode of *Medical Center*, which would air right after Reed's two-parter. Production on episodes two and three overlapped. She was playing against her *Brady* type, too: Her character, a nurse named Jenny, was in love with, and pregnant by but not married to, a much older man.

One day, Henderson was sitting in a makeup chair on set and looked over at the tall woman sitting beside her. She thought the woman looked familiar, but she couldn't quite place her. It was Reed, getting into hair and makeup for his post-operation scenes as Dr. Caddison. Neither of the former *Brady* marrieds knew the other was also making an appearance on the show.

Another surprising entry on Reed's post-*Brady* résumé was a 1984 guest appearance on *Hotel*, the Aaron Spelling–produced primetime soap set in a luxury hotel in San Francisco. He guest-starred in three episodes of the ABC drama, but in season two's "Transitions," he played sportscaster Larry Dawson, who was in town for a working vacation. His wife, Maggie (played by daytime soap legend Deidre Hall), and son Kevin (played by River Phoenix) were going to meet up with him, and Maggie decided to show up early to surprise her husband.

She got a bellhop to let her into his room at the St. Gregory with her luggage. Hearing the shower running, she decided to stretch out on the bed and greet her husband when he walked out of the bathroom. Maggie was the one who was surprised, though, when Larry walked out of the bathroom wrapped in a towel...with another man in a towel, his producer, Biff, right behind him.

Maggie would soon find out that not only was her husband having an affair, he'd been involved with Biff for two years. The *Hotel* story had far more drama than a whole lifetime of *Brady Bunch* episodes could have served up, but it did have one thing in common with *The Bunch*: Just as the Bradys could resolve any problem in half an hour, *Hotel* wrapped up the Dawsons' marital meltdown in just twice the time, the drama series equivalent of the Bradys' quick-fix closure. Larry wanted to maintain his marriage and continue his relationship with Biff. Though heartbroken, magnanimous Maggie told Larry he should be with Biff, and only Biff. Then she checked out of the St. Gregory and Larry's life, wishing him happiness on her way home.

Robert Reed, meanwhile, remained in the closet as far as the public was concerned. But maybe these roles on *Medical Center* and *Hotel* weren't just about trying to shed his Mike Brady image (a futile effort, as nothing that has emerged about the actor's professional or personal life has canceled his legacy as one of TV's all-time favorite fathers). Maybe they were also his way of honoring his own life, of injecting some reality, some of the more modern storytelling he tried to get Sherwood Schwartz to inject into *The Brady Bunch* for all those years into his work. Maybe?

* * *

As *Brady Bunch* fans continue to obsess about how a man who played the quintessential problem solver and family man on-screen could have felt so differently behind the scenes about what he was sending out over the airwaves, the ultimate question about Robert Reed remains: If he hated the original series and the experience of making it so much, why did he keep returning for all the spin-offs?

The answer to that question becomes even more puzzling when you consider just how dramatically production on the final episode of season five, which turned out to be the *Brady Bunch* series finale, unfolded.

Reed's complaints about the script for "The Hair-Brained Scheme" carried over into rehearsal for the episode, where the actor refused to say his lines. Sherwood Schwartz was beyond frustrated. Ratings for the show had been sliding, the network had forced him to add Cousin Oliver to the final six episodes of the season in an (unsuccessful) attempt to boost those viewership numbers, and a sixth season of *The Brady Bunch* on the ABC schedule was far from a guarantee. The last thing he wanted to deal with, on the last episode of the season, was another battle with Reed. So he decided he wouldn't.

If Reed didn't want to read the words Schwartz had written, he wouldn't have to. The producer wrote Mike Brady out of the script, sending the architect on a business trip. He told Reed to stay home, take the week off.

Reed had gotten what he wanted. He didn't have to read Schwartz's words that he found so ridiculous. But he wasn't happy. The solution, he felt, wasn't to remove him from the equation, it was to remove the script, the storyline. He, in fact, was not *going* to be removed. He showed up to Stage 5 on filming day, telling Schwartz he was interested in what was going on. Florence Henderson recalled how strange it was: Reed sitting in the background, watching the episode proceed without him, realizing he'd pushed Schwartz too far this time.

Schwartz asked him to move to the side, out of the cast's eyeline, as it would be awkward for them, especially the kids, to see him as they were filming. They had gotten the new script, in which Mike/Bob was no longer involved. They knew *something* was going on.

Paramount executives had even offered to send a pair of security guards to Stage 5 and carry Reed off the set if necessary. Schwartz told them, emphatically, that was not to happen. He would not have the children traumatized by seeing this man they respected and adored taken away like that.

Finally, after one more plea by Sherwood Schwartz, Reed retreated to his dressing room.

In what is perhaps the only made-for-TV movie that is a dramatic reenactment of a TV series finale, Fox's 2000 film *Unauthorized: Brady Bunch—The Final Days* mashed up selections from *Growing Up Brady* with *Brady* lore and played out the production of the final episode, focusing mostly on Reed's meltdown about the storyline and his refusal to stay away from the set when he was told to stay home. Also included were nods to cast romances and the kids' demands to have their singing featured more prominently and regularly throughout the series. As the title warns, there is no official *Brady*-related involvement in the movie, though it is a guilty-pleasure must-see.

But back in the reality of 1974, Schwartz had had enough. He told Paramount and ABC that if the show were to be greenlit for a sixth season, it would be without Robert Reed. He was going to fire his leading man and replace him with a new actor.

Lloyd Schwartz had a thought about who might be a good fit for the part: "Robert Foxworth. I thought he looked a lot like Mike Brady." The future *Falcon Crest* and *Six Feet Under* actor was never approached about the role, because the Schwartzes developed an alternative scenario for a potential sixth season.

They were going to kill off Mike Brady.

Carol would become a widow (again?), and the kids would spend the next year helping their mom find new love. (Remember, in *Brady* Standard Time, where troubles are resolved in thirty minutes, minus commercials, it shouldn't take more than a summer hiatus to mend a widow's broken heart.)

Lloyd Schwartz confirmed Cousin Oliver also would have returned in season six. Instead, the whole *Brady* family learned they'd just finished their final episode together—temporarily—and it had all ended in such an ugly way.

In the end—the messy, dramatic end—it all came back to family. Robert Reed had never wanted to be a part of the Brady family to begin with. He continued to want out of the family throughout the series. But, after he finally got what he wanted, after he was relieved of his duties as Mike Brady, father of six, husband of Carol, employer and friend of Alice, he couldn't make himself actually leave the gang behind.

And that's because of family. He loved his castmates, kids and adults.

The angriest, most bitter stories Sherwood or Lloyd Schwartz would tell about how impossible Reed was to deal with were always tempered by a recognition that he had great affection for the children playing his TV offspring.

His kindnesses toward them are *Brady* legends.

Like the Super 8 cameras he purchased for Susan, Mike, Eve, Chris, Maureen, and Barry as Christmas gifts in 1971, encouraging them to learn more about their jobs, their industry, than simply being in front of the camera (and leading to footage that would be collected for the 1995 CBS special *Brady Bunch Home Movies*). In *Brady Bunch Home Movies*, Mike Lookinland said his career as a cameraman on TV and movie projects was sparked by Reed's Super 8 gift. As a kid on the *Brady* set, he loved to hang out around the camera equipment, watching and learning how the crew operated all the fascinating tools of their trade. When he got his very own camera from Reed, he had the chance to make his own movies (clips of which were shown in the special) and realized his love for being behind the camera as well as in front of it. He even showed Susan Olsen that he had kept the Super 8 for more than two decades...and it still had a roll of film in it.

He once planned and hosted an all-day fishing trip for them.

And there was the incredible post-season-four trip to New York and London, which Reed booked, paid for, and chaperoned. With all six kids, his parents, and *Brady* set teacher Frances Whitfield along, he wanted to expose his young co-stars to the city he'd loved so much when he attended the Royal Academy of Dramatic Art. On the way to London, the group stopped in New York City for a sleepover at the Plaza hotel, then spent four days on the *Queen Elizabeth 2* en route to England, where (as was also included in the *Brady Bunch Home Movies* footage) they toured Stratford-upon-

Avon (home of William Shakespeare's birthplace and gravesite), watched the Changing of the Guard at Buckingham Palace, and shopped at the famous Harrods department store.

Despite his problems with *The Brady Bunch* as a show and with the Schwartzes as those with creative control of it, the *Brady* bunch had become his ersatz family. And not just in a "we play one on TV" kind of way. "I firmly believe that we were his family," Florence Henderson said. "We were his real family."

Reed had a daughter, Karen, born during his five-year marriage to his college sweetheart, dancer and fellow theater student Marilyn Rosenberg. The couple married in 1954 and moved to London while Reed attended RADA, then to New York City while he worked in the theater. After a brief stint in Chicago, in 1957 they moved to Los Angeles, where many young actors were heading as they became more and more in demand for television roles.

Karen was born in 1958. But the next year, Reed came home from work one day to find that Marilyn had left with Karen and all the furnishings in their home. "Her leaving was a big surprise," Tam Spiva said in a 2001 A&E *Biography* episode on Reed (hosted by Barry Williams). After the Reeds' July 1959 divorce, Marilyn and Karen moved to Chicago, where Marilyn remarried and her new husband adopted Karen. "At first, he thought that would be the best thing for [Karen]," Spiva said, "and I know that's what he was trying to think about: her." Reed didn't see Karen as often as he would have liked, Spiva said, and that frustrated and saddened him.

An only child, Reed also had a complicated relationship with his parents. His mother and father owned a ranch in Oklahoma, but they lived with him for large periods of time in his home in Pasadena. When his father died in 1975, his mother stayed with him for several more years, until they had a falling-out. Because of how private he was, he didn't share the details of their quarrel, but his mom, Helen, moved back to Oklahoma, and Reed told

Florence Henderson he hadn't spoken with his mother in more than half a decade. Helen, who died in 2002, did not visit Reed in the hospital before he died.

The Bradys, then, were the most constant presence in his life, for the longest period of time. He was a part of the young cast's lives for a key period in each of their childhoods, and he came to think of himself as a true father figure to them. They loved and respected him, and these relationships came without the complicated feelings he had about missing his daughter and trying to make decisions that would create a stable childhood for her, free from being torn between two parents who lived two thousand miles apart.

"I often felt guilty…all the love he wanted to give to [Karen], we got," Susan Olsen said.

So when it came time to do *The Brady Bunch Variety Hour* on ABC, and *The Brady Girls Get Married* reunion movie and the short-lived spin-off series *The Brady Brides* at NBC, Reed signed on as quickly as everyone else. The *Variety Hour* was a Sherwood Schwartz–less venture. But both Sherwood and Lloyd were *Brady Brides* producers. Despite the script wars of the original series, Reed agreed to the reunion, saying no one else was going to walk his (TV) daughters down the aisle. He even gave up a week of pay for a Broadway show he was doing—the comedy-thriller *Deathtrap*, in which he played another gay character—to fly back to Los Angeles and appear in the 1981 reunion movie.

Ditto *A Very Brady Christmas* TV movie (1988), a *Brady*-themed episode of the NBC comedy *Day by Day* in 1989, and *The Bradys*, a 1990 spin-off dramedy series. Reed returned for them all, even when some of his TV children didn't.

He liked to work. But he really liked to work with his *Brady Bunch* family.

Their reunion on *The Bradys* lasted for just six episodes in 1990, and it would be the final time Reed would work with the kids and Florence and Ann B.

The experience was like old times in many ways. Reed once again fought with Schwartz about storylines. He complained so much that Henderson, finally fed up with his attitude, snapped at him. She and the rest of the cast had experienced the highs and lows of post–*Brady Bunch* career opportunities (for some, a lack thereof), and she reminded him that some of them were happy to be there, together, and well paid for the project. "I think had he not been forced to lead a double life, it would have dissipated a lot of his anger and frustration," she said.

But she also noticed he looked frail and tired. She worried something might be wrong with his health.

In the meantime, he reunited with Karen, and after his HIV and cancer diagnosis, spent most of his time with her and his friend Anne.

When, in May 1992, he had to admit he wasn't going to beat the diseases, he reached out to his TV wife. Reed and Henderson had not only kept in touch after *The Brady Bunch*, they had continued to occasionally work together. The two guest-starred on *The Love Boat*—as Carol and Mike Brady, in a 1987 episode that also featured TV stars from *Leave It to Beaver* and *Father Knows Best* playing their characters from those classic family sitcoms—and in 1989, they co-starred at the La Mirada Theatre in La Mirada, California, in *Alone Together*, a play about middle-aged marrieds who don't get to enjoy their empty nest because their adult children move back into the family home. That they kept playing a married couple spoke not only to typecasting but also to their comfortable friendship and genuine affection and respect for each other. Reed broke the news about his devastating prognosis to Henderson himself. And then he asked her to help him break the news to the rest of their family. Reed asked Henderson to call Maureen, Barry, Eve,

Chris, Susan, and Mike, and let them know he was sick. Each Brady kid had the chance to talk with him on the phone before he passed away.

Sherwood Schwartz and Robert Reed never worked together again after *The Bradys*. There were plenty of times when each of the men wished they had never worked together in the first place.

Schwartz, though, ultimately acknowledged that Bob Reed starring as Mike Brady had been the right thing for the TV family.

"Mike Brady was there for his kids, offering wisdom and guidance," Schwartz wrote in *Brady, Brady, Brady*. "Robert Reed brought qualities of integrity and honesty to the role. That cannot be denied, so as much pain as he caused us, I'm glad Robert Reed was Mike Brady."

CHAPTER SEVEN

Keep on Groovin'

Production of *The Brady Bunch* series finale certainly did not lack drama.

But the episode itself, aired on March 8, 1974, was anticlimactic. Greg graduated high school and his dad wasn't in attendance. Cousin Oliver uttered the word "sex"—only the third time it was said throughout the entire series—and also said the final words of the series. Not bad for a character who's accused of ensuring *The Brady Bunch* jumped the shark before jumping the shark was even a thing.

Some members of the cast didn't feel so blasé about the series end, though. Ann B. Davis, always the most laid-back, happiest-to-be-working member of the cast, would have loved to continue the show for several more seasons. And Maureen McCormick, who got a call about the show's cancellation from Sherwood Schwartz one evening just as her family finished dinner, broke into "uncontrollable sobs" when she learned the Bradys were splitting up. "The years I did *The Brady Bunch* were five of the happiest years of my life. It was a marvelous show, and I loved everyone involved with it," she told *16* magazine.

Of course, there was sadness for everyone that this production that had been such a major part of their lives for half a decade—during which time they had celebrated marriages, babies, real-life graduations, and worn enough polyester to stretch from the Grand Canyon to Kings Island—was over. But there was also more than a little relief, and not just on the part of Robert Reed.

The last year of the series, even aside from Reed's finale fit and the cold reception to Cousin Oliver, had been a strained one for the once-happy TV family. With a sixth-season renewal looming, contracts would have to be renegotiated. The *Brady* kid stars and their parents were excited about those prospects, as they imagined there would be raises all around. Sherwood Schwartz, as the producer, worried that too many demands by the cast's representatives could factor negatively into Paramount and ABC's decision about whether or not there would be a sixth season.

After all, ratings were respectable, and *The Bunch* still had a loyal fan base on Friday nights, but their time-slot competition, NBC's *Sanford and Son*, had finished the 1972–73 season as the second-highest-rated show on television, just behind *All in the Family*. *Mission: Impossible* and *The Sonny & Cher Comedy Hour*, which shared the 8:00 p.m. spot on CBS, pulled away their fair share of viewers, too. And with the *Brady* kids aging—only in Hollywood is twelve, the age Susan Olsen was during season five, considered "aged"—studio and network executives worried the show wouldn't maintain the same appeal to as wide a group of young viewers. Hence: Welcome, Cousin Oliver, who, the thinking went among ABC executives, would open up storyline possibilities that would once again appeal to the youngest-of-the-young demographic. Viewers were unimpressed.

A long list of demands in new contract negotiations, then, might tip the show over into the cancellation heap, Schwartz worried, and rightly so. As Barry Williams put it, the Brady kids were about to start feeling their oats.

Before *The Partridge Family* became a hit on TV and the music charts, the Brady kids recorded an album. *Merry Christmas from the Brady Bunch* (also known as *Christmas with the Brady Bunch*) was just what it sounds like: an album filled with the kid cast warbling covers of classic holiday songs like "O Come, All Ye Faithful" and "O Holy Night," "Jingle Bells" and "Silver Bells," "Frosty the Snowman" and "Rudolph the Red-Nosed Reindeer." The music, released just before Christmas during the show's second season, was not...good. There is something charming about hearing Susan Olsen's cute little voice chirping about Frosty and Mike Lookinland doing a delightfully off-key version of "The First Noel." But it's pretty safe to assume a major selling point of the album was its cover, with the Brady kids in the Brady living room, wearing their PJs, opening gifts around the Christmas tree. Even Tiger is in the photo, with a bow on his head.

The Christmas album failed to break into the *Billboard* 200 album chart, but, with the record sales of the *Partridge Family* band in mind, executives at Paramount's record label, Famous Music, decided it was silly not to have the *Brady* gang release more music. After all, unlike the Partridges, *all* the Brady kids were actually doing their own singing. This was considered a good thing, even if Christopher Knight was not at all comfortable with or confident in his vocal prowess.

Meet the Brady Bunch and *The Kids from the Brady Bunch* followed in 1972, with covers of contemporary pop songs, but more importantly, the Bradys singing the tunes they'd performed on the show. "Baby I'm-a Want You" and "American Pie" covers were not the reason to purchase *Meet the Brady Bunch*—they were mere fillers, and added to the fun of hearing the *Brady* kids sing pop hits—but it was the place to find recordings of "Time to Change" and "We Can Make the World a Whole Lot Brighter," the songs "The Brady Six" recorded in one of the true classic *Brady Bunch* episodes, "Dough Re Mi" from season three. The album peaked at 108 on the *Billboard* album chart.

The Kids from the Brady Bunch album, with a cover that used rebuses to indicate the song titles found on the vinyl inside and drawings of the cast from their spin-off cartoon series *The Brady Kids*, included Bradyized versions of "Saturday in the Park" and "Love Me Do" alongside Brady gems "Keep On" and "It's a Sunshine Day," from what is arguably the best *Brady Bunch* episode, season four's "Amateur Nite." The album was heavily promoted, with the record label running an ad in *Billboard* magazine that declared: "When the *Brady Bunch* launch an album, they do it on TV!"

The Kids from the Brady Bunch didn't chart, but it did help spark more rock-star dreams in the Brady kids' heads. Backed by a group of parents eager to see their children maximize their profits, the cast—calling themselves the Brady Kids—hired a pair of producers, Joe Seiter and Ray Reese, to help them prepare a tour show. They spent weeks learning a setlist of songs, along with choreography for each tune, rehearsing at Barry Williams' house one day and Maureen McCormick's the next. The mothers sewed the kids' costumes, plenty of bright colors and fringes included. During their hiatus after season three, they planned to tour the country.

But first, their official debut as the Brady Kids came, appropriately enough, on television. On January 14, 1972, a Friday night (the same night the "Dough Re Mi" episode of *The Bunch* premiered on ABC), CBS aired *The Entertainer of the Year Awards*, a special hosted by Ed Sullivan and honoring Hollywood stars chosen by the American Guild of Variety Artists. Carol Burnett, Flip Wilson, Barbra Streisand, and the Carpenters were among the recipients at the event, taped at Caesars Palace in Las Vegas, and the Brady Kids joined Sonny & Cher, Don Rickles, and Tanya the trained elephant (who has her own IMDb.com page) in saluting the winners with performances. The Bradys, in mismatched outfits that included everything from suit jackets and ties to shorts and go-go boots, sang "Time to Change," after they had waited for the stage to be cleaned after Tanya's appearance.

When season three came to a close, the Brady Kids took their show on the road. On Memorial Day, 1972, the group performed at the National Orange Show in San Bernardino, California. The nearly two-week-long festival celebrated the citrus industry, and Bob Hope, *Bonanza* star Michael Landon, *Gunsmoke's* Ken Curtis, and *McCloud* star Dennis Weaver were other big acts performing in free stage shows throughout the May 18–29 event. Dozens of friends and family members were in the crowd cheering the Brady Kids on, as were almost two hundred members of the Barry Williams and Maureen McCormick fan clubs. The group sang Mac Davis's "I Believe in Music" and Ray Stevens's (the "Everything Is Beautiful" guy) "Can We Get to That."

An appearance on *American Bandstand* followed. During the next year, the Kids played the Minnesota State Fair with Tony Orlando and Dawn, who had the number one song in the country with "Tie a Yellow Ribbon Round the Ole Oak Tree" (in her book *Here's the Story*, Maureen McCormick professed a crush on Orlando, joking he could tie that yellow ribbon around her). The group also shared a bill with the 5th Dimension, did a string of shows at Knott's Berry Farm, and by the summer of 1973 was the headliner for a "World of Sid & Marty Krofft Presents" showcase at the Hollywood Bowl (*Bugaloos*, *Lidsville*, and *H.R. Pufnstuf* characters co-starred).

They were enjoying this new layer of *Brady*-related success. After several seasons of spending most of their time on Stage 5, they were out and about, getting to experience *Brady* fandom up close and personal. Sometimes *too* up close, and too personal, as fans would chase them, pulling at the fringe (there was so much fringe) on their costumes, and even yanking out patches of their hair. Their appearances in teen fan magazines became more frequent, with features like "Chris: Is He Your Knight in Shining Armor???" and "Eve Plumb Plays 20 Questions."

With a fifth season of the series on the horizon, the Kids and their parents got together and hired a manager, Harvey Shotz, who they thought could take their singing careers to the next level. Shotz encouraged them to demand their singing efforts become a bigger part of the series. Egged on by the high of live performances and immediate audience feedback and, as Williams would later admit, feeling emboldened, the Kids and Shotz requested a sit-down with Sherwood and Lloyd Schwartz to share their thoughts on season five.

It did not go well.

Father and son producers were both blindsided by their young stars' requests, which included salary increases, more exposure for the singing group (they wanted to sing in roughly half of all upcoming episodes), and more input into the storylines. Basically, with heads full of opinions of their own, and plenty shared with them by their parents and Shotz, the Kids made clear to the Schwartzes that they wanted the direction of the show to change, and they wanted some control over how it changed. Negotiations for a sixth season might become very difficult if their requests were not met.

Sherwood, ever the peacemaker, ever the diplomat, even after all those years of Robert Reed denigrating his long, successful career, played nice again. Though visibly stunned by what the kids were demanding, he put a strained smile on his face and assured his cast he'd think about everything they said.

But, as Williams himself summed up, "We had stabbed him in the back...six times."

The united front of the Brady Kids (and the Parents of the Brady Kids) soon fell apart. The Brady girls decided they didn't want to perform as a bubblegum pop group any longer, and the parents, who had once been good friends as they spent all those days together on Stage 5, no longer were one big happy family behind the family. Interests and priorities had diverged. Though the kids continued to get along well enough to film season five, the attempt at Partridge Family–like music success had caused a softening of the once-tight connection the actors and the Schwartzes had spent years building.

When Sherwood and Lloyd found out *The Brady Bunch* was being canceled—news delivered to them during an industry lunch by Paramount executive Bruce Lansbury (brother of *Murder, She Wrote* star Angela, and the name featured in the *Brady Bunch* end credits as "Vice President, Creative Affairs")—they were sad, but also relieved. For a series that wrapped up every episode with a happy ending, this particular chapter of the *Brady Bunch* history was unusual: It was going to just fizzle out.

* * *

With the household at 4222 Clinton Way closing its front doors to primetime audiences, it seemed likely that *The Brady Bunch* would fade out of viewers' consciousness pretty quickly, never to make a lasting impact on TV or pop culture history. But a funny thing happened on the way to obscurity: syndication.

Once again, *The Brady Bunch* owed a big debt of gratitude to Lucille Ball.

It was the success of Lucy's 1968 movie, *Yours, Mine and Ours*, that helped Paramount and ABC decide Sherwood Schwartz's long-gestating TV show about a blended family could be a hit.

And it was Lucy and husband Desi Arnaz's entrepreneurial plans for *I Love Lucy*, via their Desilu Productions, that paved the way for television reruns and syndication.

When *I Love Lucy* premiered in 1951, most television shows originated from New York. Lucy—pregnant with first child Lucie—and Desi were committed to remaining in Los Angeles, which meant the show would be performed live in LA and taped for broadcast to the rest of the country. Taping meant kinescope, a method that involved using a film camera to record a program as it was displayed on a TV monitor. The quality was not good, and no one on the Desilu team or at *I Love Lucy*'s network, CBS, was happy that the majority of the viewing audience would have to watch the program via this shoddy picture. Ball and Arnaz instead wanted to use a three-camera system and shoot the show directly onto 35 mm film, which would not only produce a better picture for airings of the show but would also preserve each episode with a quality that meant it could be rebroadcast. Thank you, Desilu, for making reruns possible.

This production method was more expensive than kinescope, however, something CBS and *I Love Lucy* sponsor Philip Morris would not support, until Lucy and Desi agreed to take a huge chunk—$1,000 a week (equal to nearly $10,000 a week in 2019)—out of their own paychecks and funnel it into the production. As compensation, they shrewdly demanded they retain ownership of the show, and they later sold reruns as syndication packages, for which they reaped millions of dollars in profits.

I Love Lucy was a huge ratings success during its original run, finishing four of its six seasons (including its final season) as the top-rated show on TV. It continued to be successful in reruns on

CBS and when it was sold into syndication markets. More than sixty years after the show ended, CBS (which now holds the rights to the series) continues to make more than $20 million a year in profits from *I Love Lucy*.

Desilu's legacy as the television syndication pioneer benefitted shows like *Leave It to Beaver*, *The Odd Couple*, *Star Trek*, and *The Brady Bunch* to a degree Lucy and Desi could not have imagined when they were simply trying to make sure viewers saw their show in as high-quality a picture as possible.

Those aforementioned series, unlike *I Love Lucy*, were not huge hits during their original airings, but all became classics when fans had the chance to catch them in syndication. *Leave It to Beaver* was never a top 30 show, but beginning with off-network syndication airings—when a show is licensed to networks other than the one it originally aired on—the 1957–63 comedy gained new generations of fans. The retro TV gem became a favorite on TV Land, TBS, and now MeTV, and because of its syndication success in the 1970s and '80s, sparked a 1984–85 sequel/revival series, *Still the Beaver*, on the Disney Channel, retitled *The New Leave It to Beaver* when it moved to TBS from 1986 to 1989.

The Odd Couple, which aired as *The Brady Bunch*'s Friday night lineup companion on ABC, also never finished a season among the top 30 highest-rated shows, despite three Emmy nominations as Outstanding Comedy Series, and Emmy wins by stars Jack Klugman and Tony Randall as lead actors. The Neil Simon–penned story of two radically different roommates had already been a successful Broadway play and movie hit when Garry Marshall developed it for Paramount Television. After its 1970–75 run on ABC, the show lived on even more successfully as a syndicated series, cementing its place as a genuine classic that was included on *Rolling Stone*'s list of the 100 greatest TV series of all time, the list of the 101 best-written TV series of all time from the Writers Guild of

America and *TV Guide*, and *Time* magazine's 100 best TV shows ever. *The Odd Couple* has been remade as a TV series twice: a 1982–83 series (titled *The New Odd Couple*) with *Sanford and Son* star Demond Wilson and *Barney Miller's* Ron Glass, and a 2015 version starring *Friends'* Matthew Perry and *Reno 911!* co-creator Thomas Lennon. The series even spawned a short-lived 1975 Saturday morning cartoon remake, *The Oddball Couple*, about polite, well-organized writer cat Spiffy and his rude, messy roomie, photographer Fleabag the dog.

Star Trek, meanwhile, is the only other moderately rated series to build the same kind of decades-spanning, multimedia fandom via syndication as *The Brady Bunch*. The original *Trek* series ran on NBC from 1966 to 1969, and never finished a season among the top 30 series on TV. The show lived on for three seasons in large part because of an ongoing fan letter-writing campaign that included written messages of support from Isaac Asimov and New York governor Nelson Rockefeller. When the show began airing in syndication in 1969, a large fanbase was all set to watch the series again, and love it even more the second, third, twentieth time around (never underestimate the devotion of the most devoted Trekkies).

Syndicated viewings, in fact, can be seen as the earliest form of binge-watching. Where, during these shows' original runs, viewers had to wait at least a week—longer during summer hiatus—to see a new episode, syndication meant they could often see a new episode every day (strip syndication, or daily airings in the same time slot, is the syndication format in which most series thrive).

In the case of *The Brady Bunch* in syndication, several episodes often aired in mini blocks during after-school hours. Even with 117 episodes total, one-per-day airings meant the strip would be repeated at least twice a year. If stations aired two episodes a day, Monday through Friday, which many did, viewers could potentially see each episode four times each year. Add in marathon airings, and it's no surprise that you'd be hard-pressed to find anyone who grew up in the 1970s, '80s, and '90s who doesn't know the lyrics to the *Brady* theme song, who hasn't used the phrases "something suddenly came up," "Marcia, Marcia, Marcia," and "pork chops and applesauce," or who can't tell you, in detail, why the Silver Platters needed to come up with $56.23, tout de suite.

It's also no surprise that, as of the show's thirtieth anniversary, it was estimated all 117 episodes of *The Brady Bunch* had already aired more than 100,000 times…*each*. One hundred thousand chances for the earworm that is the theme song to get stuck in your head, one hundred thousand times to be comforted by the sight of Alice stirring something on the stove in her familiar blue dress, one hundred thousand times to wish you were a Brady. These airings were chances for viewers of every changing age group to memorize the show, identify with the characters and their problems, and allow *The Brady Bunch* to become a permanent part of their culture and their childhood memories.

In his 2008 book on the use of popular culture in counseling, author and professor Lawrence C. Rubin wrote that, from the time *The Brady Bunch* began its syndication run in September 1975 through 2007, "at least one episode of the show has been broadcast in some United States location every day of every year."

With more recent syndicated series, especially those still on the air in first run, syndication success can mean a boost of viewership and fandom for the show's current seasons. *The Big Bang Theory*, which ended its twelve-season run on CBS in May 2019, began airing syndicated repeats multiple times a week on TBS and local Fox stations in September 2011. That coincided with the fifth season of the show's CBS run, which saw a significant jump in ratings: a 16 percent increase in the average number of viewers from season four.

Syndication success on the scale achieved by *Star Trek* and *The*

Brady Bunch has meant nearly fifty years each of spin-off series, stage shows, big-screen movies, books by and about the cast members and the productions, national fan conventions, merchandise from cookie jars to interactive Hallmark ornaments, adult film parodies, amusement park rides, and Saturday morning cartoons.

But only one of the syndication superstars had its own variety show.

* * *

The Brady Bunch was an immediate hit as a syndication offering. In an ad in *Broadcasting* magazine before the 1975 NATPE (National Association of Television Program Executives) convention in Atlanta, Paramount Television Sales boasted that the show had drawn more than twenty-six million viewers every Friday night on ABC, and 85 percent of them were under the age of fifty. The syndicated *Brady Bunch* had already been sold in the New York, Los Angeles, Chicago, Philadelphia, Boston, San Francisco, Detroit, St. Louis, Pittsburgh, and Washington, DC, markets, so if buyers elsewhere wanted to snag the top new syndication offering for attracting young women in the 18–49 and 18–34 age groups, the PTS ad invited them to visit suite 1736 at the Hyatt Regency Hotel to seal a deal.

Other markets quickly signed up for the show, and viewers tuned in in big numbers, much to the surprise of media reporters. "Incredible as it may seem," *Toledo Blade* reporter Norman Dresser wrote, *The Brady Bunch* was the number one show in local ratings in November 1975 when it aired in the 7:00 p.m. time slot on WTOL-TV in Toledo, Ohio. Dresser quoted a WTOL executive saying "Toledo is a funny town" to explain how, in Dresser's words, this "ancient and rather hokey series" snagged four spots in the top 10 ratings of local programming. *The Brady Bunch* was airing five days a week in nearly 150 markets, and by the time presidential debates were aired in 1976, ratings for the syndicated *Brady Bunch* topped ratings for the vice-presidential debate—the first vice-presidential debate in history—between Bob Dole and Walter Mondale. In a poll conducted shortly before the debate, roughly 50 percent of voters said they didn't know what either candidate stood for. And apparently, finding out, at least during this televised meeting between the two, was less important than *Brady* reruns.

A newspaper columnist summed up *Brady* success for a young reader from Connecticut who wrote in to say she hoped the series would go away because her sister watched it all the time. "*The Brady Bunch* has done very well in syndicated reruns, and it looks like the show will be around for some time," the *Brady* skeptic was told. "Plan your outdoor activity around the time your sister watches the adventures of the Bradys."

Another young *Brady* viewer was much happier about the syndicated Bradys' ubiquitous presence on his TV set, even though it cost him his allowance.

Tommy Russell was a second-grader at Edison Elementary School in Hammond, Indiana, in 1975. He spent his afternoons, as so many children did during *The Brady Bunch*'s syndicated airings on local TV stations' after-school schedules, happily parked in front of his family's television set, catching up with the adventures of the Brady six.

In season five's "Mail Order Hero," Bobby Brady got himself into a pickle with his friends when he told them he knew NFL superstar Joe Namath personally. (Apparently Bobby had learned nothing from Marcia's Davy Jones promises in season three.)

It just so happened that Namath was in town to play in an exhibition game, which was bad news for Bobby: His friends expected him to introduce them to the Super Bowl MVP quarterback. Bobby called the stadium to try to talk to Namath, and left a message with his phone number—555-6161—asking that Namath return his call.

"I was sitting there, and I'm like, 'Well, if he's sitting by the phone, and he's waiting on Joe Namath to call him, then he's not doing anything,'" the all-grown-up Tom Russell said. "So I decided to give him a call."

Tommy tried the number several times; five, according to the phone bill his surprised mom would soon receive, with long-distance charges totaling $3.50. He never got to connect with Bobby, but he did pay for the attempts. Mom Janie made him give up a few weeks of his allowance to cover the cost.

"Back then, I had no clue that things were being taped and aired later, or that the episode [originally] aired a year earlier," said Russell with a laugh. "I was under the impression that if I'd seen him, and he was giving out his phone number, then I could talk to him."

Mrs. Russell teased him about the calls from time to time, and his grandmother was so tickled by his efforts to chat with his favorite fictional friend that she shared the story with a reporter at the *Times* newspaper in Hammond. On January 8, 1976, a *Times* headline read "Boy 'Lives' TV Series," with details on how Tommy "lives and dies with *The Brady Bunch*," and how he'd also lost phone privileges for making those unapproved long-distance calls. A clipping of the article is saved in one of his late mom's photo albums.

Tom remained a *Brady* fan, even while he had to make up for his lost allowance by shoveling snow for neighbors, sometimes earning a dollar in cash, sometimes an orange and a pack of Juicy Fruit gum. "I couldn't relate to the older [Bradys], but Bobby, being younger, I could kind of relate to him. I'm a middle child. I could relate to him because you still had to deal with older people. I've got a brother that's four years older and a sister seven years younger than I am."

Today, the Nashville-based truck driver still watches the show when he catches an episode on MeTV. "I was telling my girlfriend the other day that I can barely remember things that happened two or three weeks ago, but I got all the *Brady Bunch* names down. I can't tell you what I ate a week ago, but I can tell you all about *Brady Bunch.*"

Does he remember what he would have said to Bobby if he could have talked to him on the phone?

He laughed. "I have no clue. Maybe just, 'I'm a big fan. How's everything going? What are you doing? I see you on TV.'"

* * *

This runaway syndication success meant new fans were drawn to the series, and then–ABC president Fred Silverman took notice. Maybe, he thought, *The Brady Bunch* had life left in it. And if it did, he wanted the show back on his network. In 1976, less than two years after the show's series finale aired, he had the perfect idea for a test run.

Seeking to lure the young demographic to ABC's Friday nights (the same primetime spot that had been reserved for the Bradys), Silverman had matched teen-heartthrob singer Donny Osmond and his sister Marie with kids TV producers Sid and Marty Krofft to create *Donny & Marie*. Both Osmonds had released hit records— Donny with "Go Away Little Girl" and "Puppy Love," Marie with "Paper Roses"—and after Silverman saw them co-host *The Mike Douglas Show* for a week in 1974, he thought a variety show was the perfect spotlight for the duo.

Donny & Marie was an instant hit, with its combination of Donny-and-Marie musical duets (always accompanied by cheesy choreography and color-coordinated outfits sometimes designed by Bob Mackie), even cheesier comedy bits with guest stars like Ruth Buzzi, Suzanne Somers, and Paul Lynde, and, cheesier still, a giant ice skating rink on which the Osmond siblings and the Ice Vanities skaters performed themed routines.

The show featured a who's who of seventies entertainers as guest stars, including Lucille Ball, Milton Berle, Farrah Fawcett, the Harlem Globetrotters, Redd Foxx, Olivia Newton-John, Betty White, the cast of *Happy Days*, Kristy McNichol, and the Bradys.

Four Bradys, to be exact: Florence Henderson, Maureen Mc-Cormick, Susan Olsen, and Mike Lookinland, who appeared on the October 8, 1976, episode. Henderson sang with "I'm a little bit country" Marie and "I'm a little bit rock 'n' roll" Donny, while all the Bradys participated in a spoof of the soap opera spoof *Mary Hartman, Mary Hartman* and sang in the show-closing Renaissance Faire–themed song-and-dance number that also included fellow guest star Chad Everett.

The *Brady* cast's appearance on *Donny & Marie* was such a success that, less than two months later, they'd be debuting their own variety show on ABC, *The Brady Bunch Hour* (also known as *The Brady Bunch Variety Hour*).

The *Brady* cast had filmed the *Donny & Marie* episode in September, and by Thanksgiving week in November, a set that included a 50,000-gallon swimming pool had been constructed at KTLA Studios (the same studio that hosted *Donny & Marie*) for the *Brady Variety Hour*. Bruce Vilanch, the future Emmy-winning writer of the Oscars, was a writer on *Donny & Marie* and began penning material for *The Brady Bunch Hour*. Sid and Marty Krofft, the producing brothers (even in this bizarre chapter of the *Brady*verse, family was a continuing theme) who'd worked with the Brady Kids on the Hollywood Bowl concert in 1973, were asked by ABC executive Michael Eisner to create the series. But neither the producers nor the network bothered to ask Sherwood Schwartz and Paramount, who jointly controlled rights to *The Brady Bunch*, for their thoughts or, more importantly, their permission to create this new family adventure.

This could have turned into a legal brouhaha that absolutely would have prevented ABC from getting the variety show on the air in two months, but it was prevented because, even though Schwartz only found out about the new show when he read about its impending premiere in *TV Guide*, the Brady creator and Paramount agreed to let *The Brady Bunch Variety Hour* happen in exchange for a small fee. Paramount had a lot of joint projects with ABC, and they didn't want to endanger the relationship. Schwartz, who wasn't happy about his TV family being spun off in this new version without his permission or involvement, signed off on the show for two reasons: He thought it would help boost the Bradys' continuing popularity (i.e., continuing royalties), and he didn't want to deny his cast the chance to earn a paycheck. He had no involvement with the show, however, including its concept or ongoing storylines.

The concept was a crazy idea from the beginning, and the resulting show was far more out there than the premise suggests. In a show-within-a-show idea, the Brady family left their Clinton Way house behind and moved to a beach house in Malibu, because Bobby Brady wanted them to star in their own variety television series. Mike Brady, the once-sensible, down-to-earth paterfamilias, not only agreed to the pursuit, but gave up his job as an architect to sing and dance and get punny with the other seven Bradys (and Alice!), in glittery costumes, on a stage with a giant swimming pool.

Even more incredible was that Robert Reed, who'd complained out loud and in writing for five seasons about playing Mike Brady and about the hackneyed hokum of Sherwood Schwartz's family-friendly storylines, happily signed on to do the show. *This* show! This show, which would see him, among other things, don a Carmen Miranda outfit—complete with a bowl of fruit on his head—and sing "Hooray for Hollywood," because guest star Milton Berle said it would be funny. This is the same actor who had refused to participate in a pie fight at the end of *The Brady Bunch* episode "Welcome Aboard," because he thought it was too silly.

Reed said yes to the show because, well, because he wanted to get paid, but also because he was always eager to try something he hadn't done before in his career. He wasn't particularly good at singing or dancing, something his co-stars, and watching the show, confirm. But Marty Krofft said no one put forth a bigger effort than Reed, who really seemed to enjoy himself during the musical numbers and the ridiculous narrative that surrounded the fake show within the show. He also, Susan Olsen said, was happy to have the opportunity to reunite with his TV family. Most of it, anyway.

The fake show wasn't the only famous fake in *The Brady Bunch Variety Hour*. There was also Fake Jan.

The rest of the Brady household had signed on for the variety series without much fuss. Florence Henderson was the one with the most experience doing this exact kind of work. Barry Williams, now twenty-two, had starred in *Pippin* on Broadway and in the touring show. He initially said no to the variety series, until Marty Krofft explained that, as the only other cast member besides Florence to be an experienced singer and dancer, he would be spotlighted, with solo numbers in each show. That was enough to get him to resign from *Pippin* and join his *Brady* cohorts. Maureen McCormick, twenty years old, always had plans to pursue a singing career, so she signed on. Chris Knight, who celebrated his nineteenth birthday in the summer of '76, enjoyed singing and dancing less than anyone in the cast, but agreed to do the show when producers told him they'd keep his musical performances to a minimum (which turned out not to be true). Mike Lookinland, who would turn sixteen just before Christmas that year, didn't really want to do the show, either, so he demanded double the salary, thinking that would get him gracefully out of the series.

Instead, he got the extra dough, for himself and the rest of the cast. Fifteen-year-old Susan Olsen, a big comedy fan, hated everything a variety series of this type was about, but she liked the idea of reuniting with the cast, and the paycheck. Ann B. Davis had retired from Hollywood after *The Brady Bunch* ended and moved to Denver to work as a volunteer in a vicarage with the Episcopal Church. She didn't miss show business, but she did miss her old castmates, and she'd enjoyed her theater work in her pre-*Brady* days, so she signed on to guest-star in the first episode. That turned into her appearing in all nine over-the-top installments—blue dress, white apron, and all.

That left one open square in the tic-tac-toe board, the one belonging to Jan Brady.

Eve Plumb, now eighteen, didn't say no to the variety show immediately. In fact, she initially said yes. The actress, who has a reputation for being the Brady kid least likely to continue Bradying, was pursuing acting, and had recently starred in the 1976 NBC movie *Dawn: Portrait of a Teenage Runaway*. The movie, starring Plumb as the titular teen who runs away to Hollywood and becomes a prostitute, was a ratings winner for the network, and there was already talk of a sequel. But she had also, the previous year, briefly toyed with starting a band—the Brady Bunch Three—with Olsen and Lookinland. She liked performing and thought the variety series might be fun. What she didn't like was the idea of signing a contract that would potentially tie her to the series for five years. Okay, sure, in hindsight, it seems unlikely *The Brady Bunch Hour* ever would have run for five seasons. But who would have predicted in 1969 that fifty years later *The Brady Bunch* itself would remain one of the most influential sitcoms in television history?

So Plumb countered that she'd be willing to sign on for five of a planned thirteen episodes; *Brady Bunch Hour* producers said no, fearing special accommodations for Plumb would rankle the rest of

the cast. Neither side budged, so, with less than a month to go before the series premiered, and two weeks until production would
begin, the search for Fake Jan began with a casting call.

Fifteen hundred FJWs (Fake Jan Wannabes) descended upon
KTLA Studios, where producers were looking for, literally, a faux
Jan. Not someone sorta like Eve Plumb's Jan, not someone to put a
new spin on the Jan Brady character, but a copycat Jan, who looked
like Eve and who could also sing and dance. The lot of 1,500 was
whittled down to 300 by the second round of auditions.

Among the three finalists: then-seventeen-year-old Kathy
Richards, whose family members, daughter Paris Hilton and sisters
Kyle and Kim Richards, would become reality TV superstars. Kathy
had several TV guest spots on her résumé, including *Happy Days*,
Bewitched, and *The Rockford Files*.

But her experience paled in comparison to that of Geri Reischl,
a sixteen-year-old from the Los Angeles suburb of Lakewood, who
not only looked like long-haired, blond Eve Plumb, but could sing,
dance, had starred in more than three dozen commercials, was a
model for Mattel dolls as a younger child, fronted her own country
music band, and had spent the summer of 1976 as a backup singer
for Canadian pop star René Simard.

Just one day after her final meeting with the Kroffts, Geri was
called to her guidance counselor's office at school. That's where she
found out her life was about to be changed forever by nine episodes
of television. She'd won the role of Fake Jan. She was now, and
would always be, a member of the Brady family.

Even with the main cast in place—comedian Rip Taylor would
join as Jack Merrill, the Bradys' meddling Malibu neighbor and love
interest for Alice (poor, cast-aside Sam the butcher)—making the
Thanksgiving Sunday premiere date seemed like an impossible feat
with a mere two weeks to go.

Dancers (the Krofftettes) and swimmers (the Krofft Water Follies) had to be hired. That giant fifty-foot swimming pool had to be constructed from individual pieces brought into the studio, then filled, which proved to be a big challenge. And the cast had to go through intense rehearsal sessions to prepare for the first show. With guest stars Donny and Marie Osmond and Tony Randall, the pilot featured fourteen musical numbers and a "plot" that finds the kids worried that Mike isn't a gifted-enough singer or dancer to do a family variety show. Bobby's solution: Replace him with guest star Randall (so very un-Brady-like).

Mike remained head of the family and the family act, of course, which meant he was part of a Brady medley of "Baby Face" and "Love to Love You Baby"; a duet of "Cheek to Cheek" performed with Henderson; and *Brady*fied disco performances of "The Hustle" and "(Shake, Shake, Shake) Shake Your Booty." There could not have been a flake of pink or orange glitter or a single sequin left in the rest of Los Angeles after the episode was completed, for it had all been used on Brady costumes or the sets.

One particular delight from the pilot: Ann B. Davis, in a white pantsuit, shake, shake, shaking her booty right along with the family, looking like she was having more fun than anyone.

The Brady Bunch Hour hosted an impressive lineup of celebrity guests, including Redd Foxx, Tina Turner, Vincent Price, and then-marrieds Lee Majors and Farrah Fawcett.

But, as excited as viewers may have initially been to catch up with the *Brady* bunch, the novelty of seeing them in this trippy new setting wore off quickly. Three-a-day dance workouts and rehearsals weren't enough to mask the lack of skills of those who simply weren't comfortable with all the dancing. And ABC's Silverman, whose enthusiasm and hopes for a new *Brady Bunch* hit waned quickly after the November 28, 1976, premiere, moved the variety show all around the schedule, airing it every fifth week.

Reviews, as was almost always the case with any Brady project, were not positive. *St. Petersburg Times* critic Charles Benbow: "Such pap offers another reason for joining the national boycott 'Pull the Plug on TV Week.'" Gannett News Service writer Buck Biggers wanted more comedy, fewer of "those big production numbers... they look like MGM musical numbers shot in someone's garage."

Variety mustered up the most positive review, calling the show "hardly world-shattering... nevertheless qualified as painless entertainment."

TV Guide put the show in historical perspective in a 2002 cover story that ranked the fifty worst series of all time. *The Brady Bunch Hour* was number four on the list, worse than *Manimal* ("half-man, half-animal"), worse than *Cop Rock*, worse than *Celebrity Boxing*, but still better than the XFL football league, *My Mother the Car* (literally, star Jerry Van Dyke as attorney Dave Crabtree purchased a car that was the reincarnation of his mama), and *The Jerry Springer Show*.

The final of nine episodes aired on May 25, 1977, and *The Brady Bunch Variety Hour* officially became a thing that really did happen, a guilty-pleasure viewing experience that should be remembered for:

—Providing the most surreal scene in *Brady* history. In the first episode after the pilot, McCormick, Williams, Knight, and Rip Taylor don *Wizard of Oz* costumes to sing and dance Rose Royce's *Billboard* chart-topping disco hit "Car Wash." McCormick was Dorothy, Williams was the Scarecrow, Knight was the Tin Man, and Taylor was the Cowardly Lion at the Emerald City Carwash, where Kroffttettes were dressed up like sudsy brushes and rags, and balloon bouquets represented soap bubbles. At the end of the production, Ann B. stepped in as the Wicked Witch, demanding Dorothy's ruby slippers, until a team of Kroffttettes dressed like water streams vanquished her. It's unforgettable, no matter how hard you might try.

—Giving cheeky writer Vilanch the chance to corner guest star Milton Berle backstage and ask Uncle Miltie to prove the legend about Berle being the, ahem, *biggest* star in Hollywood. "He just laughed it off," Vilanch said. "I did try. He said, 'Why do you want to see it?' and I said, 'Because I want to feel closer to Marilyn Monroe.' He thought that was funny, because he used to go around talking about how he'd schtupped Marilyn Monroe." So, ultimately, no proof to confirm or disprove this long-running Hollywood urban legend? "No, he just laughed it off. We actually had a poll [among the writers] to see who could do it, who would ask him. They decided that I, as the out gay person, could [get the answer]. Didn't work out that way."

—Bringing Fake Jan into the *Brady*verse. The delightful Geri Reischl embraced her *Brady*hood from the moment she was cast as the Jan replacement, and said she was embraced by the friendly cast, including Robert Reed. "After a day or two, [he] came up to me and, what a sweet gentleman, he said to me, 'Geri, it feels as if you've been a part of this family the whole time.' That broke the ice. I had worked with Susan before on commercials. They all were very nice to me. I think they liked that I could hold my own with some of the singing and the dancing."

Reischl went on to record an album titled *Fake Jan Sings for Real*, and in 2008, her friend Lisa Sutton (co-author, with Susan Olsen and Ted Nichelson, of *Love to Love You Bradys*, the fantastic oral history book of *The Brady Bunch Hour*) declared January 2 officially "Fake Jan Day." Why that date? Because Geri was the second Jan. The annual fake holiday must include the official food of Fake Jan Day, a cheeseball. Reischl usually makes her own, sometimes from the recipes friends and *Brady* fans use to make their own Jan Day treats.

—Being such a happy experience for the oft-grumpy, perfectionist Robert Reed that he actually shared a positive review of the original *Brady Bunch* series. When asked by a reporter to explain why the series was such a hit in syndication, Reed responded, "It is one of the few shows the family can watch together. I hadn't noticed this when the show was running [originally]...I think I am the only father on a television series who sits down and discusses problems with the family. On *The Brady Bunch*, we talk things over."

—Proving that, even though the cast was horribly mismatched with this particular genre (the variety show genre would die out altogether by the end of the decade) for its first TV comeback, viewers do still love to love you, guilty-pleasure *Brady Bunch Variety Hour*. Just maybe not in a beach house in Malibu instead of the iconic Brady residence on Clinton Way.

* * *

Neither the Brady Kids nor *The Brady Bunch Hour* had long lives in the *Brady*verse, but music has always played a significant role in the show's history and pop culture influence.

"The theme song is perhaps even more iconic than the actual show," *Brady* fan Al Yankovic said. "It's one of those brilliant theme songs that encapsulates the show's entire concept at the start of each episode. It's basically the elevator pitch for *The Brady Bunch* in song form.

"I loved theme songs like that...*Gilligan's Island*, *Green Acres*, *Beverly Hillbillies*, *Mr. Ed*. They don't write theme songs like that anymore. That's why when I was given my own network kids' show on CBS in the late nineties [*The Weird Al Show*], I wrote a retro-styled theme song for it, wherein I go into excruciating detail about the stupid reason why the show exists."

Yankovic's song "Brady Bunch" contains a lyrical, though not musical, adaptation of the *Brady* opener, and other entertainers have been just as inspired by Sherwood Schwartz and Frank De Vol's seminal theme song.

Oscar and Grammy winner Jamie Foxx's 2002 HBO stand-up special *I Might Need Security* included a segment during which the performer sat down at a piano and talked about his special way of using a wholesome TV theme song to get romantic with his girlfriends on his grandmother's living room couch, without offending the sensibilities of his strict grandma. He treated the audience at the Paramount Theatre in Oakland, California, to his slow-jam cover of the *Brady Bunch* theme—taking "a song off the TV and making it sound good enough to make love to." In the ultimate unique *Brady* theme mash-up, Foxx employed his pitch-perfect impersonation skills to sing the song in the style of fellow Grammy winners Babyface, Luther Vandross, and Prince.

Sesame Street employed the theme song and the opening-sequence format to teach young viewers how *Street* resident Telly had a "hunch" that ingredients like bologna, lettuce, cheese, and a loaf of bread could form a healthy lunch in the 1996 segment "Telly's Lunch."

A 1995 *Sesame Street* segment called "The Braid-y Bunch" parodies the *Brady* theme and tic-tac-toe board opener to spotlight kids who love wearing braids in their hair. The adorable little girl with braided pigtails who's occupying the square where Mike Brady usually resides: Lindsay Lohan.

In the season eight "Secret of the Flushed Footlong" episode of *Robot Chicken*, a *Brady* theme song and checkerboard opening-sequence parody offers a harsh theory about what really happened to Carol's first husband. It's an irreverent tale, involving radiation poisoning, an exploding face, and falling out a plate glass window.

Credit for the most star-studded *Brady* theme homage goes to *The Tonight Show Starring Jimmy Fallon*. In 2018, the late-night series premiered the instant viral video and song "The Marvel Bunch," featuring the cast of *Avengers: Infinity War* singing the origins story of the MCU (Marvel Cinematic Universe). Robert

Downey Jr.'s Tony Stark ("Here's the story of a playboy genius"), Chris Hemsworth's Thor, Chris Evans as Captain America, Scarlett Johansson as Natasha Romanoff, Chadwick Boseman as Black Panther, Benedict Cumberbatch as Doctor Strange, Anthony Mackie as Falcon, and Chris Pratt as Star-Lord summed up their backstory— "So then one day all the heroes were assembled, to fight a villain who packed much more than a punch, and this group was labeled the Avengers, that's the way we all became the Marvel Bunch"— before the punch-packing villain himself, Tom Hiddleston's Loki, pops into the center square.

The Brady Kids even adapted the *Brady Bunch* theme song themselves, for the 1972–73 Saturday morning cartoon *The Brady Kids*. The first spin-off of the mothership series was created by Sherwood Schwartz and featured the *Brady Bunch* kid cast voicing animated versions of their characters, who didn't live with Carol, Mike, and Alice, but instead were surrounded by Marlon, a talking magic mynah bird; Mop Top the dog; and a set of twin panda cubs named Ping and Pong.

The *Brady Kids* theme song, performed by the Brady cast, maintained the original *Brady* music and opening-sequence squares, as the brothers introduced their sisters ("Meet three sisters"), the sisters sang about their brothers ("Now meet their brothers"), and they all urged viewers, "Let's get set now for action and adventure, as we see things we never saw before...The Brady Kids, the Brady Kids, here's the world of your friends the Brady Kids."

The twenty-two-episode series found the kids in appropriately cartoonish stories like taking on jewel thieves (in two episodes), mistaking the world's richest man—Nick L. Dime—for a poor man, and being magically transported to Greece to hang out with Wonder Woman (the first time that superhero was ever shown as a character on-screen). The toon Bradys also performed as a singing group ("Time to Change" was featured in the second episode) in sequences that had a lot in common with *The Archie Show*, and it was no coincidence. Filmation was the studio behind both shows, and certain animation scenes from *Archie*, including the band performance sequences, were simply repeated in *The Brady Kids*.

Though the *Brady* cartoon was short-lived, it was, unlike *The Brady Bunch Hour*, an officially authorized Sherwood Schwartz project. It also spawned its own spin-off series.

Mission: Magic! starred Rick Springfield, who still had a thick Australian accent, as Rick Springfield, a rock star who went on magic-fueled journeys with schoolteacher Miss Tickle (a character who had first appeared on *The Brady Kids*) and her after-school Adventurers Club. Tickle and the students communicated and rendezvoused with Rick via a magic gramophone and a ceramic cat named Tut-Tut, who came to life via Tickle's magic. It was as kooky, even by Saturday morning cartoon standards, as the description hints, but *Mission: Magic!* had one very special selling point: actor and future Grammy-winning "Jessie's Girl" singer Springfield wrote and performed original songs just for the series.

* * *

The Brady Bunch Hour was ultimately a flop, but it did reveal one important thing: Bob Reed could rock a fruit basket headdress. Okay, two things: Viewers' love of the Bradys was not limited to syndicated reruns; they also wanted to check in with the fictional family on an occasional basis, and that's what led to the next *Brady Bunch* spin-off, *The Brady Brides*.

Originally conceived by Sherwood and Lloyd Schwartz as a TV reunion movie for NBC (the second broadcast network to host the Bradys) called *The Brady Girls Get Married*, the 1981 series is most notable for being the last *Brady* project in which the original cast, including both parents, all six kids, and Ann B. Davis, starred.

In *The Brady Girls Get Married*, everyone reconvened at the Clinton Way home for the weddings of Marcia and Jan, who were marrying Wally (Jerry Houser) and Philip (Ron Kuhlman). NBC—now run by Fred Silverman, who had moved over from ABC in 1978—had bigger plans for the reunion, though. The network wanted to break the movie into three pieces and run them across three weeks, and then continue the storyline as a new series called *The Brady Brides*. The Schwartzes had been trying to sell an unrelated comedy (titled *Full House*) about two newlywed couples who cohabit when neither can afford a home on their own, and *Brides* seemed like a great way to see that premise play out, via the newly hitched Brady women.

The *Brady Brides* series, including the *Brady Girls Get Married* movie broken into three parts, would last just ten episodes (which was probably seven too many), but it was a proper reunion, as the story opened on a pan across the Brady backyard, into the house, through the living room (the staircase! the horse statue! the double front doors!) to the arrival of Mike and Carol, who were returning after dropping off Cindy at college.

Schwartz had insisted the Brady house set be rebuilt for the series, even though it took a $200,000 chunk out of his budget. "The house is a character," he said. "Kids remember every room in the house...I said, 'There's no way I can put these people in a different house.' [The network] said, 'People move.' I said, 'Not the Bradys.'"

We'd find out what was up with the rest of the family, too: Mike was still architecting (as was Jan), Carol had become a real estate agent, Marcia was a fashion designer, Greg was a doctor, Peter was in the Air Force, Bobby was also in college, and Alice finally, after all those self-deprecating spinster jokes she made during the original series, was married to Sam!

They all came home for what ended up being a double wedding (inside the Brady home), and then the two *Odd Couple*–ish couples moved into a house together. The fun goes downhill from there. The *Boca Raton News* review that *Brides* is the "worst show ever" was a gross exaggeration, but the highlight of the post-wedding episodes was a guest appearance by Bob Eubanks, who invited Marcia and Jan and their hubbies to be contestants on *The Newlywed Game*.

The "delayed spinoff," as *TV Guide* termed *The Brady Brides* and a series of *Gilligan's Island* reunion movies Schwartz created for NBC, performed well in the ratings…for the initial three episodes. But once again, after viewers got a good dose of "where are they now" details on the Bradys, they were satisfied. *The Brady Bunch* had always focused on the core family (and Alice!), with the occasional guest star who stirred up some excitement. *The Brady Brides*, after the double wedding, turned much of the focus on Marcia's and Jan's husbands, who were not compelling characters. There was also not enough chemistry between the actors to compensate for the fact that it was weird to see Marcia and Jan, characters we'd watched grow up on the original series (for more than a decade thanks to the reruns), married to strangers. A date with Doug Simpson? Sure. Jan's crush on Clark Tyson? Groovy. But a new Brady series where four of the six kids and dad disappear after the first three episodes, leaving viewers with two new guys and occasional pop-ins by the mother-in-law and the former housekeeper-in-law? Nah.

But never count the Brady family out, as TV land would learn time and time again.

And there's no time like the holidays for yet another *Brady Bunch* reunion.

A Very Brady Christmas, a two-hour movie that gathered the whole family back at the Clinton Way house, moved the franchise to CBS (*The Brady Bunch* is the only TV series to air, in some version, on all three major broadcast networks). That's where the show found its biggest ratings success ever.

Premiering on December 18, 1988, the movie was not only the second-highest-rated TV movie of the year, but *A Very Brady Christmas* scored a 39 share rating, meaning that 39 percent of all television sets in use on that Sunday night were locked in on the Bradys.

What does a very *Brady* Christmas look like? In the original series, we saw the family's holiday unfold only once (in season one's "The Voice of Christmas"), when Carol lost her voice and Cindy asked Santa (Hal Smith, who later played the Kartoon King in season two's "The Winner") to make her all better so she could sing "O Come All Ye Faithful" at Christmas church services.

That syrupy celebration (which was referenced with a clip in *A Very Brady Christmas*) gave way to a more realistic (still covered in lots of syrup) family gathering in the 1988 reunion movie, as all the Brady kids, Mike, and Carol (and Alice!) reunited with a slew of adult problems. Jan and Philip were on the verge of divorce. Peter was dating his boss and was too embarrassed by the situation to ask her to marry him. Bobby didn't tell his parents he'd dropped out of grad school to become a race car driver. Marcia's husband, Wally, didn't want the family to know he'd lost his job as a toy salesman. Mike was working on a construction project with a businessman who cared more about money saving than safety. And Alice showed up on the Bradys' doorstep with news that Sam had left her for a younger woman (and told her via a letter, written, of course, on butcher paper). It was strange, yet somehow also comforting, that as Mike and Carol's houseguest, Alice still chose to wear her blue dress and white apron around the house. Oh, Alice!

Mike and Carol, as they were wont to do, helped solve everyone's problems, though it took a whole two-hour block of time versus the old twenty-two-minute sitcom solution. Peter and boss Valerie got engaged at the Christmas dinner table, Mike helped Wally with a new job prospect, Jan and Philip made up, and Bobby fessed up about his new passion.

It was up to the whole family to help solve Mike's problem, when he was trapped inside a collapsed building on Christmas Day after he'd gone to investigate trouble at the construction site of that weaselly businessman, Ted Roberts. A crowd gathered at the site, news teams covered rescue efforts, and the whole Brady family left their dinner to wait outside the building and hope for Mike's safety. Well, they did more than hope: Carol led the entire crowd in a sing-along of "O Come All Ye Faithful" (you have to love a callback), which, in true Brady miracle style, brought him climbing safely out of the building.

The movie, as always with *Brady* projects, earned scathing reviews from critics. How bad was the movie? New York *Daily News* reviewer David Bianculli asked, and answered, "So bad that, as Columbus redefined the edge of the world, *A Very Brady Christmas* redefines the bottom of the barrel." The movie was "blather for the mindless, a series of well-dressed, good-looking people strutting across the screen, mumbling inanities which, when strung together, were supposed to suffice as plot." Though that may sound like one of Robert Reed's infamous rants at Sherwood Schwartz, it was actually a review from *Boston Herald* critic Beverly Beckham.

TV Guide simply wrote, "One reason to go abroad for the holidays...CBS-TV is presenting *A Very Brady Christmas*."

And even with the incredible ratings, there were things for fans to complain about. Chiefly there was the missing Susan Olsen as Cindy. The movie's production schedule conflicted with Olsen's honeymoon plans for a trip to Jamaica, though Olsen later revealed there were money issues, too. Eve Plumb and Maureen McCormick were offered higher salaries for the project because they had starred in *The Brady Girls Get Married* and *The Brady Brides*. Olsen rejected the lesser amount she was being offered, and then found out there would be a replacement Cindy when her agent saw casting notices. Jennifer Runyon, best known as Gwendolyn Pierce, the love interest of the titular manny played by Scott Baio on *Charles in Charge*, became Fake Cindy.

Also missing: Allan Melvin, the actor who played Sam the butcher. At the end of *A Very Brady Christmas*, Santa showed up at the front door with a gift for Alice: Underneath the red suit and beard, it was Sam, begging for Alice's forgiveness, which she all too easily and quickly gave. But it was a Fake Sam under that fake beard. Actor Lewis Arquette stepped in for Melvin, whose schedule of voice-over work conflicted with filming on the movie.

A personal nitpick: The Brady house was mostly the same structurally (save a picture window that was added to the kitchen above the sink). But the house had been redecorated, eighties style, with the family room turned into a workout room for Carol and Mike's exercise bikes, the iconic staircase now painted white, and those gorgeous colored glass panels in the living room replaced with clear glass bricks. There was nary a splotch of avocado green or orange anywhere, and if not for the horse statue and the sideboard it sat on, every bit of retro mid-century decor would have been as MIA as Susan Olsen.

The ratings trumped whatever issues critics or some viewers may have had with the movie, though, and CBS, like ABC and NBC before, failed to heed the lesson of *Brady* reunions past. Fans love the occasional update on the Brady family, but even if that spins into Nielsen gold, it doesn't mean they should spin off a new series.

Critic Richard Hack wrote in the *Hollywood Reporter*, "What [CBS] neglected to realize is that much of that 39 share of audience who tuned in [for *A Very Brady Christmas*] has already gotten their

Brady charge. They have already caught up with the family...the mystery is gone."

But Sherwood and Lloyd Schwartz, who wrote the Christmas movie, had an idea when CBS executives came looking for more Brady content: How about a series of reunion movies, centered around various holidays? CBS, with *60 Minutes* and *Murder, She Wrote* the network's only series in the top 20 for the 1988–89 season, wanted more, though, and the Schwartzes agreed to develop a new Brady series, 1990's *The Bradys*.

The good news: Susan Olsen returned as Cindy. But now it was McCormick's turn to sit out a family reunion, deciding that this was just one *Brady Bunch* spin-off too many for her. That meant there would officially be fake versions for all three daughters in the *Brady*verse now—none as beloved as Geri Reischl, the only fake commemorated with her own fake holiday. The Fake Marcia: Leah Ayres, who had starred on the daytime soap *The Edge of Night* and the movie *Bloodsport* with Jean-Claude Van Damme.

The bigger issue with *The Bradys*, which ran for just six episodes before the ratings-beleaguered CBS canceled it, was the tone. It was serious...way, way too serious. Viewers fell in love with the Bradys as a sitcom family. CBS, Paramount, and the Schwartzes had mistaken the success of the more serious-tinged *Brady Christmas* as fans' desire to see the adult Bradys dealing with real-world angst on a weekly basis. Furthermore, even if viewers were into seeing Marcia tackle a drinking problem (in a scene that was accompanied by a laugh track) or Bobby paralyzed in a racing accident, those very serious problems couldn't be solved by the end of an episode, even if the dramedy was now an hour long. But that is exactly what happened in "Bottom's Up," the penultimate episode of *The Bradys*; Marcia was stressed out and started drinking too much. By the next episode, "The Party Girls," she was opening a catering business with Greg's and Bobby's wives, and the problem with hooch wasn't mentioned.

Viewers weren't having fun watching the show, and it didn't come across on-screen that the cast was, either. Most had signed on for yet another spin-off because, well, broadcast network money is *good* money, and the Brady kids who were still regularly pursuing acting work weren't exactly filling their résumés with new projects. Robert Reed was crankier than ever, fighting again about the minutiae of the scripts. At one point he angered the easygoing Ann B. Davis when he argued about how quickly birthday cake candles could be lit, then said he had worked too long and hard to be "doing this shit" at this point in his career.

"Maybe it's time you got a new career," Ann B. snapped.

Florence Henderson had also grown impatient with Reed's complaining, and reminded him at one point that even if he didn't want to be there, the rest of them were happy to have a job. Both she and Leah Ayres noted they knew Reed's health was in decline at that point, too. Henderson saw him taking pills he dismissed as being for stomach trouble, and Ayres said he would have to conserve his energy, retiring to his trailer for rest breaks throughout production.

This dramedy version of the family's lives, which was nicknamed "*bradysomething*" in reference to ABC's hit drama *thirtysomething*, also ran up against bad time-slot competition. CBS scheduled *The Bradys* in *The Brady Bunch*'s old time slot, Friday night at 8:00 p.m. Now airing in that hour-long spot on ABC: *Full House* and *Family Matters*, two shows with more than a little of the *Brady Bunch* family sitcom DNA floating around in them. Uncle Jesse, the Olsen twins, and Steve Urkel kicked off ABC's TGIF (for "Thank God It's Friday" or "Thank Goodness It's Funny," depending on your opinion of those shows) lineup, a night that was a hit with ABC's younger viewers. *The Bradys* was being clobbered in its time slot by two series benefitting from the fact that *The Brady Bunch* had helped make Friday nights in front of the television a destination for younger viewers.

Producers suggested to CBS that *The Bradys* move to a later spot, owing to the series' less kid-friendly vibes (nine-year-olds probably weren't so interested in Jan's fertility issues or the fact that Mike was being blackmailed by the opposing campaign manager in his bid to win a seat on the city council).

But CBS's schedule for the rest of the night was filled by *Dallas* and *Falcon Crest*, neither of which the network was prepared to shift at the time. If *The Bradys* couldn't hang with the competition at 8:00 p.m., then, they weren't going to stick around for long.

And that is how the last attempt (so far) at a scripted *Brady Bunch* spin-off ended.

father of all things Brady: Sherwood Schwartz, whose prime-time work earned him an Emmy, a star on Hollywood Walk of Fame, and entry into the Television Academy Hall of Fame. *Alan Levenson*

Robert Reed and Florence Henderson played Mike and Carol Brady for five seasons on *The Brady Bunch* (*ABC/Photofest*), but for more than twenty years in TV land, where they reprised the characters for *The Brady Bunch Variety Hour*, *The Brady Girls Get Married*, *A Very Brady Christmas*, *The Bradys* (*CBS/Photofest*), *Love Boat*, and *Day by Day*.

Ann B. Davis had already won a pair of Emmys for her performance on *The Bob Cummings Show* when she took on the role of endearing live-in housekeeper Alice Nelson, the Brady kids' friend, confidante, and bonus parent. *ABC/Photofest*

Paramount executives wanted the young *Brady Bunch* cast to be kept on their set. But producer Lloyd Schwartz insisted they be allowed to explore the Paramount lot and behave like any kids who would be excited to ride their bicycles around the lot and visit fellow Paramount series like *Star Trek*, *The Odd Couple*, and *Mission: Impossible*. *ABC/Photofest*

In "Amateur Nite," one of the most beloved episodes of *The Brady Bunch*, the kids perform as the Silver Platters on *The Pete Sterne Amateur Hour*. Their mission: to keep on groovin', of course, but also to try to win enough cash to pay for an anniversary gift for their parents. *ABC Photo Archives/Walt Disney Television via Getty Images*

All the queen of Middle Child Syndrome Jan Brady ever wanted was to get out of the shadow of her sisters. In the season two episode "Will the Real Jan Brady Please Stand Up?" that meant donning a wig to wear to Lucy Winters's birthday party, but Jan learned her friends already thought she stood out because of her own beautiful hair. Classic *Brady Bunch* happy ending. *ABC/Photofest*

What's making the Bradys (and Alice!) so happy? Needlework. No, really. Ann B. Davis's crafting hobbies caught on with the rest of the cast as a way to occupy their downtime on the set. The gang was even featured in an issue of *Aunt Suzy's Needlecraft Journal. ABC/Photofest*

It seems perfectly appropriate that the show's 100th episode ("Peter and the Wolf") celebration cake paid homage to the famous opening sequence tic-tac-toe grid, but the cast members didn't find their frosting likenesses flattering. *Hulton Archive via Getty Images*

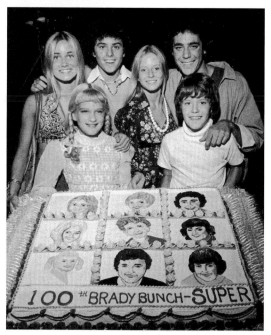

Jeffrey Hunter, who played origi- nal *Star Trek* captain Christopher Pike, tried to convince Sherwood Schwartz that he would make the perfect Mike Brady. But Schwartz thought he was too perfect—too per- fect looking—to play the architect and dad of the blended Brady family. *Paramount Television/Photofest*

Twins? No, but Robert Foxworth (*20th Century Fox/Photofest*), the actor best known for his role on the 1981–90 CBS drama *Falcon Crest*, certainly wouldn't have been a shocking choice to replace Robert Reed (*ABC/Photofest*). *Brady* father and son produc- ers Sherwood and Lloyd Schwartz had decided Reed would not return if *The Brady Bunch* had been renewed for a sixth season, and Lloyd thought Foxworth would make a fine replacement Brady paterfamilias.

Did *The Brady Bunch Variety Hour* really happen or was it just a sequin-filled, musical dream? It was real, or rather surreal, and one of the most bizarre but undeniably fun slices of *Brady* history. *ABC/ Photofest*

The whole family gathered on the staircase for the 1981 reunion movie *The Brady Girls Get Married*, as the Bradys moved from ABC to NBC. The movie, which turned into the short-lived series *The Brady Brides*, was the last time the entire original *Brady Bunch* cast worked together. *NBC/Photofest*

Future Emmy-winning *Glee* star Jane Lynch (top row, middle) and Melanie Hutsell (middle row, left) were among the cast members of *The Real Live Brady Bunch*, the stage show in which episodes of *The Brady Bunch* were performed, verbatim, in Chicago, New York, Los Angeles, and on a national tour. Hutsell, who played Jan, would go on to play her version of pop culture's favorite middle child as a cast member on *Saturday Night Live*. *Paul Natkin/WireImage via Getty Images*

A *Brady Bunch/Partridge Family* showdown never happened in real life, but in Stephen Garvey's musical *The Bardy Bunch*, the two clans meet, leading to a drama (and dark comedy) with Shakespearean consequences. *The Bardy Bunch keyart design by Amanda Spielman*

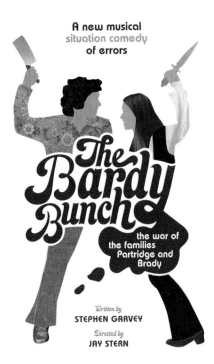

A new musical
situation comedy
of errors

the war of
the families
Partridge and
Brady

Written by
STEPHEN GARVEY

Directed by
JAY STERN

The Brady Bunch was G-rated, which made it a perfect candidate for a XXX parody movie. Producer and director Will Ryder, who also made XXX spoofs of *Bewitched*, *M*A*S*H*, and *Three's Company*, made five *Brady* porn parodies, including *Not the Bradys XXX: Marcia, Marcia, Marcia* and *Not the Bradys XXX: Bradys Meet The Partridge Family. Jeff Mullen/All Media Play*

Confirmation that *The Brady Bunch* characters remain pop culture royalty: In 2018, they were immortalized in plastic as Funko Pop! figures. The initial batch of releases included Greg, Marcia, Peter, Bobby, Cindy, and Alice, but Funko cleverly gave middle child Jan (and her imaginary boyfriend, George Glass) their own debut at New York Comic Con. *FUNKO*

As iconic as the Brady house, staircase, horse statue, and theme song, the blue tic-tac-toe board of smiling faces has inspired homages from a diverse pop culture lineup, including *Sesame Street*, *The Avengers*, and *Claws*. *ABC/Photofest*

CHAPTER EIGHT

Bradys vs. Partridges

The Bradys' primetime contemporaries that fared far better in the ratings, with critics, and with Hollywood awards recognition have not in most cases enjoyed the enduring popularity and multiple decades of pop culture presence *The Brady Bunch* can claim.

During the 1969–70 season that featured the debut of *The Brady Bunch*, *Family Affair* was TV's top-rated family sitcom. Revolving around three orphans—adorable twins Buffy and Jody and their teen sister, Cissy—who were being raised by their wealthy Uncle Bill in Manhattan, *Family Affair* finished that season at number 5 among Nielsen's top 30 programs. In five seasons, the show, which, like *Brady*, focused largely on the younger characters, earned two Emmy nominations as Outstanding Comedy Series. But by its fifth and final year on CBS, *Family Affair* was nowhere to be found in the Nielsen top 30, and a remake that premiered on The WB in 2002 (with *The Brady Bunch Movie*'s Mike Brady, Gary Cole, as Uncle Bill) lasted just one season.

All in the Family, Here's Lucy, Mayberry R.F.D., and *Sanford and Son* were all top 25 Nielsen hits during *The Brady Bunch*'s 1969–74 original run, but none of those series went on to match the Bradys' longevity and continuous rebirths (unless someone secretly produced a *Mayberry R.F.D. Variety Hour*, if so, please provide video evidence).

There was one hit family comedy that had much in common with *The Brady Bunch*, and that show was not only the Bradys' Friday night lineup cohort on ABC, it was also the Bradys' TV and pop culture rival. It was, of course, those singing, Mondrian bus–riding siblings of *The Partridge Family*.

Headed by brief Carol Brady contender Shirley Jones as mom Shirley Partridge, *The Partridge Family* joined ABC's Friday night—following the Bradys at 8:30 p.m.—during the 1970–71 season (the Bradys' second season). Widow Shirley and her bunch, including Jones's real-life stepson David Cassidy as oldest Partridge son Keith, were half–*Brady Bunch* and half–*The Monkees*, splitting their time between suburban life in California and pursuing their pop star dreams on the road, traveling to and fro in the aforementioned de Stijl art–covered bus.

Unlike the Bradys, the Partridges were an instant ratings grabber. *The Partridge Family* finished season one in the top 25 shows in the Nielsen ratings, and just as importantly, the band-within-the-show, led by the vocals of rocker Cassidy and his stepmama, landed a song at number 1 on the *Billboard* Hot 100 chart. "I Think I Love You," which was featured twice on the show during season one, topped the Hot 100 on November 21, 1970, a little less than two months after the series debut on September 25. It remained atop the chart for three weeks, and even though Cassidy and Jones were the only cast members who actually sang on the TV show and on the recordings, *The Partridge Family* as a show and as a band were one of the year's biggest successes.

And the hits kept on coming. The Partridge Family, the band, was nominated for Best New Artist at the 13th Annual Grammys (losing out to another sibling act, the Carpenters). *The Partridge Family*, the TV series, was nominated for Best Television Series—Comedy or Musical at the 1971 and 1972 Golden Globes. The second season of the series finished as the sixteenth-highest-rated show of the year, when *The Brady Bunch* reached its all-time year-end Nielsen ratings peak, number 31, for its third season. In the Partridges' third season, they were still going strong, as the nineteenth-most-watched program.

The band had four more top 20 singles, four albums that made the top 20 on the *Billboard* 200 album chart, breakout performances by Susan Dey as oldest sister Laurie and kid star turned adult star/tabloid magazine magnet Danny Bonaduce, and an impressive lineup of guest stars that included Richard Pryor, Jodie Foster, Rob Reiner, and Johnny Cash. There were *Partridge Family* comic books, a board game, a monthly magazine, a short-lived animated series (*Partridge Family 2200 A.D.* ran for sixteen episodes), countless teen magazine covers, and—a must-have for any TV series with a large kid fanbase in the seventies—a metal lunchbox.

Then came season four.

By this time, David Cassidy was a full-on, screaming teenage girl–attracting, nationally touring singer. He had reached this level of fame quickly, but he was just as quickly burning out. Partially turned off by teen pinup stardom when he really wanted to be taken seriously as a rocker, and completely exhausted from a schedule that had him filming the TV series all week and flying across the country to perform sold-out concerts in arenas on the weekends, Cassidy wanted to pull the plug on something. He decided the bubblegum heartthrob image was the thing that should go, so he posed for an Annie Leibovitz–shot cover of *Rolling Stone*, in a strategically cropped nude photo that shocked his younger fans only slightly less than the revelations inside the magazine. The May 11, 1972, feature detailed his drunken and stoned state, his desire to leave fame behind and live on an island, and his own indelicate description of the "thousands of sticky seats" his excited teenage girl fans left behind after his concerts. Network executives were unamused, and Coca-Cola dropped out of sponsoring a TV special that was to star the singer/actor. He was on the way to getting his wish to end his Keith Partridge existence.

Unfortunately for the rest of the cast, the end was nigh for all of them. To make room for a new comedy based on the movie *Adam's Rib*, ABC moved *The Partridge Family* from its Friday-night, post-*Brady* time slot to Saturday night at 8:00 p.m. The crooning clan had been the only major hit in the Friday night roster, but it was part of a strong lineup that included the Bradys, the future classic *The Odd Couple*, and viewer favorites *Room 222* and *Love, American Style*. In its new Saturday night home, network brethren weren't the issue; network competition was. CBS's Saturday schedule for the 1973–74 season was one of the best nights of programming in television history: *All in the Family*, followed by *M*A*S*H*, *The Mary Tyler Moore Show*, *The Bob Newhart Show*, and wrapping up the evening with *The Carol Burnett Show*. All future classics, CBS's 8:00–9:30 block was back-to-back-to-back top 10 hits. The Partridges were up against Archie Bunker in his fourth season, *All in the Family*'s third consecutive year as the number one show on TV.

Between the ratings crash (the Partridges went from nineteenth place in 1972–73 to seventy-eighth for their fourth season) and the fact that Cassidy did not want to spend another season singing sugary pop tunes and having to play out storylines like getting trapped in a ghost town or accidentally arranging two dates for the same night or being stuck in a remote cabin (had the show returned for season five, Rick Springfield was going to become the replacement heartthrob), *The Partridge Family* was canceled. The series finale aired March 23, 1974. *The Brady Bunch* had aired its series finale earlier in the month, on March 8, ending the show's five-season run.

What else did the Partridges and the Bradys have in common, besides their network home, being family shows popular with young viewers, a relatively short run for each series, catchy theme songs, and unhappy leading men who wanted to be anywhere but on the sets of their TV series?

Bringing in a precocious kid to try to boost ratings in the later seasons.

Season five of *The Brady Bunch* introduced Cousin Oliver, Carol's adorably bespectacled and curious nephew who upped the show's cuteness factor but also became the patron saint of the TV trope in which just such characters are added to aging series for a quick storyline jolt, a.k.a. Cousin Oliver Syndrome. The Partridges had an Oliver of their own. In season four, they befriended new neighbor Ricky Stevens (Ricky Segall), a four-year-old aspiring performer who liked to hang out with the family and sing. As the Partridges would sit around listening to Ricky with smiles plastered on their faces, these scenes were akin to being forced to listen to, well, your neighbor's four-year-old singing. Mercifully, after appearing in ten episodes, Ricky disappeared, with no explanation, halfway through the season. In 1973, Bell Records released *Ricky Segall and The Segalls*, a ten-track album that included many of the songs the tot had sung in *Partridge* episodes.

Both TV families were also dependent on help and advice from their unofficial family members, live-in housekeeper Alice Nelson for the Bradys, and Reuben Kincaid (Dave Madden), the Partridge family's band manager.

Alice, try as she might to pretend she wasn't a softie who was wrapped around the Brady kids' fingers, not only helped Carol and Mike keep the chaotic household running smoothly; she was also effectively a third parent for the siblings, doling out advice as often as sack lunches and always ready to drop her mop to listen to a kid's problems.

Reuben, despite his protestations that he didn't even like children, was always there for the Partridges' professional and personal dilemmas, and had a special father figure–like bond with Danny, Shirley Partridge's droll, entrepreneurial offspring.

Brady producer Lloyd Schwartz recalled a time a fan thought the Bradys were the Partridges. "We were in the Grand Canyon and I was in an elevator with the six kids and Florence. A woman got on and looked at everybody and said, 'I can't believe it, it's the Partridge Family.' She looked at Florence and said, 'Shirley, I love you in the show,' and she thought that I was Reuben."

Henderson took the mistaken identity in stride. "Florence would never correct," Schwartz said. "She would just sign 'Shirley Jones' if people asked for an autograph."

Finally, the two shows had several episode plotlines in common. It's not surprising, given that both series appealed to young viewers and families, and that many of those storylines were written to resonate with as broad an audience as possible. Like...

...Both families were involved in fender benders that resulted in them being dragged into legal proceedings by would-be scammers (the Bradys in season three's "Fender Benders," the Partridges in season one's "The Sound of Money").

...Marcia Brady (season one's "Brace Yourself") and Laurie Partridge (season one's "Old Scrapmouth") were unhappy about the consequences of wearing braces.

...Both families spent more time than they planned in ghost towns (the Bradys in season three's "Ghost Town, U.S.A." and the Partridges in season two's "Don't Bring Your Guns to Town, Santa").

…Oldest Brady son Greg craved independence and his own bedroom (first in Mike's den, then in the Brady attic) in season two's "Our Son, the Man" and season four's "A Room at the Top." Keith Partridge craved independence and sought it by moving into a room in the house next door in season two's "Waiting for Bolero."

…Freckle-faced middle child Jan had a crush on Clark Tyson, who liked her big sister Marcia instead in the season-two *Brady Bunch* episode "The Not-So-Ugly Duckling." Freckle-faced middle child Danny had a crush on Gloria Hickey, who liked his big brother Keith instead in the season-two *Partridge Family* installment "Promise Her Anything, but Give Her a Punch."

…Cindy accidentally donated Marcia's diary to a charity in season one's "The Possible Dream" episode of *The Brady Bunch*; Danny accidentally donated Laurie's diary to a school auction in season two's *The Partridge Family* episode "The Partridge Papers."

…The whole Brady family visited Kings Island amusement park in Ohio in season five's "The Cincinnati Kids." The whole Partridge family had been there in season three's "I Left My Heart in Cincinnati."

…The *Brady* bunch filmed a television commercial for Safe brand laundry detergent in season three's "And Now, a Word from Our Sponsor." The *Partridge* posse filmed a television commercial for Uncle Erwin's Country Fried Chicken joint in season three's "Bedknobs and Drumsticks."

…And in the season-one *Partridge Family* episode "Star Quality," a bit of positive press gave Danny a swollen head. That's something every Brady kid went through, from Peter buying into his own heroics after saving a little girl from getting crushed by falling boxes in season one's "The Hero," Marcia demanding star treatment in her school play in season three's "Juliet Is the Sun," and Bobby's power trip as school safety monitor in season four's "Law and Disorder," to Cindy's case of "televisionitis" that wrecked her quiz show success in season four's "You Can't Win Them All," Greg's rock-star ego in season five's "Adios, Johnny Bravo," and Jan's pooped out popularity in season five's "Miss Popularity."

Both shows also featured music, of course, and it's that particular detail, more than any of the other similarities, that sparked a still-persistent rumor of a *Brady* vs. *Partridge* rivalry.

Inspired by the Cowsills, a popular touring and recording group made up of six siblings and their mother, *The Partridge Family*'s inherent premise revolved around the characters as musicians. Forming a sibling act to compete on a TV talent show and to record brother Greg's songs was just one ambition for *The Brady Bunch*. When Paramount saw the success of *The Partridge Family*—as a TV series and a recording act—the studio realized there might be moneymaking potential for the *Brady* kid cast to record spin-off albums, too. The *Brady* cast suddenly had visions of pop star success dancing in their heads, and that resulted in four group albums and a series of concert performances at county fairs and festivals around the country. Eve Plumb, Barry Williams, and Mike Lookinland made solo recordings, and Maureen McCormick and Chris Knight released a whole album of duets, but none of the *Brady Bunch* singles or albums landed on *Billboard* or other national music charts.

The Partridge Family was, then, the clear winner in the race for TV ratings and music sales. But *The Brady Bunch* ran a season longer and was an immediate and enduring hit in syndication, unlike the Partridges.

But did a *Brady* vs. *Partridge* rivalry ever really exist?

Probably not. Not organically, anyway.

In *Come On Get Happy: The Partridge Family Story*, a 1999 ABC TV movie produced and narrated by Danny Bonaduce, a memorable, if not at all believable, scene found the *Partridge* cast—in their trademark maroon velvet suits—boarding their colorful bus and driving off to Paramount Studios. A *Partridge* producer had arranged the visit, and members of the press just happened to be there when the Partridge bus pulled up to Stage 6. The *Brady Bunch* cast also just happened to wander outside as the Partridges disembarked. The two groups stood on the lot, facing each other, as reporters and photographers watched the tense showdown unfold, and the theme from *The Good, the Bad and the Ugly* scored the scene.

Words were exchanged. Danny Bonaduce asked *Brady* actor Christopher Knight if he wanted to fight. They argued about which show had better ratings. They turned to their TV moms for backup, which led to a catty exchange between Shirley Jones and Florence Henderson. A reporter confused the two actresses—a frequent occurrence in real life, as Henderson confirmed—and Mom Brady announced she was "the mother of the TV family that *acts*."

Responded made-for-TV movie version of Shirley Jones: "Yes, and *I'm* the mother who happens to have won an Oscar," as she and Henderson held their TV sons back to avoid a physical fight, and the youngest female cast members of *The Brady Bunch* ran excitedly toward David Cassidy.

The problem? The scene never actually happened.

Jones and Henderson were longtime friends who even performed concerts together in their post-*Brady* and post-*Partridge* years.

The Brady Bunch was filmed at Stage 5 at Paramount (a detail that should have been correct, given that the movie aired on ABC, original network home to both the Bradys and the Partridges).

The germ of the idea for the scene likely came from Cassidy's 1994 memoir, *C'mon, Get Happy: Fear and Loathing on the Partridge Family Bus*. In it, he described walking on the Paramount lot one day and being spotted by the *Brady* girls. "When they saw me, they dropped to their knees and screamed," he wrote. "It didn't matter that they were featured in a popular TV show themselves."

The *Come On Get Happy* TV movie scene is the continuation of the idea that these two shows, so alike in so many ways, *had* to be in competition with each other. Especially since the Partridges did score higher ratings and the Brady kids' musical plots did pop into their series after *The Partridge Family* premiered, network executives and producers saw no reason to discourage the whispers of a rivalry.

In the years since the shows ended their original runs, the steady increase of the love of retro programming (on Nick at Nite, TV Land, MeTV, and other networks of their delightful ilk) has presented opportunities for the rivalry to be perpetuated even further.

Danny Bonaduce and Christopher Knight never scrapped as child stars on the Paramount lot, but as adults, the two did go Partridge vs. Brady in a 1994 exhibition wrestling match. At the WCW Spring Stampede pro wrestling event in Chicago, "The Partridge Family Fiend" (sporting a Viking hat and a fur coat) stepped into the ring against "The Brady Bunch Bruiser." Despite an opening clothesline by the Brady Bruiser, who also slammed the Family Fiend's noggin against a turnbuckle, the Fiend rebounded with some kicks, some punches, and a flying elbow drop that clinched victory.

Eight years later, on Fox's short-lived *Celebrity Boxing* series, Danny "Boom Boom" Bonaduce once again beat up on a Brady. This time his fightwear included a tattooed ad for GoldenPalace .com across his back, as he battered "Barry Da Butcher" Williams to a TKO in less than two rounds.

Williams got his revenge in 2012's *Bigfoot*, one of Syfy's trademark low-budget TV flicks, which pitted the two actors against each other in a story involving the titular monster, a rock music festival, Mount Rushmore, and Williams' chance to shove Bonaduce around some rocky terrain.

Those are all things the actors have done for paydays, though, and Williams and Bonaduce admit there isn't, and has never been, a genuine rivalry between the casts of their classic seventies TV shows. Boxing matches and reality-TV trash talking aside, no Bradys or Partridges were harmed in the building of this pop culture legend.

"If there was a real rivalry in those days between who was the heartthrob, David Cassidy or Barry Williams, the clear winner was [Cassidy]," Bonaduce said. "I'll go flat on the record, though: *The Brady Bunch* is a much nicer group of people than *The Partridge Family*."

Williams thinks the Partridges are better than the Bradys in one regard. "The biggest problem was who sang better and who were the better dancers. I've always felt the Partridges sang better, but, of course, the Bradys did all their own choreography."

* * *

Try as Williams and Bonaduce might to snuff out those exaggerations of a feud among Friday-night family sitcom stars of the past, there is one playwright who's put a clever, Shakespearean twist on the alleged rivalry.

Stephen Garvey mashed up one part *Brady*, one part *Partridge*, and one part Bard to create *The Bardy Bunch*, an Off-Broadway musical subtitled *The War of the Families Partridge and Brady*.

The 2011 New York International Fringe Festival hit was sparked not just by Garvey's deep knowledge of the sitcoms and Shakespeare—though he certainly has both—but by his imagining of Keith Partridge and Marcia Brady as star-crossed lovers Romeo and Juliet.

One day the writer was doing laundry, separating the colors from the whites, when his mind wandered and he started sorting Bradys and Partridges into Shakespearean plots.

Mike and Carol Brady became Macbeth and his Lady, Danny Partridge was Hamlet, and Jan Brady, the oft-maligned middle child, became Ophelia. At last, Jan was the tragic drama queen she always thought herself to be, in *The Bardy Bunch*.

Rage, revenge, and the use of Sunflower Girl cookies as a murder weapon ensued. The play is heavy on familiar music and laughs, too. Garvey secured the rights to songs from both comedies, and mixed "I Think I Love You," "It's a Sunshine Day," "I Woke Up in Love This Morning," "Keep On," and the two series' theme songs with the Bradys' dunk tank, Laurie Partridge's pal Snake, and plenty of quips from Reuben Kincaid and Alice. There's even a Cousin Oliver twist, and it involves a body count.

Simple but crafty stage design and props recall the stained-glass designs of the Brady living room and the family's bike rides. The Silver Platters' blue-and-white costumes pay homage to the Bradys' love of polyester for every occasion, and even the show's poster—featuring Laurie Partridge in her maroon velvet pantsuit holding a knife up to a bell-bottomed, cleaver-clutching Greg Brady—is a little work of *Brady/Bardy/Partridge*-y art.

A Brady/Partridge war had played out before, on TV. *Partridge Family* star Susan Dey (by then an Emmy-nominated, Golden Globe–winning star of *L.A. Law*) hosted a February 1992 episode of *Saturday Night Live*. Featured player Melanie Hutsell, in her first year on the show, had quickly become a viewer favorite with her impersonation of a hyperexcitable Jan Brady.

Hutsell had been playing Jan to much acclaim in the stage show *The Real Live Brady Bunch* at the Annoyance Theatre in Chicago. When that production, in which episodes of *The Brady Bunch* were reenacted verbatim for sold-out audiences, moved to New York City, Hutsell went with it, and caught the attention of *SNL* producers. She was hired, and when producer Marci Klein told her they expected something special from her the week the *Partridge Family* alum hosted, Hutsell knew this was a chance to impress her new boss and co-workers, and to live out a childhood fantasy at the same time.

She was one of the very young *Brady Bunch* fans during the show's ABC run. She watched the Partridges, too, immediately following the Bradys on Friday nights. And in her toddler's mind, she wondered, were the two TV fams neighbors? With that, and a whole lot of *Brady* and *Partridge* trivia filed away in her mental Rolodex, she wrote a sketch that pitted the two families against each other in a battle of the bands.

After sharing her "Marcia, Marcia, Marcia" woes, Jan learned the Partridges had problems, too. Laurie shared how they all had to take tomato juice baths because Danny let a skunk inside their tour bus. Then they invited Jan to jam with them.

Shocked to learn most of the Partridges (with Mike Myers playing Danny and Dana Carvey as Keith) didn't actually sing or play their instruments, Jan rounded up her siblings—Kevin Nealon, Adam Sandler, and Rob Schneider as Greg, Peter, and Bobby— from across the street, and the sing-off began.

The Bradys sang "Sunshine Day." The Partridges countered with "I Think I Love You."

"What am I so afraid of..." Keith crooned.

"I know what you're afraid of...this next song," Greg said, as the Bradys launched into "Time to Change," complete with Sandler's voice cracking on Peter's "Sha na na na na."

The sketch was a fun shout-out to favorite memories from the shows, but no rivalry was settled. The Partridges just confirmed what viewers had been surprised to learn, that only David Cassidy and Shirley Jones were truly musical among the TV family. The Brady kids established, meanwhile, that they all did their own singing, for better or worse.

The Bardy Bunch's spin on a Brady/Partridge rivalry went beyond reenactment, and wittily melded the families' best moments with some of the worst tragedies from Shakespeare's works, turning classic TV moments into their own bloody, darkly funny narrative, with music and dancing. And it finally proved to every high schooler who has griped about having to dive deep into Shakespeare that there was a purpose to studying the Bard.

The musical, which won the award for Outstanding Ensemble at the Fringe Festival, ran at New York's Theatre at St. Clement's in 2014. Bryan Cranston was earning his first Tony Award eight blocks away, with his performance as Lyndon Johnson in *All the Way*. On *The Bardy Bunch*'s closing night at St. Clement's, the curtain was held so Cranston could finish his Sunday show at the Neil Simon Theatre and go show his support for the feuding *Bardy Bunch* families.

In 2016, Chicago audiences proved the Windy City is a *Brady*-friendly town, too. *Bunch* devotees once waited in lines wrapped around the Annoyance Theatre to see *The Real Live Brady Bunch* in 1991, and in 2016 they gleefully took a gander at those same characters making mincemeat (spoiler: *literally*, in one instance) when *The Bardy Bunch* played at the Mercury Theater for more than a month in the fall.

In *The Brady Bunch*'s golden anniversary year, *The Bardy Bunch* was being licensed to theaters and schools all around the world. Garvey hopes its surprisingly sweet (there's *a lot* of murder) ending will continue to resonate with fans who are still invested in these characters fifty years after they first arrived on America's TV sets.

"There's this shared experience that people that grew up with these shows [have]...It's like a little brother that you make fun of, but at the same time you actually adore and would fight to defend," Garvey said. "That's what I wanted the show to be, to capture that feeling of, 'Yes, we know these shows are corny, but there is something beautiful about them, too.'"

CHAPTER NINE

Something Suddenly Came Up

Brady Bunch viewers initially tuned in for a comforting look at a happy family with two devoted parents and an equally attentive, nurturing housekeeper, who were there to greet the kids when they came home from school, to listen to their problems and make it their priority to help solve them.

Viewers repeatedly returned to the show throughout the years—which turned into decades—because of their nostalgic affection for a series that had provided them with the hope of a *Brady*-like home environment of their own: parents who made the home a safe landing and instituted a set of guiding rules and principles that gave them a sense of security. *The Brady Bunch* became a beacon in particular for Generation X viewers, a group of young people who glommed onto after-school syndicated *Brady* reruns.

There is no standard definition of the Generation X demographic, but counting those born between 1965 and 1984 covers the majority of birth years researchers from MetLife to the Pew

Research Center have incorporated in the wide range of ages they've used when studying Gen X.

This is the generation of divorce, of parents whose focus was sometimes turned away from child rearing, be it because of work or the stresses of managing single-parent homes. As a result of divorce, children often suffered fractured relationships with at least one of their parents. Shuttling between two households meant a lot of time spent alone when school ended and before their primary caregiver came home. TV and processed snacks became a latchkey child's babysitter, and Pop-Tarts and Pringles never tasted as good as they did while watching Marcia and Greg and Jan and Peter and Cindy and Bobby deal with bullies, braces, and boyfriends.

The Bradys were among the few contemporary examples of a large family on television (*The Waltons* being the other main one), and the only specific example of a blended family. Post-divorce, that was becoming a more prevalent household configuration, and *The Brady Bunch* was a place where young viewers could turn to see how the dynamics of such a household worked, however idealized an example of family in general, and a blended family in particular, *The Brady Bunch* proved to be. The Brady kids enjoyed constants in their lives, including people and places and things, and for that half hour they showed up on our TVs on Friday night—and every afternoon when the syndicated reruns began—they were a constant in ours.

Not that all Gen-X *Brady* fans were unhappy latchkey kids who wanted nothing more than to swap the Bradys in for their own parents and siblings. Young viewers from happy homes loved the show, too, and continued to into their young adult years. For them, it was a throwback to their happy childhoods, not a replacement for sad ones.

Aside from the sociological aspects of the Bradys' impact on viewers, a big part of their pop culture legacy is simply being a fun common reference so many people—but especially those who've seen the 117 episodes over and over again after school in the seventies, on TV Land, Nick at Nite, DVD, and MeTV since—delight in sharing.

Raise your hand if you're a Gen Xer and you've busted out your best Silver Platters dance moves or your long-perfected, Marcia-related Jan Brady meltdown in front of a group of like-minded Bradyholics, or if you can't eat or even hear the words "pork chops" and "applesauce" without doing your best impersonation of Peter doing his (worst) Humphrey Bogart impersonation.

Who among the *Brady* devoted hasn't played show-related games, like competing with friends to guess which episode is airing on TV just from the opening few seconds or seeing who can name the most *Brady* plots, the most celebrity guest stars, all the lyrics to Greg's groovy love song "Till I Met You"?

For *Brady* trivia experts, do you know who wrote that little ditty about clowns never laughing, beanstalks never growing, ponies never running before Greg Brady met his dream girl? It was a collaboration between Barry Williams and Lloyd Schwartz. And now that you've just thought about the song, good luck getting it out of your head for the next three days.

Such is the mental storage space *The Brady Bunch* claims for those who are well versed in the many details of the *Brady*verse. Which is why, with so many Gen X viewers already obsessed with the original show and craving even more of the Bradys, the 1990s became a comeback decade for the show that never really went away.

It began with a pair of *Brady*-obsessed fans and their friend's wicked impression of Marcia.

Jill Soloway, the creator of Emmy-winning Amazon series *Transparent*, and sister Faith Soloway, a writer and producer on *Transparent*, "lived and breathed" *The Brady Bunch* when they were growing up in Chicago, getting themselves to sleep every night by playing a game where one of them said a line of *Brady* dialogue and the other had to say which episode it was from.

"When you're young, in real life, when you go to somebody's house and you just see the way that they do family, it sticks with you, because it's so foreign to you that you keep studying it or wonder why your family is *this* way," Faith Soloway said. "Not in any kind of negative comparison, even. I just remember those feelings of going to people's houses and going, 'Wow, that's the way they do dinner, play with each other, speak to each other.' That first sort of culture shock. Television is the same thing. Certain sitcoms speak to you as a young one.

"Boys living with girls together and sharing a bathroom, that was like, 'Huh?' Thinking of the family dog, everything that we didn't have...it drew me in. Then [the Brady kids] started singing, they performed as a family. You're growing up with them and they keep changing, their lives changed. You're literally growing up with them, and it feels like you want to see what's going on with your best friends, the Brady Bunch."

In 1990, Jill and friend Becky Thyre were watching TV one afternoon, and the "Her Sister's Shadow" episode (a.k.a. "Marcia, Marcia, Marcia") of *The Brady Bunch* came on. Becky launched into a spot-on imitation of Marcia. When the two met up later in the day with Faith, the three were cracking each other up as they continued riffing on the Bradys and Thyre's perfect Marcia.

Faith, a longtime member of the Annoyance Theatre improv group in Chicago, thought the trio was onto something special. The Soloways and Becky couldn't stop laughing at this impromptu re-creation of one of *The Bunch*'s most classic episodes. What if they took it a step further and got actors to play each member of the Brady family and acted out an entire episode, verbatim, on stage?

With expectations of nothing more than a fun night of comedy in the 110-seat theater in an old Chicago storefront, Annoyance artistic director Mick Napier gave a thumbs-up to the performance, and even agreed to play Bobby. Becky Thyre, who not only sounded like Marcia but also looked like her, played the oldest Brady sis. Faith asked her friend Jane Lynch if she'd like to play Alice, but life-long *Brady* fan Lynch opted to play Carol instead, fashioning the perfect Carol do with a wig and several pieces of yellow yarn. Future late-night sidekick Andy Richter would soon become the perfect Mike Brady, and future *Saturday Night Live* star Melanie Hutsell would start a Jan revolution with her performance as the middle female Brady in a constantly irritated, stressed-out state.

Using videotapes of old *Brady* installments, the Soloways wore out their VCR rewind button as they meticulously transcribed the episodes to create scripts. Costumes were retro seventies clothing scrounged up from thrift stores around the city. The set consisted of little more than a chair and a table, and Jill would direct the production while Faith played the laugh track (there *had* to be a laugh track) and performed all the music, including those little transitional gems that Frank De Vol had written for the TV series.

Aside from passing out some flyers, the group did nothing to promote the show, and they didn't know how many people would pay seven dollars a ticket for something that seemed, for the most part, a goof that would amuse the cast for an evening.

What they got was confirmation that a whole lot of other twenty-somethings in Chicago felt the way they did about the Bradys. *The Real Live Brady Bunch* sold out on the June night it opened, and it continued to sell out two shows every Tuesday night for the next fourteen months. There was no air-conditioning in the small, crowded theater, and no concessions, either, so audience members were encouraged to bring their own beer and pizza. It was prime-time, after all, and they were all grown up. No longer did they have to watch the adventures of *The Brady Bunch* unfold with Nestlé Quik and Ding Dongs, though that would have been fine, too.

The cast spent the first few weeks going up to the roof of the theater building before showtime, so they could see the audience line wind around the block. The show was actually making money, even with the bargain tickets. New episodes were transcribed and performed every two weeks, so fans came multiple times.

The audience knew the lines before the actors said them, so sometimes they said them right along with the cast. And sometimes they didn't, because they didn't want to miss the performances from reenactments of episodes like "Adios, Johnny Bravo," "The Subject Was Noses" ("Oh, my nose! Oh, my nose!"), "Amateur Nite," "Dough Re Mi," and "Confessions, Confessions" ("She always says, 'Don't play ball in the house'").

The audiences laughed at and with every familiar line and character entrance, as if the stories were playing out live in their living rooms. Seeing this performance art made them love the show, the characters, and the stories even more, and also realize just how silly the show and characters and stories had been when they watched them with the limited experiences of children. Best of all, and the real reason people came back multiple times, was the communal experience of enjoying this little show, and how this live version, even performed verbatim, exaggerated every aspect of what they'd watched on a TV screen. It was bigger, and still beloved, but also much clearer to the adult fan how unreal much of Brady life had been.

"All of our generation knew it. It was the one show that everybody knew verbatim, the episodes, and everybody had a favorite Brady. I look at all the fads from back then, they would come on for two or three years, but *The Brady Bunch*, it just kept going, and not just in posters and records. It was in your mind, in your recall, when you're talking to people," Faith said. "There was always a reference—'Don't play ball in the house'; Alice the maid, an iconic character; Bobby Brady, he's the obnoxious one; Jan Brady, the tortured middle child. The characters became archetypes for family, especially the kids and how they related to the world. Each had a different color, a different way of being in the world. I remember even looking forward to whose story [would be featured]. Was it going to be a Peter story, which means it would be more madcap, or a Marcia, where it was going to be more emotional? You think of Cindy, and you think of Buddy Hinton, the bully who made fun of her, so she brought Peter along to help. Each character had lots of traumatic moments, and it was like it was *your* traumatic moment."

Later, *The Real Live Brady Bunch* had successful runs in New York and Los Angeles, and the show visited thirty cities with a touring version. More than twenty-five different episodes had been reenacted by the time they went on tour, including "Getting Davy Jones," in which the real Monkees singer once again played himself and performed "Girl" on stage. On the *Real Live* tour, Alice was played by Kate Flannery, *The Office*'s Meredith, and it's worth Googling to read her essay about her on-the-road fling with co-star Jones. It's funny, and Michael Scott–level cringeworthy. Future *Saturday Night Live* star Ana Gasteyer also played Alice later with the touring company (though there's no indication she had anything more than a strictly professional interaction with the Monkee).

Jones wasn't the only celebrity who stepped on stage with the *Real Live* cast. Eve Plumb was so amused by the show that she agreed to play the record producer one night in Chicago when the Annoyance crew did "Adios, Johnny Bravo." Other *Brady Bunch* cast, including Robert Reed, saw the show in various cities, too. Reed even participated in the show's opener, *The Real Live Game Show*, which plucked audience members to be contestants in a game show spoof. Susan Olsen saw performances in Chicago, New York, and LA. Longtime *Brady* fan Tom Hanks brought his daughter Elizabeth to see the show in the Windy City.

Ann B. Davis was invited but did not attend a performance. That's especially sad since every live show wrapped with a coda featuring Carol singing Faith Soloway's spoof version of Jefferson Airplane's "White Rabbit"—with the line "Go ask Alice"—which always earned a standing ovation. All those kids who'd watched Alice and been entertained by her mugging and self-deprecating remarks were now, as adults who were experiencing the harsher realities of adulthood themselves, much more appreciative of just how vital a role Alice played in the Brady household. In the Brady *family*.

Then again, while Carol sang, the kids smoked pot and engaged in various other activities than were un-Brady-like, so maybe Ann B. wouldn't have enjoyed that part of the show so much.

The boss of all things *Brady* himself, Sherwood Schwartz, did pay a visit to the show, and the Annoyance gang thought it was going to mean trouble.

By October 1990, *The Real Live Brady Bunch* was making headlines in newspapers and magazines across the country, and Paramount and Schwartz, who had joint say on *Brady Bunch* licensing matters, noticed. No one with the show had asked for permission to reenact Schwartz's scripts or perform as the characters he'd created. They hadn't expected it to become such a hit, and by the time they had a chance to realize word of the show was spreading, word had already spread to Hollywood.

Paramount's legal department was all set to send a cease-and-desist letter when Schwartz told them to hold off. He was going to be in Chicago soon anyway, so he'd check it out before they took any action. He *was* prepared to take action, though.

Until he saw the performance, sat among the zealous *Brady* fans who sang along with the theme song and shouted out lines of dialogue like they were at *The Rocky Horror Picture Show*. When Schwartz himself was introduced, the crowd began shouting, "Sherwood! Sher-wood!" He'd expected *Real Live* to be a real poke at his show. Instead, he saw that the audience and the cast had great affection for him and his work. "It was the most incredible experience I've ever had," he told the *Chicago Tribune*. "I felt like a rock star, at my age" (seventy-three at the time). When he returned home to Los Angeles, he told Paramount he would sign off on allowing *The Real Live Brady Bunch* to continue, for a token fee.

Schwartz called it a satire, but "a gentle satire," something he could appreciate. So much, in fact, that the Soloways—who paid subtle homage to *The Brady Bunch* in the 2019 musical series finale of *Transparent*—did some consulting work on the next big *Brady* project, the family's journey to the big screen.

* * *

TV sitcom, syndication dominance, a very…well, *a* variety show, two TV reunion movies that each led to a spin-off series, and a stage show that used the original series scripts to bring together old-school *Brady* fans all across the country. All that was left for *The Brady Bunch* to tackle was the big screen, which is exactly what the Schwartzes and Paramount had in mind.

Not only had the family behind the Brady family and the powers that be at the studio noted the success of *The Real Live Brady Bunch*, they had noted specifically that a major reason for the stage show's popularity was its tone. It embraced how millions of fans were feeling about the show at the beginning of the nineties: lovingly irreverent. It was cool to acknowledge that, though the Bradys were uncool, you loved them in spite of it (and a little bit because of it).

So while initial ideas for *The Brady Bunch Movie* included such

high-concept loglines as the Bradys entering witness protection after reporting a crime, and the Bradys being taken hostage inside
their house by escaped convicts, Schwartz absolutely drew the line
at a script that would have found Marcia in a lesbian love affair,
Mike flipping burgers, and Alice sleeping with every male visitor to
the Brady home. Paramount had final approval on the movie script,
but he made it clear: A movie that chipped away at the established
TV family he'd created would not only not have his support, he'd
actively, publicly, campaign against it.

The plot everyone could finally agree on was a simple one: The
Bradys were going to lose the family home if they didn't come up
with $20,000 to pay their back taxes. The movie would film on
Paramount Stage 5, and the old sets would be resurrected for the
movie. Even some iconic *Brady* items, like that horse statue from
the living room and the beds in the girls' upstairs room, were found
preserved in Paramount lot storage.

That main storyline was a familiar riff on "Amateur Nite," of
course, one of many movie nods to the best-remembered and most-
loved plots from the TV series, but the success of the film would
come down to how craftily the writers, director Betty Thomas, and
especially the new cast playing the Bradys, embraced one main concept: The family was still living like it was 1970, while the rest of
the world was living in 1995.

Brady clothes, hair, home decor, mores, and lingo were straight
outta the seventies (the *Brady*'s version of the seventies, which was
already uncool in the seventies), and they were blissfully unaware
they were living in a time warp. Even when their neighbors—
especially the plotting Larry Dittmeyer (Michael McKean)—
schoolmates, and random strangers poked fun at their Bradyness,
Mike, Carol, Greg, Marcia, Jan, Peter, Bobby, and Cindy continued
to live in their cozy, sheltered, retro universe. Architect Mike designed all his projects to look like the Brady house, Marcia was still

chasing Davy Jones, and Cindy skipped right through any sign of danger, including live electrical wires.

The movie's script resulted in a film that was a box-office success—earning $46.6 million on a $14 million budget—and an almost instant cult classic. Betty Thomas, the Emmy-winning actress (*Hill Street Blues*) and director (*Dream On*), didn't want to direct a TV-inspired movie for her first feature film initially, until her agent encouraged her to read the first ten pages of the screenplay written by Bonnie and Terry Turner, the marrieds and former *Saturday Night Live* writers who also penned the scripts for *Wayne's World* and the *Coneheads* movie and created *That '70s Show* and *3rd Rock from the Sun*. The Turners' script was already strong on satire, Thomas said, but she also brought in Stan Zimmerman and Jim Berg, *Roseanne* and *The Golden Girls* writers who were *Brady Bunch* fans and helped her focus in on the *Brady* TV moments that should be included in the movie. And moments that shouldn't; the original ending, which Thomas filmed and then called a mulligan on after various test screenings, found the Bradys not coming up with the cash to save their house, which was then torn down by a giant wrecking ball Alice (Henriette Mantel) was riding on. Oh, Alice!

Like a wave of other boob-tube-to-big-screen movie hits in the first half of the nineties, *The Brady Bunch Movie* strived to be more than a hastily thrown together remake of a TV show. *The Addams Family* and *Wayne's World* preceded *The Brady Bunch Movie* in not catering only to fans of a TV show. The humor was specific and callback-loaded enough to satisfy *Brady*philes, but clever enough to entertain the average moviegoer and even draw some new fans to the *Brady*verse.

"The reaction on that first Friday night it was released [February 17, 1995], it was so fun, because there were people packed into the theater, standing room only in the back against the walls," Thomas said. "There were younger people giggling like crazy and older people going, 'Oh my God.' That's just exactly what I was try-ing to do, not make it stupid in earnest, but also not break the bond that the characters had with the people who were still in love with them. I think the actors...Come on. The actors were great. They made it happen."

That included *Cheers* alum Shelley Long as Carol, Christine Taylor (who'd played Marcia in *The Real Live Brady Bunch* show in Los Angeles) as the hair-flipping oldest sister, Christopher Daniel Barnes as wannabe hipster Greg, and the movie's biggest scene stealers, Gary Cole as advice-spouting Mike, and Jennifer Elise Cox as Jan.

Original *Brady Bunch* cast—three Bradys (and Alice!)—also ap-peared in the movie. Florence Henderson, after tough negotiations and Thomas's insistence that she had to be in the film, showed up at the end as Grandma Brady, whose tough love was the only thing that seemed to soothe the angst-ridden Jan. Barry Williams played a record producer who dashed movie Greg's Johnny Bravo dreams, and Chris Knight played a high school coach who helped protect movie Peter from bullies. Susan Olsen, Mike Lookinland, and Maureen McCormick filmed scenes (as a lemonade lady, cop, and reporter, respectively) that were deleted from the final cut, and Eve Plumb declined to participate at all.

Of the new Bradys, Cole was best known at the time for more dramatic roles, as a cop turned talk-radio host on the NBC drama *Midnight Caller* and for portraying Jeffrey MacDonald, a doctor and US Army officer convicted of murdering his wife and children, in NBC's Emmy-winning, fact-based miniseries *Fatal Vision*. It was this impression of Cole that made Thomas pass when Cole's agent asked the director to let him audition to play Mike. Thomas, who had directed Cole in an episode of *Midnight Caller*, loved working with him, but thought he simply wasn't right for the part of Mike Brady. His agent persisted. Thomas said okay.

"He comes in, without the wig, but comes in and plays Mike, and he *is* Mr. Brady!" Thomas said. "We have fifty million people come in; every person in the world doing comedy came in and read for that role, and I said, 'I'm sorry, no one's ever going to beat the Gary Cole audition.'"

Kevin Spacey, Beau Bridges, David Strathairn, Kevin Nealon, Peter Gallagher, Paul Reiser, Ed Begley Jr., Barry Williams (Greg as Mike!), and Cole were among the actors on the studio's initial Mike Brady wishlist, but Thomas went to bat for Cole with Paramount president Sherry Lansing. Lansing wasn't convinced Cole was the right guy to lead a comedy. Thomas made a deal with her: Allow Cole to film one day of scenes as Mike Brady. If, after seeing the dailies, Lansing remained opposed to the idea, Thomas said they'd figure out an alternative (even though she had no second choice). Lansing agreed.

"Of course, after the first day, when he put the wig on, everybody said, 'That's it. It's over. He's Mike.'"

Cole later said the key to his Mike was simply embracing the character as Robert Reed had played him for all those *Brady* incarnations. "Mike hardly ever made sense, but that didn't seem to bother him. Robert Reed had a distinct delivery, and I tried to match that. He was very earnest, always the teacher. 'The moral of the story is...' was his whole thing."

The performance, which Cole reprised for *A Very Brady Sequel* and the TV movie *The Brady Bunch in the White House*, was the start of what has been a prolific comedy run in his career, including *Veep, Dodgeball, Talladega Nights, Family Guy*, and another cult classic film, *Office Space*.

As for the actress who played his middle Brady daughter, Jennifer Elise Cox, her performance as Jan brought a new level of fan respect and affection for a character who had been the subject of much derision. In playing the middle child always in Marcia's shadow as a more than a little disturbed, always stressed-out teen, Cox made Jan the sympathetic figure she always was, but entirely more relatable in this portrayal. Jan was so distraught by the constant rivalry with the perfect Marcia that she was hearing voices in her head! The wackier Jan behaved, the more likable she was, and Cox's performance was truly a breakout one.

She also happened to be one of the biggest *Brady Bunch* fans in the movie cast. While even Thomas had to do a *Brady* series watch before the movie, Cox said she and Christine Taylor—whose "Sure, Jan" and quirky pronunciation of "school" as "skule" are *Brady* movie memes—already knew the show by heart. Hundreds of people were considered for the various family roles for the movie, and Jan was one of the toughest to cast. But Cox earned the role in just two meetings with Thomas and the producers, because she really embraced being Jan.

"I had a friend who's a hairdresser, and she did my hair, but with those little blonde ringlets at the front. I had a great outfit on that my mom gave me, a seventies outfit. I had so much fun, and then I was like, 'I think I'm going to get this part,' and I never think that in an audition," said Cox, who was twenty-five at the time. "I really wanted it. I really wanted it, and I was like, 'Either they're going to give me this part, or they're going to have me teach the girl they cast how to play Jan,' like teach her how to do the breathy voice and everything.

"Then the second time I went in, because I didn't have glasses, Betty Thomas gave me hers. I couldn't see through her bifocals, so I was just stumbling around the room, and they thought it was so funny. I was like, 'That wasn't acting.'"

Cox said she "went Method" on the set, which amused and concerned one of her co-stars. "I was very young, early in my career, and I was very concerned that I did a good job. I would go back to my trailer talking like Jan a lot... It's embarrassing. I think [my castmates] thought I was a little cuckoo for Cocoa Puffs. I remember RuPaul going, 'I'm a little bit worried about you, Jennifer.'"

The actress was especially proud to be playing Jan, one of her favorite Bradys and the one who often had the most dramatic storylines on the original series. "Sherwood Schwartz, before he died, told me that Eve Plumb was the best actress of the bunch, and that's why they gave her the difficult storylines," Cox shared. "The part I love about Jan is that women have complicated emotions, and especially when you're a teenager, it's all over the place. People love to make fun of it, but also you love her, because she's just misunderstood."

Cox handily won the role of Jan, and she did so with some tough competition for the part. Future Oscar winner Natalie Portman read for Jan, as did future *Transparent* Emmy nominee Gaby Hoffmann. *Blossom* star Jenna von Oy passed on the chance to play Jan.

Casting documents for the movie reveal that a who's who of nineties Hollywood read for various roles or were on the studio's wish list. In the interest of *Brady* trivia fodder, a few of the most interesting names and the Brady characters they could have played:

CAROL BRADY: Julia Duffy, Blair Brown, Patricia Heaton, and Judith Ivey read for the role, while Beverly D'Angelo and Patricia Wettig passed. Paramount wanted *Brady Bunch* series guest star Rita Wilson to read, but she was unavailable at the time.

MIKE BRADY: Barry Bostwick, Robert Hays, Steve Guttenberg, Tim Matheson (who would go on to star in *A Very Brady Sequel*), David Morse, Michael O'Keefe, Bruce Davison, and *Saturday Night Live* star Charles Rocket read for the part. John Slattery and Scott Bakula passed.

ALICE NELSON: Margo Martindale and Dana Ivey read, Elayne Boosler and Kathy Najimy passed.

LARRY DITTMEYER: Austin Pendleton and Steve Guttenberg read; Eric Bogosian, Terry O'Quinn, Kevin Pollak, and Robert Klein passed, and Peter Gallagher and Jeff Fahey were deemed too expensive for the role.

GREG BRADY: Paul Rudd and *Who's the Boss?* star Danny Pintauro read; Fred Savage, Matthew Lillard, Sean Patrick Flanery, and Mark-Paul Gosselaar passed.

MARCIA BRADY: Katherine Heigl and Danica McKellar read; Alicia Silverstone passed.

PETER BRADY: Joshua Jackson read; Ben Savage passed. The role was played by Paul Sutera.

CINDY BRADY: Michelle Trachtenberg, Kaley Cuoco, and Elisabeth Moss read; Tina Majorino passed. The role was played by Olivia Hack.

BOBBY BRADY: David Gallagher, Brian Bonsall, and Adam Wylie read. The role was played by Jesse Lee (who now goes by Jesse Lee Soffer).

DENA DITTMEYER: Andrea Martin, Nora Dunn, Rita Rudner, Julia Duffy, Priscilla Barnes, and Cathy Moriarty read; Joan Allen passed. Jean Smart played the role.

ERIC DITTMEYER: Joey Lawrence and Danny Masterson read; Johnny Galecki, Jake Busey, and Devon Gummersall passed. Jack Noseworthy played the role.

NOREEN: Julie Bowen and Alicia Witt read; A. J. Langer passed. Alanna Ubach played the role.

DOUG SIMPSON: Jared Leto and Casper Van Dien read; Noah Wyle passed. Shane Conrad played the role.

* * *

Coinciding with the Gen X–led *Brady Bunch* resurgence in the nineties, the show became more than a TV property, or a TV property that sparked a theatrical movie release. *The Brady Bunch* became a full-on pop culture phenomenon, one that was an obsession for many fans, and for others, one that deserved a deeper examination.

Brother and sister *Brady* fans Erin and Don Smith started one of the first publications that would take that deep dive into Brady-dom with their zine *Teenage Gang Debs*. Named after a 1966 movie of the same name about a young femme fatale from Manhattan who stirred up serious trouble with a Brooklyn gang, *Teenage Gang Debs* the zine debuted in 1988 with an issue that teased the *Brady Bunch* treasures that would continue throughout the DIY publication's existence. An article on Robbie Rist's Cousin Oliver character and reviews of *Brady*-related music, like the Lunachicks' ode to the patron saint of middle children, "Jan Brady," set the tone and subject matter the Smith sibs cared about most: seventies television and music, with a special focus on the Bradys.

Erin Smith was a high school sophomore when she and Don started *TGD*. They always had a special interest in history and television (their parents allowed them to watch as much TV as they wanted). Smith's favorite book to pore over and use to fill her near-photographic memory with minutiae on TV series and casts was Tim Brooks and Earle Marsh's TV bible, *The Complete Directory to Prime Time Network and Cable TV Shows*. It influenced how she saw other pop culture coverage, and what she saw was missing from most of it.

"I was familiar with music fanzines and punk fanzines and doing DIY, writing and layouts and things like that...I wanted to share my weird take, different take, on our culture and TV, and *Brady Bunch* was the thing I was an authority on," said Smith, who was also an intern at iconic *Sassy* magazine and the guitarist for the influential riot grrrl band Bratmobile. "I just thought all TV writing basically was overly dry or dumbed down, like joking about bell-bottoms or calling it 'groovy,' the dumb stuff that everybody says.

"I thought [*Brady Bunch* coverage] should be totally different and reverent and really respectful…I think anything that pervasive in the culture is important to study, whether you think it's realistic or not. You can learn about what's not shown. I was really interested in episodes about women's lib or hippie culture. I certainly did papers in college about it."

TGD, then, was not to be confused with fluffy teen magazines that featured pullout mini posters of celebrities and features on how *you* were the girl of their dreams. The Smiths had actually watched every episode of *The Brady Bunch*, and not just from syndicated reruns. They had videotaped all 117 installments (Erin said her collection—copies of her tapes—was the source for Jill and Faith Soloway's transcriptions for the scripts for *The Real Live Brady Bunch* performances).

The Smiths were superfans who had long-gestating opinions on *The Brady Bunch*, and very specific questions about the show and its stars. They landed a rare interview with Eve Plumb for issue number four, and drove six hours from their home in Maryland to Pennsylvania, where she was appearing in a stage production of *South Pacific*, to talk to her about filming the opening sequence of the *Bunch*, those Brady vacation episodes, and the Brady Kids concert tour. Plumb was also the issue's cover girl, via one of *TGD*'s trademarks: a screengrab from a *Brady* episode, enlarged in all its black-and-white graininess. The issue also included a review of "Top Secret" (the one where Bobby and Oliver think Sam the butcher is a Russian spy), with references to several other *Brady* eps. It's a review with far more thought and insight than most "professional" reviewers ever gave the show.

Other *Teenage Gang Debs* highlights include interviews with Barry Williams and Robbie Rist (who respected the Smiths' pop culture knowledge and fandom so much that they became pals), and a wonderfully detailed account of Erin and Don's trip to New York to appear on *The Sally Jessy Raphael Show*. The theme was obsessed TV fans, and celebrity guests included Williams, Florence Henderson, Charlotte Rae and Lisa Whelchel from *The Facts of Life*, and Kathy Garver and Johnny Whitaker from *Family Affair*. Erin and Don even showed a copy of *Teenage Gang Debs* to Williams, who—clearly a zine naïf—asked why they used photos they took from a TV screen. Erin's response (delivered via an issue of *TGD*): "Because we don't have access to Paramount vaults, dumbass."

The same issue, number five, which would be the zine's last hurrah, included a four-page interview with Williams, a screenshot of Chris Knight on the cover, and the publication's most exclusive feature ever. Elizabeth Moran, author of the 1992 book *Bradymania!*, wrote about her experience attending the 1992 memorial service for Robert Reed in Pasadena. Bradys aplenty were in attendance, and, aside from the obviously sad occasion that brought them together, Moran observed some of the more dysfunctional aspects of *Brady* cast member dynamics.

The service was organized by Williams at the Pasadena Episcopal Church, and Moran estimated fifty people were in attendance, including Williams; Florence Henderson and her second husband, John Kappas; Mike Lookinland and his mom; Susan Olsen and her parents; the *Brady Bunch* on-set teacher, Mrs. Whitfield; Chris Knight's parents (minus Chris Knight); Reed's friend, actress Anne Haney; Brady Kids producer Joe Seiter; and, sitting in pews on the other side of the church, Maureen McCormick and Eve Plumb. "Later, I found out that Susan went over to her 'sisters' and basically told them to get a life," Moran wrote. Post-eulogy, given by Williams, the group went into a private room, where McCormick let Williams know she was not a fan of his *Growing Up Brady* book, and she and Plumb refused to be in a group photo for Mike Lookinland's mom, suggesting that it would just be sold to appear in another book.

Teenage Gang Debs treated *The Brady Bunch* like a subject worthy of examination on multiple levels. All the websites, blogs, Twitters, Instagrams, recaps, and aftershows that came afterward owe a debt to this photocopied treasure (with a circulation of two thousand copies an issue at its peak, all designed and copied at Kinko's, folded, stuffed into envelopes, and hand-mailed out by the Smiths).

"Gen X finally got some control over the press," said Erin Smith, who now works for a performers' rights organization. "Before that, the baby boomers were like, 'Well, if you'd seen [*The Brady Bunch*] back in the day, you would hate it, you don't understand.' We would get some nasty comments like that, people that were angry about it, but we finally got to talk about what we wanted to talk about.

"I can hardly think of [the show] in a normal way at all, because it's such a thing for me. It's still perfect, it's still great when I see it, there's still always something new you can make out in the background. It holds up, and it's pointless to say it's dated. If you're studying classic film, you're not going to say it's dated or 'What are they wearing?' Definitely, anything that pervasive in the culture is worthy of study."

* * *

The Brady Bunch was not getting all its Gen-X love from Xeroxed sources. Those original 117 episodes continued to thrive in TV land and on TV Land. The reruns became a part of the Nick at Nite lineup. Egged on by a call from *Lifestyles of the Rich and Famous* TV host Robin Leach, who was seeking *Brady*-related footage for a TV special he was producing, Susan Olsen produced the 1995 CBS special *Brady Bunch Home Movies*, which featured videos filmed by the *Brady* kids themselves, using the Super 8 cameras Robert Reed gifted to them during the series. The sweet special ended with a tribute to their late TV pops.

That same year, Nick at Nite celebrated the release of *The Brady Bunch Movie* with a mockumentary—Ken Burns–style—called *Brady: An American Chronicle*. Complete with narration, and commentary on the show's cultural impact from the likes of George Plimpton (who had lots of thoughts on Jan), the tongue-in-cheek special compared the Bradys to key figures in the Civil War. "Jefferson Davis was central to the Confederacy's hopes...Ann B. Davis was the center square," the narrator said. "Mathew Brady was a brilliant Civil War photographer whose stark portraits...spoke eloquently of a national tragedy. But it was Greg Brady who took the photograph of the cheerleader Lynette that revealed that Westdale High's receiver was, in fact, inbounds when he caught the game-winning touchdown," the narrator continued, referencing the season-three *Brady* episode "Click."

The 1993 MTV Movie Awards saluted that year's top films, and the Bradys at the same time, by having the cast reenact memorable movie scenes. Florence Henderson stood in for Jack Nicholson in the courtroom scene from *A Few Good Men*, as son Greg (Barry Williams) interrogated Carol Brady about whether or not she ordered the grounding of Marcia. "I have neither the time nor the inclination to explain myself to a kid who rises and sleeps under the blanket of the very bunk bed I provided, then questions the manner in which I provide it!" Carol shouted, as Peter (Chris Knight) and Cindy (Susan Olsen, in Cindy curls) looked on.

A spoof of *The Bodyguard* riffed on Williams' infamous story about his "date" with Henderson, as he took over for Kevin Costner as the titular security detail who fell in love with singer Rachel Marron (Henderson subbing for Whitney Houston). The scene ended with—yes, they really went for it—a kiss between the pair who'd played TV son and mother.

And Henderson got even naughtier in the police interrogation scene from *Basic Instinct*. As cops played by Williams, Knight, and Olsen looked on, Henderson repeated Sharon Stone's lady biz–flashing move, and then revealed she'd gotten busy with Sam the butcher: "He gave me a lot of pleasure. And a 30 percent discount on rump roast."

In other movie-related *Brady* fun, 1996's *A Very Brady Sequel* featured the return of the cast from *The Brady Bunch Movie* and a storyline that finally answered, sorta, what had happened to Carol's first husband. Roy Martin (Tim Matheson, a contender for the role of Mike in the first movie, finally got to be a Brady daddy, kinda) was thought by his wife and daughters to have died. Instead, he claimed, he was injured, suffered from amnesia, then had plastic surgery. The gullible family believes his tale, until they discover he is an imposter after that damn horse statue in the living room, which is really an ancient artifact worth a cool $20 million.

Betty Thomas didn't return to direct the sequel, which failed to make the critical and box-office impact of the first movie, but it did touch on one other entry in the *Bradypedia* that had become a particular favorite of Generation X fans. Roy Martin's return meant Carol and Mike's marriage wasn't legal, hence Marcia and Greg weren't related at all. And that gave them the freedom, at least secretly, to act on all those frisky moments their real-life counterparts from the series, Maureen McCormick and Barry Williams, had engaged in as per Williams' *Growing Up Brady* tales.

Back to the TV set, the greatest Gen-X *Brady* moment may have come at the end of the previous decade. A sweet but short-lived 1988–89 NBC sitcom called *Day by Day* should be best remembered for two of its cast members, who were about to become major breakout stars on *Seinfeld* (Julia Louis-Dreyfus) and *Melrose Place* (Courtney Thorne-Smith). Instead, the show's spot in TV history was sealed with a February 1989 story called "A Very Brady Episode."

Revolving around a couple, Brian and Kate (Doug Sheehan and

Linda Kelsey), who quit their jobs and opened a child daycare program in their home so they could spend more time with their own kids, the show also included the couple's teen son, Ross. Ross was much more interested in repeat viewings of *The Brady Bunch* than he was in studying or writing a history paper that was worthy of anything above an F. His parents freaked out about his flunking grade, which he deemed very un-*Brady* of them.

Later that night, while up late, ostensibly to study, he fell asleep while watching *The Brady Bunch* on his Sony Watchman. Ross dreamt he was in the Brady household (which was re-created for the episode) as "the lost Brady" brother named Chuck (a nod to the *Happy Days* brother who went MIA after the second season of that show). Cue the Brady cameos: Florence Henderson, Robert Reed, Chris Knight, Mike Lookinland, and a very pregnant Maureen McCormick showed up to play Ross/Chuck's Brady brethren. Oh, and Alice! Ann B. Davis entered the living room sporting boxing gloves, so she could spar with Chuck to prepare him to defend himself against that bully Buddy Hinton. Other *Brady* tributes: Chuck kept hearing the theme song (though no one else did); Chuck was opposing his sister, Marcia, for student council president; and Marcia's cheerleader friends performed the same routine that won guest star Rita Wilson the head cheerleader position in the *Brady* episode "Greg's Triangle" ("One, two, tell me who are you, the Bears! Three, four, tell me who's gonna score . . .").

When the Bradys started repeating the same things over and over, Ross/Chuck was horrified to learn he'd actually stumbled into a repeat, and he woke up.

The cheeky episode featured the *Brady Bunch* theme song being sung by the five main cast members, including Christopher Daniel Barnes, the Ross/Chuck portrayer whose stellar, enthusiastic performance was so memorable he went on to play Greg in *The Brady Bunch Movie* and *A Very Brady Sequel*.

* * *

No chronicle of the *Brady*liciousness of the late 1980s and 1990s is complete without a look at Barry Williams' *Growing Up Brady: I Was a Teenage Greg*. Less celebrity memoir than biography of a show, the book stands as a unique, refreshingly open remembrance of the making of a beloved TV series.

Williams conceived the idea of the book in 1989, while starring in the Broadway musical *Romance/Romance*. "I was getting a lot of attention, and I was excited to tell everyone interviewing me about my new musical," Williams said. "Everyone would ask me two questions about *Romance/Romance* and forty questions about *The Brady Bunch*. I suddenly realized this is what people really wanted to know. I better write a book."

Collaborating with TV writer and author Chris Kreski, who'd authored three books with William Shatner, was head writer for *The Daily Show*, and worked on the aforementioned 1993 MTV Movie Awards, Williams made the decision to let *Brady* family secrets fly. On-set romances, the war between the Schwartzes and Robert Reed, the shocking truth about what happened to the dog who played Tiger (he was run over by a truck)...all fine fodder that grabbed headlines and sparked a whole new desire for information on the show and its cast. The most scandalous revelation of all, that Williams went out on an ultimately innocent "date" with his TV mom, Florence Henderson, was even the subject of a Johnny Carson monologue on *The Tonight Show*.

Those stories about Cindy and Bobby smooching in Tiger's doghouse and Marcia and Jan trying to appear on camera without their bras were clickbait before that was even a thing. If that's all a reader was looking for, a quick perusal of the tome at a bookstore would have satisfied the desire for *Brady* trivia that could be swapped at a party.

The real joy of Williams' book for the most devoted *Brady Bunch* fans was the detailed recollections of time on the set, the particulars of how the show was filmed, and the behind-the-scenes details on the relationships between the cast and crew and producers, as he and his castmates had experienced them. Williams interviewed his castmates and producers Sherwood and Lloyd Schwartz, and his is the most two-sided, up-close account of the decades-long clash between Sherwood Schwartz's commitment to his vision of the series and Bob Reed's desire to make a very different show. His respect, and that of his *Brady* siblings, for both their TV dad and the father of the Brady universe was clear. Reed not only wrote the foreword for the book but also allowed Williams to print, verbatim, several of his scathing memos about *Brady* episodes like "The Impractical Joker" and "The Hair-Brained Scheme."

Aside from how tickling it is to know the actor had *kept* copies of his notorious screeds for decades, readers learn that revisiting the past and the memos apparently gave him a chance to reflect on his part in the *Brady* production strife. Reed died less than two weeks after the release of *Growing Up Brady*, but his friend Anne Haney told Williams that Reed had read the book before he passed. His response was to ask, "Was I really that difficult?"

Growing Up Brady was not a book to be skimmed at Barnes & Noble, but to be taken home, savored, and chased, of course, with a *Brady Bunch* marathon.

The paperback, a *New York Times* best seller that sold 100,000 copies in its first month of release in May 1992, was also adapted as a made-for-TV movie in 2000, with Williams as a co-executive producer.

The *Growing Up Brady* movie, like every *Brady* project, had extra family connections, too. Williams cast Scott Lookinland, Mike's son, to play Mike/Bobby in the NBC movie; Mike Lookinland played a cameraman; Sherwood Schwartz made a brief cameo as himself; and Susan Olsen—who all the *Brady* kids name as the one who has the best, most detailed memories of their TV childhoods—was a consultant. Future stars Adam Brody (*The O.C.*) and Kaley Cuoco (*The Big Bang Theory*) played Williams and Maureen McCormick, and exaggerated re-creations from the book included Greg and Marcia's bedroom scene from "A Room at the Top," the one that prompted Lloyd Schwartz to, well, Brady block when his young cast members were making goo-goo eyes at each other. In the *Growing Up Brady* movie, there is no such interruption; the TV siblings proceed to make out while filming, ruining take after take.

CHAPTER TEN

When It's Time to Change, You've Got to Rearrange

Vietnam, the Manson Family murders, Watergate—reel life inside the Brady residence acknowledged no such turmoil. Richard Nixon, whose presidency spanned the length of the show's original run, was never mentioned. But saccharinity of Brady escapades aside, the series was trailblazing in many ways.

By the end of the 1970s, the decade most episodes ran in originally, *The Brady Bunch* had aired thousands of times, in hundreds of markets across the United States and internationally. Repeats of the show, and other syndication powerhouses like *Star Trek* and *I Love Lucy*, grew viewers' love for rewatching an entire series, not just individual favorite episodes. This essentially gave birth to our love of DVD box sets and streaming *Seinfeld*, *The Office*, and *Friends* like they're shows still in production on new episodes.

The enduring success of *The Brady Bunch* also has a hand in the recent trend of television series reboots. When the series was canceled in 1974, no one would have guessed viewers in the 1980s and '90s would be looking to check in again with the family (on TV, stage, in books, and on the big screen). Even in 2019, fifty years after the show debuted, HGTV spent millions of dollars to buy "the *Brady Bunch* house," renovate it to match the interior seen on the show, and then package the whole project as a new TV series, starring…the surviving cast members of *The Brady Bunch*. The fact that *The Brady Bunch* and *Star Trek*, in particular, have continued to thrive in multiple media has helped feed the belief among entertainment executives with the power to green-light that viewers might also want to see new or updated versions of TV series like *Murphy Brown*, *One Day at a Time*, *Roseanne*, *Full House*, and *Beverly Hills 90210*.

* * *

Speaking of *Full House*…For a different generation of TV viewers, that comedy, via its spot in ABC's Friday night TGIF lineup, is the definitive blended-family sitcom. Unlike the Bradys, the Tanner/Katsopolis/Gladstone household was not created by remarriage but as a result of the death of Danny Tanner's (Bob Saget) wife. With three daughters to raise on his own, sportscaster turned talk-show host Danny looked to his brother-in-law Jesse (*General Hospital* star John Stamos) and his best friend, comedian Joey (Dave Coulier) to play house in his spacious, gorgeous (and out of the salary range of a local morning talk-show host) Victorian home in San Francisco. Uncle Jesse and Joey shared with Danny the day-to-day and big-picture responsibilities of taking care of D.J. (Candace Cameron), Stephanie (Jodie Sweetin), and baby Michelle (Mary-Kate and Ashley Olsen), who were—similar to *The Brady Bunch*—a big focus of the show's storylines.

But where the teen magazine coverage came courtesy of the Brady kids on the *Bunch*, Stamos was the heartthrob on *Full House*, and the Olsen twins, once they were old enough to talk and create their own catchphrases ("You got it, dude," "You're in big trouble, mister," and "owce cream"), were the cute breakouts who became a billion-dollar industry as very merchandise-able child stars.

The storylines were Schwartzian in nature, though, especially when it came to the kids' problems and the inordinate amount of time and attention the adults focused on them. Among the kid dramas both the Bradys and the Tanners tackled were sibling squabbles over shared rooms, first-day-of-school jitters (all three men in the household accompanied Stephanie to kindergarten), middle-child angst, and a nose injury that had one of the Tanner girls (Stephanie) trying to avoid showing her face at school, just like Marcia.

Ratings-wise, *Full House* was a bigger hit than the Bradys. *The Brady Bunch*'s highest finish for a Nielsen season was number 31; *Full House* never finished lower than number 30, and was a top 10 hit for its fifth and sixth seasons. *Full House*, like *The Brady Bunch*, has been a hit in syndication.

It's the overall flavor of both shows that connects them most. The problems of the children and adults in that big Victorian house were just as quickly resolved as those of the Bradys, and the emphasis of both comedies was on how these very different people, some—like Joey, and Jesse's wife, Rebecca (Lori Loughlin)—with no biological connections, could form familial bonds as strong as those of any household.

Full House even paid proper homage to the blended family that came before it. At the end of the series' season-six episode "Grand Gift Auto," a credits sequence found the whole family, plus D.J.'s best friend and boyfriend, looking around at each other and waving to the audience from inside a blue tic-tac-toe box.

Plenty of other hit comedies about families created by circumstance rather than biology owe a debt to *The Brady Bunch*, too— *Modern Family*, *Drake & Josh*, *Diff'rent Strokes*, and even younger-aiming series like *Sofia the First* and *Dog with a Blog*—but only one was deemed such a direct knockoff by Sherwood Schwartz that he toyed with the idea of a lawsuit.

Step by Step was another ABC TGIF sitcom, joining that block of family-themed programming in September 1991. *Dallas* star Patrick Duffy and *Three's Company* alum Suzanne Somers played divorced contractor Frank Lambert and widowed hair-salon owner Carol Foster, who impulsively got married during a Jamaican vacation. Complications ensued when they returned home and broke this news to their children—they had three each—who didn't even know they were dating.

Because they weren't.

In an origins tale that almost makes you happy we never got the backstory on how Carol and Mike Brady met, it unfolded that Frank had been a client of Carol's at the salon she ran out of her home. He was attracted to her, and when she mentioned she was planning a solo vacation to Jamaica, he went to her travel agent, found out exactly where she was staying, and booked the same trip for himself. They ran into each other, coincidentally she thought, and sparks flew. After an intense week of vacay romance (i.e., booze and beach nights), they decided to get married before they returned home to Port Washington, Wisconsin.

Never mind that Frank left his three children to fend for themselves while he stalked his next wife, a scheme she found romantic. When Carol and Frank first saw each other after returning home, they locked lips and fell onto her kitchen island in a display of affection that certainly never would have happened on that tangerine countertop in the Brady kitchen.

In short, aside from each of them having three kids and moving them into one house (hers) to live as one big family, Carol and Frank had little in common with Carol and Mike. The Fosters and the Lamberts did not bond easily (most of the children didn't like each other at all much of the time). Carol had two girls and one boy, while Frank had two boys and one girl. Frank was hardly the responsible, advice-spouting father (see above, leaving the children on their own to go on vacation). And the Foster and Lambert children were definitely not the respectful young citizens the *Brady* bunch were. Schwartz must have been horrified at how these teens and younger children spoke to their parents and each other, and that—one of his cardinal sins of TV families—the children often appeared to be, or think they were, smarter than the adults.

Detroit Free Press critic Mike Duffy, like nearly every other reviewer, called *Step by Step* "a '90s version of *The Brady Bunch*." He noted the series was "overrun with wisecracking kids," and quoted star Somers as saying, "Patrick and I are responsible for bringing great sex to TGIF."

So very un-Brady-like. *So* very un-Brady-like that Schwartz decided against pursuing legal action, as he was told he was unlikely to win. That's a good thing for the legacy of his blended-family comedy, that it would not hold up in court that *Step by Step* was a replica of *The Brady Bunch*.

* * *

Full House, *Step by Step*, and *Modern Family* all have one major trope in common with *The Brady Bunch*: the family vacation episodes. All four shows took family trips to an amusement park and to Hawaii, and the Bradys were the first family sitcom to pack up the whole production and head for the Aloha State.

The Bradys opened season four with a three-part adventure in Hawaii, a reward for the season-three performance that was the show's best ever. The arc, one of the Bradys' most beloved storylines, saw the whole family (and Alice!) flying to Oahu when Mike's company sent him off to check on a construction project. The cursed tiki idol, Cindy and Bobby's private Don Ho performance, that hairy tarantula that crawled up the leg of a sleeping Peter, and the boys being held hostage by archaeology professor Hubert White-head (Vincent Price) are iconic moments for viewers. And the trip to film in Hawaii was such a pleasant one that even the usually ir-ritable Bob Reed had no issues. Amazing what a free trip to the islands can do for a guy's attitude.

The cast and crew spent a week in Oahu for the episodes, which also showed them taking a hula lesson, visiting sandy beaches, and getting a history lesson at the USS *Arizona* Memorial in Pearl Har-bor. The family (plus Alice!) also took what was supposed to be a relaxed ride on an outrigger. It turned into what has become a somewhat disputed entry in Brady lore.

The oft-told story, as initially chronicled in a 1972 article in the *San Bernardino Sun*, is that an outrigger carrying the camera crew accidentally crashed into the outrigger carrying the cast. Susan Olsen, a non-swimmer, was thrown into the water, and, if not for the quick action of Florence Henderson, who grabbed her to keep her head above water, the trip to paradise could have ended in tragedy.

In *Growing Up Brady*, Barry Williams confirmed the camera boat "rammed" the cast's boat, Olsen said she ended up hanging off the side of the boat when a giant wave left her and Henderson under-water, and Henderson said she was hanging upside down under the boat (and lost her eyelashes to boot). As Henderson told the *Sun* newspaper, "It all happened so fast. After I pulled Susie back in, we headed out again and completed filming. But every time the cam-era boat angled toward us for close-ups, little Susie shivered like a parkaless Eskimo."

But in *Brady, Brady, Brady*, producer Lloyd Schwartz, who was on the boat with the camera crew, wrote that the crew outrigger merely "nudged" the cast boat. The outriggers were in water so shallow that the crew got off the boat and walked to shore, cameras held above their heads to keep them dry. "The tale has been blown out of proportion so as to rival the sinking of the *Titanic*."

All parties were on the same page with the story of the Hawaii trip's other accident, Williams' dangerous wipeout at Queen's Surf Beach—a surfing hotspot in Oahu—while filming Greg's big wipeout during a competition with a group of local surfers.

What viewers saw on-screen at the end of "Hawaii Bound," the first episode in the Hawaii arc, was what really happened. Williams was an experienced surfer, but when he fell off the board, he hit a patch of coral that nearly wreaked havoc with his head. He managed to maneuver himself around so that his feet "got turned into hamburger meat" instead, a relatively lucky break.

What's most enduring about the influence of the *Brady Bunch* Hawaiian vacation episodes is that storylines for other family shows that have trekked to the islands have largely followed the same general outline. The family goes on a very expensive vacation because someone wins a contest or it's a perk of a job—in an effort to be as relatable as possible, no one wants to posit they can afford to fly off on such a pricey trip on their own whim, which would risk alienating so many viewers who cannot afford a similar luxury. Some members of the family have an established agenda while on the trip—like a job assignment—others simply want to relax, enjoy the sights, maybe have a romantic experience; and yet another element will end up involved in hijinks that inevitably interrupt the plans of the rest of the family. Mike takes the Bradys to Oahu for work, Carol and the girls want to take hula lessons, Greg wants to surf and stare at girls on the beach, but Bobby's insistence on hanging on to the tiki idol he thinks is lucky results in the boys putting themselves in danger to return it to an ancient burial ground where they're held hostage and Mike has to save them.

On the *Step by Step* two-parter "Aloha," the family wins a trip to

Hawaii, where Carol wants to focus on a grand tour of the islands. But Frank's nephew Cody wants to hunt for treasure, and Carol's seventeen-year-old daughter Dana falls in love with a boy and wants to marry him, sparking a fight with her mother that threatens to ruin the entire vacation.

Modern Family also stretched a Hawaiian vacation across two episodes—given the hefty production costs for such a trip, most Hawaiian vacation episodes are multiparters—and the whole Pritchett clan traveled together for Jay's birthday in season one. Jay, the wealthy patriarch, paid for the excursion (so it was kind of like winning the trip for the rest of the family), during which he hoped to simply relax and eat rich, unhealthy foods. Son-in-law Phil viewed the trip as a chance for a do-over on the fancy wedding and honeymoon he and wife Claire never got to have, a plan that was temporarily interrupted when their daughter Haley got drunk and Claire had to tend to her hurling teen.

Full House deviated from the script a bit. The season-three premiere, "Tanner's Island" (a nod to Sherwood Schwartz's Gilligan), was a single episode, and the household (plus Rebecca) was vacationing in Hawaii not because of work or a contest win, but on Danny's dime, to celebrate their two-year anniversary of blended-family togetherness. (Again, that Victorian house, a Hawaiian vacation for seven, on a local talk-show host's salary? And people accuse the Bradys of living too well on Mike's architect salary!) While there, Elvis-obsessed Jesse hoped to get romantic with the future Aunt Becky via a driving tour of all the locations where the King filmed *Blue Hawaii* and *Paradise, Hawaiian Style*, and the kids wanted to swim and surf. But (back to the Hawaiian vacation episode formula) Danny's overplanning with his "Clipboard of Fun" led to the whole group being stranded on what they thought was a deserted island instead of off chasing Elvis fantasies. Uncle Jesse did get to sing

Elvis's "Rock-A-Hula-Baby," from the *Blue Hawaii* soundtrack, to end the episode, thankyouverymuch.

Similar scenarios played out for other sitcoms that packed up production and headed for Hawaiian shores, including *Growing Pains, Mama's Family, The Jeffersons* (a four-episode arc, and yes, they took Florence the housekeeper), *Sanford and Son* (a three-parter), and *Saved by the Bell*, which turned a trip to Hawaii into a two-hour TV movie, *Saved by the Bell: Hawaiian Style.*

The Bradys also spent a three-episode arc at the Grand Canyon to open season three. For such a go-to family vacation destination, the Grand Canyon hasn't been a big presence in TV-land family trips, at least not as far as location shoots. On the big screen, there's *Vacation* (that famous *Thelma & Louise* ending wasn't actually shot at the Grand Canyon because of fear by park officials that it would inspire copycat suicides), but the Bradys remain the only primetime family sitcom to visit the spot and ride mules down into the canyon. Perhaps Florence Henderson's review of the mule ride was enough to scare off future TV moms from embarking on the same adventure.

As the mules carried the cast down the trails, they would stop to eat leaves, which made them lean. "And when we started down the trail, you look straight down to the bottom of the canyon," Henderson said. "I thought, 'I can see the headlines: FLORENCE HENDERSON FALLS OFF MULE AND FALLS TO HER DEATH IN GRAND CANYON.'

"I was scared to death. By the time we got done [with] that scene, and I got off the saddle, it was *not* dry."

The Bradys survived their camping excursion at the Grand Canyon, but their final family vacation—season five's trip to the Kings Island amusement park—provided some scary moments of its own.

"The Cincinnati Kids," another of the series' most-loved episodes, found the Bradys flying off to Ohio when Mike's company was competing for the chance to build an addition at the newly opened amusement park. One important note: *The Partridge Family* aired "I Left My Heart in Cincinnati," an episode shot at the park, in January 1973, and the *Partridge* episode even featured a guest appearance by Cincinnati Reds baseball legend Johnny Bench. *The Brady Bunch* episode aired in November 1973, so score one for the Partridges in terms of being first, but the Bradys' trip is arguably the comedy more closely associated with Kings Island.

The amusement park had opened officially in May 1972, and though there were plenty of rides and attractions throughout the 300-plus acres of fun in northern Cincinnati—including the Racer wooden roller coaster and a replica of the Eiffel Tower that allowed visitors to go to the top observation deck to see as far as eighteen miles away—there was only one hotel, the Kings Island Inn, nearby. When fans learned *The Brady Bunch* was filming on location for four days in August 1973, they quickly deduced the cast was probably staying in that one hotel. And that's the way the *Brady* bunch found out just how popular they were with viewers: Fans tried to peek into their hotel rooms and would pound on their doors in attempts to meet the cast. As Barry Williams recalled in *Growing Up Brady*, he and the other Brady kids started referring to Kings Island as "The Fishbowl," because everywhere they went crowds would stop and stare.

Park officials, who had heavily promoted the event via local media outlets, weren't fully prepared to juggle the needs of the production with those of the thousands of Kings Island visitors who showed up to see the Bradys. Efforts to corral visitors to make the episode look like it was happening on any old day at Kings Island weren't completely successful. In some of the scenes where the Brady kids and Alice were racing around the park trying to return Mike's missing design plans to him before the clients left, groups of onlookers who were supposed to appear nonchalant about the filming instead could be seen watching the actors run. Still other paying park customers were angry to find that some sections were closed for the *Brady* shoot, in particular the very popular Racer.

And that ride was the source of another off-camera drama for "The Cincinnati Kids."

To capture shots of the cast riding the Racer, crew members had mounted a camera to the front of the coaster, facing backward, to get the reverse point of view. Robert Reed, who wasn't thrilled to be riding the Racer to begin with, insisted it be sent on a trial run to test the safety of the camera rig. Mark it as one time when no one could say a word about Reed holding up production. When the coaster came back after the test run, the crew discovered the camera had flown off, backward, toward the coaster cars. Fortunately, no actors were harmed during the test run of this scene. If anyone had been in the Racer at the time, they would have been injured, possibly seriously. The camera was rerigged in a safer manner, but both Reed and Susan Olsen didn't trust it. They were replaced by stand-ins, and the rest of the Bradys (and Alice!) filmed the roller coaster scenes that appear in the middle and end of "The Cincinnati Kids."

Olsen finally got her chance to experience the Racer, by the way, thirty-five years later. She, Barry Williams, and Mike Lookinland were invited to Kings Island in 2008 to celebrate the anniversary of "The Cincinnati Kids," and Olsen and Lookinland caught a ride in the front two seats of the Racer's red train. Five years later, she returned with her other TV brother, Chris Knight, and Williams to celebrate the episode's fortieth anniversary with another ride on the red train.

The Bradys' trip to Kings Island isn't just that amusement park's most memorable pop culture moment. "The Cincinnati Kids" also helped make the theme park episode—especially corporate synergy jaunts to Disney parks by the series of Disney-owned ABC—a standard for other family sitcoms.

Boy Meets World, Family Matters, Full House, Roseanne, Sabrina the Teenage Witch, Step by Step, and more recently, *Black-ish* and *The Middle* spent family vacations at Disney World, while *Modern Family* and *George Lopez* (as well as NBC's *Blossom*) got goofy with Mickey Mouse and friends at Disneyland.

* * *

One of this author's least favorite *Brady* moments: in season one's "54-40 and Fight," when the boys are arguing with the girls about what premium the family should get when they cash in the books of trading stamps they've been collecting. The girls have their eye on a sewing machine, which is of no interest to the boys. The fellas want a rowboat, which gets two big thumbs down from the girls. As the fight continues, Greg demands that Marcia give him a good reason why the girls should get to decide how to use the stamps. "Well, because they come from groceries, and taking care of groceries is a woman's job!" she answers. Another least favorite moment: In "A Clubhouse Is Not a Home," after the girls and Carol have been unsuccessful with their efforts to build the girls a backyard hangout spot of their own, Mike insists he and the boys will take over the project and build the Brady sisters a real groovy clubhouse. All he asks in return: The girls and Carol go inside and make the dudes some lemonade.

There's also "A-Camping We Will Go," when the boys don't want the girls to go camping with them; "Is There a Doctor in the House?" where the girls don't want to share the boys' male doctor, and the boys don't want to be treated by their sisters' female doctor; and "The Grass Is Always Greener," in which the battle of the sexes is fought by Carol and Mike, who each think the other has the easier job of parenting their same-sex children.

Season one, which included all those episodes, certainly had some gender equality issues, and Marcia's claim on the groceries as a woman's responsibility remains a *Brady* low point. Which is why, along with the series' previously mentioned aversion to addressing timely social issues, season two's "The Liberation of Marcia Brady" came as such a surprise. This time, a welcome one.

In the episode, reporter Ken Jones (played by Ken Jones, the first black anchorman on a Los Angeles weeknight news program) visited Marcia's junior high for an on-camera interview with "the young girls of today . . . the women of tomorrow" about the women's liberation movement.

Marcia's friend Judy Winters didn't have much to say, but Marcia answered the reporter's questions honestly. Did she think girls were the equal of boys?

Marcia: "Well, if we're all supposed to be created equal, I guess that means girls as well as boys."

Oh! So Marcia is all for women's liberation, then?

"I guess I am."

Uh-huh. Ken wondered, did Marcia have any brothers?

"Yes, sir, three."

Did Marcia think she could do everything they could do?

"Well, I think I should have the chance to try."

"Tell me this," Ken said. "Do they put you down sometimes, I mean, just because you're a girl?"

Marcia: "They sure do! And it's not fair!"

Ken, continuing to stir the stew of Brady sibling discord: "Do you think girls should do something about that?"

"We certainly should!" Marcia answered, as the group of girls who'd gathered around her clapped and cheered her on.

Ken told the girls to watch themselves on the evening news, and Judy called Marcia brave for taking a stand. Her father and brother would "clobber" her if they heard her talk like that, Judy said. Which made Marcia doubt herself; maybe she hadn't been brave.

Maybe, with the looming inevitability of facing her father and three brothers, she'd been stupid, she told Judy.

Mike wasn't the problem, though. Greg, Peter, and Bobby had plenty to say about her confident stance on girls' abilities to do anything boys could do. Greg even challenged Marcia to prove it, laughing at her as he issued the dare.

Which is how Marcia Brady became a Frontier Scout, and Peter Brady became a Sunflower Girl.

Not even Mike was supportive of his daughter's plan when she strode into Greg's Frontier Scout meeting and declared she was there to sign up. Mike and his fellow Frontier Scouts councilmaster scoured the Scouts handbook to find a reason to turn Marcia away, and apologized to Greg and his fellow Scouts when they couldn't find one.

When Marcia persisted in passing the field initiation test to officially become a Frontier Scout, Greg stepped up his opposition. He and Bobby egged Peter on to give Marcia a taste of her own medicine, to become a Sunflower Girl, the all-female equivalent of the Frontier Scouts, and go door-to-door to sell Sunflower Girl cookies.

Marcia was thrilled with the news, though, touched that Peter also believed everyone should be able to join whatever club they wanted. She even offered to lend him her Sunflower Girl uniform, and Peter's first, and last, sales effort resulted in one of the series' all-time funniest scenes. Chris Knight nailed Peter's embarrassment as he rolled up to a neighbor's front door, wearing the Sunflower Girl beret, and asked the man of the house to buy his cookies. After repeating the Sunflower oath, he shared that he would win an award if he sold the most cookies. What was this prize for cookie sales? the neighbor asked.

"I get to be blossom of the month," said a thoroughly humiliated Peter, as he cast his eyes anywhere but the neighbor's face. The guy laughed at Peter and bought a box of the cookies, but Peter yanked his hat off and told his brothers he was done with their plot to get Marcia to back off joining the Frontier Scouts.

In the end, Marcia did pass the grueling initiation test, despite Greg's efforts to make the challenge extra difficult for her. Jan and Cindy were upset they couldn't attend to see her initiation ceremony. After all, "From now on, we'll be treated the same as boys," Jan said. "At your age, that's victory, at mine, it's defeat," Alice pipes up.

Marcia decided not to officially join Greg's group, though. As she'd told Ken Jones earlier, she just wanted the chance to prove girls could do anything boys could do. She wanted to prove to herself that she could pass the initiation test. With that accomplished, she decided to stay home and read Carol's fashion magazine instead of going to the Scout meeting, while Mike and Greg were left standing in the living room, discussing how it was a woman's prerogative to change her mind (a sentiment, they dismissively said, that was probably coined by a woman).

Yes, there were plenty of mixed messages being floated in that script. The biggest of all was that while Marcia's attempt was sincere, not even Mike was above boiling her belief in equal opportunities down into a cliché when she decided to forgo becoming a Frontier Scout. It was quite insightful for a junior high school student to realize the value of making that big an effort to prove something to herself, and the episode was a highlight in Marcia Brady's character development and Maureen McCormick's performance of her.

Of all the contemporary topics the show could have tackled, this one was, in the early 1970s, a particularly polarizing one. But despite a well-maintained effort to avoid such issues across all five seasons, *The Brady Bunch*, with "The Liberation of Marcia Brady" episode, still feels ahead of its time (that time being "fifties-ish . . . *Leave It to*

Beaver time," as Paramount executive Douglas Cramer once said) because Marcia Brady got to, for a few shining moments (minus commercials), strike a blow for young girls of today and women of tomorrow.

* * *

Remember the *Brady Bunch* episode where Mike and Carol help their friends with raising three boys of their own? It was season five's "Kelly's Kids," a story written by Sherwood Schwartz with the intention of developing it into the first live-action spin-off series from *The Brady Bunch*.

The backdoor pilot starred Ken Berry and Brooke Bundy as Ken and Kathy Kelly, Brady family friends and neighbors who were inspired by the happiness of the Bradys to adopt their own child. Eight-year-old Matt (played by Mike Lookinland's equally adorable brother Todd) was a sweet boy who was thrilled to live with his new mom and dad, except for one thing: He had to leave behind his two best friends, Dwayne, an African-American child, and Steve, an Asian-American boy, at the orphanage.

Because it was a Sherwood Schwartz project, the episode went into overdrive on the themes of family and happiness, with Ken and Kathy almost immediately deciding to adopt not just Matt but his two best friends, too. The new family was all but destined for happily ever after, until their bigoted neighbor, Mrs. Payne, started making hateful comments about the diversity of the Kelly family. "She makes Archie Bunker sound like a liberal," Kathy said, as she and Ken discussed the many ways Mrs. Payne was threatening to make their lives difficult.

Dwayne (William Attmore II) and Steve (Carey Wong) overheard the Kellys talking, and decided to run away with Matt instead of causing their new parents any trouble with Mrs. Payne. Fortunately, the boys only made it as far as the Bradys' backyard, and when Greg discovered them sleeping on a lounge chair, he and his parents warmed them up inside with mugs of hot cocoa until Ken and Kathy arrived and assured them they were no trouble. Together, they were the five musketeers, and they were a family.

Sadly, despite the very charming cast's chemistry and three instantly endearing kid actors, ABC passed on the show. The concept did eventually make it to primetime in the Sherwood Schwartz–produced comedy *Together We Stand* in 1986. Elliott Gould and Dee Wallace starred as David and Lori Randall, marrieds who decided to adopt two children, an African-American girl and an Asian-American boy, into their family, which already included a biological son and an adopted daughter. CBS pulled the plug on the show after six low-rated airings, killed off Gould's character in a car accident, then renamed the series *Nothing Is Easy* and returned it to the network lineup in 1987 with Lori Randall as a single mom.

Nothing Is Easy aired just seven episodes before CBS canceled it permanently.

* * *

Though *The Brady Bunch* has been mocked for its lack of addressing current affairs when so many of its TV contemporaries wove social and political commentary into their storylines on a regular basis, the series owes its legacy in no small part to the fact that the show did ignore what was unfolding on the evening news. Revolving the Brady family's lives around more evergreen topics is what kept the show fresh—avocado kitchen, bell-bottoms, and the occasional tossed-off "groovy" aside—and allowed it to thrive in syndication and attract millions of new visitors who bonded with their TV age group counterparts.

Fifty years later, and the world is in a similarly polarized state, and the 24/7 news cycle floods us with even more chaos, terror, political strife, and social unrest. An episode of *The Brady Bunch* still hits the spot.

CHAPTER ELEVEN

Sunshine Days

This is why Vince Gilligan built an episode of *The X-Files*, the penultimate episode of the original run of the sci-fi drama, around a 1970s family sitcom.

"I thought about things I loved as a child, and I remember loving *The Brady Bunch*. My brother Patrick and I loved watching *The Brady Bunch* when we were kids," the *Breaking Bad* creator said.

The 2002 *X-Files* episode "Sunshine Days" was the series' 200th installment, and the thirteenth one written by Gilligan. It would be the final episode penned by the executive producer, and as the drama's final trademark "monster of the week" story—meaning it had no connection to the show's overall mythology—"Sunshine Days" could spend its forty-four minutes making sentimental, insightful comments about the medium to which it had drawn so many devoted fans of its epic storytelling across nine seasons.

"I was interested in telling a story about someone who was very powerful and yet was very childlike and had a very deep core of loneliness at his center," Gilligan said. "That was a good thing to build the plot around, the idea of a grown man who was very child-like and had fond memories of a favorite sitcom, *The Brady Bunch*."

Said lonely *Brady* fan was Oliver Martin (Michael Emerson, who would go on to earn Emmy and Golden Globe nominations for playing Ben Linus on *Lost*), a man who lived alone in a house that sometimes looked exactly like the interior of the Brady family's home. *Sometimes*, because Oliver had the power of psychokinesis, meaning he could imagine into existence physical transformations of objects and spaces, and even use his mind to conjure up people. When he was lonely, he imagined his house was filled with that iconic *Brady Bunch* living room staircase and a family-size dining room table that could seat all the Brady kids, who Oliver imagined into existence. Alice was there, too, taking dinner out of the oven and serving the meal (including applesauce) to a rowdy Brady brood.

Oliver, as *X-Files* investigators Dana Scully (Gillian Anderson), John Doggett (Robert Patrick), and Monica Reyes (Annabeth Gish) uncovered, was born Anthony Fogelman. Thirty years earlier, Anthony's psychokinetic abilities had been the subject of a research project by the ambitious Dr. John Rietz (John Aylward), who spent six months with the young boy and his mother. As the months wore on, Anthony's abilities waned, and Dr. Rietz eventually abandoned the research, and Anthony, altogether.

As an adult, still lonely Anthony/Oliver's psychokinetic abilities were stronger than ever, and that led to the accidental deaths of two young men—Mike (David Faustino) and Blake (Tyson Turrou)—who discovered Oliver's *Brady Bunch* secret. When Doggett and Reyes investigated the deaths, they made the connection between Oliver and Anthony and reached out to Dr. Rietz to ask if Oliver could be dangerous.

A reunion was in order, and when Dr. Rietz (whose name was an homage to Robert Reed's birth moniker) visited Oliver, he learned just how powerful his former test subject had become. Fearful that Oliver's abilities would cause him to hurt others again (and eager to study him herself), Scully asked him to accompany her back to Washington. Then the team learned another secret about Oliver: He was dying.

His abilities were so intense that the more he used them, the sicker he became. His powers, as Doggett put it, were eating him alive. Oliver had been utilizing them more frequently, because he was completely alone. Bringing the Bradys and their home into his was all he had in the world. When the X-Filers got him to Washington and his health began to decline rapidly, Oliver telekinetically summoned the Brady family to gather around his hospital bed. "To say goodbye," he told Doggett.

Scully and Reyes were *Brady Bunch* fans. It was Reyes who realized Anthony had chosen the name Oliver Martin because he saw himself as that character, Cousin Oliver, a pest, or "jinx," as Scully pointed out. Doggett was completely unfamiliar with the *Brady*verse, however. Why, he asked his colleagues and Rietz, was Oliver still obsessed with *The Brady Bunch*, a show that was thirty years old?

"Because they're the family everyone wishes they had," Reyes told her partner. "Loving parents, lots of brothers and sisters, everybody getting along..."

Scully added, "They're the perfect family. And since Oliver didn't have one as a child, he created one."

"Why *The Brady Bunch*?" Doggett persisted. "Why not *The Partridge Family*? Why not *Eight Is Enough*?"

The answer to that question was Dr. Rietz. During the six months Anthony spent with Rietz, the boy always asked Rietz to watch the program with him on Friday nights. As the months wore on, and they spent more significant time together, Anthony's loneliness faded. So did his powers. Then, so did his friendship, his sense of a family, with Dr. Rietz.

Oliver re-created—literally, with his abilities—*The Brady Bunch*, because for that brief time as a child when he and Dr. Rietz were close, watching the family show together, Anthony felt like he had a family. His powers didn't manifest themselves at all.

The cure for what ailed Oliver, Doggett told Dr. Rietz, wasn't experimental drugs or plasma transfusions. "(*a*) Oliver's going to die if he continues to use his power, (*b*) his power goes away when he's happy, and (*c*) you're the father he never had, and he loves you. *a* to *b* to *c*."

Rietz took responsibility for the role he'd played, and then quickly abandoned, in Oliver's life. He apologized for treating him like a lab rat, and then told him, in a stern, fatherly way, that he forbade him to use his powers ever again.

"I don't want to be alone," Oliver said.

Rietz promised him he wouldn't be. "You've got me. Can you forgive me, Oliver?"

"Anthony," the man formerly known as Oliver corrected, renewing his friendship with the good (or aspiring to be better) doctor.

The ending was more bittersweet for Dana Scully, who, in Anthony/Oliver, finally had before her concrete evidence of the paranormal phenomena she had been investigating (sometimes skeptically herself) for years. But to force Anthony to share his abilities with the world would have meant the death of him, and Scully accepted she'd made the best decision she could after Doggett told her he was sorry she didn't get her proof. "Me, too. Well, maybe I've had it these past nine years," Scully said. "If not proof of the paranormal, then of more important things."

Vince Gilligan, who also directed "Sunshine Days," said the show's producers felt pretty sure season nine would be the series' final one, and he had that in mind when he wrote that last scene between Scully and Doggett in the hospital. "I wanted a valedictory sort of a moment between Scully and Doggett. I liked the idea of her saying what she said in that final moment," Gilligan said. "That was my farewell to the fans of *The X-Files*, which, of course, as we were creating it...We all want our work to live on forever. We wanted our show to be as iconic and to last as long as *The Brady Bunch* has."

Meanwhile, Doggett's final words in the episode—"Here's hoping the TV stays off and [Anthony] learns how to love the real world"—could be misconstrued as a criticism of television and fandom. Does being a *Brady Bunch* fan, seeing the fictional Bradys as the epitome of family life, mean a viewer is ignoring the realities of how messy, complicated, contentious, and often still lonely most families' lives are at some point? Are *Brady* fans, and devotees of other fictional television shows and characters, in danger of replacing interaction with real humans by indulging deeply in fictional worlds? That is a topic worthy of its own book-length discussion. But with the "Sunshine Days" episode of *The X-Files*, a series with its own passionate fanbase, such criticism was not Gilligan's intention.

"It was meant to be a comment on the idea of loneliness and the sadness of being lonely, of living a lonely life," Gilligan said. "It's people who make us complete, it's friends and family who make us complete, and not television shows.

"Again, it wasn't a ding on television in general, it was just a kind of wish fulfillment on my part, the idea of people having the real thing in terms of family and love and warmth and companionship instead of having to find it from a TV show, even a really good TV show like *The Brady Bunch*."

* * *

This is why many people believe future NFL Hall of Fame quarterback Tom Brady was a cast member of *The Brady Bunch*, even though he wasn't born until after the show's original run.

September 23, 2001: It was week two of the NFL season, and the first game the New England Patriots had played since the September 11 terrorist attacks. Quarterback Drew Bledsoe was leading the Patriots to a 10–3 loss against the New York Jets, on the Patriots' home turf, Foxboro Stadium. Late in the fourth quarter, while scrambling for a first down, Bledsoe ran toward the sideline and collided with the shoulder of Jets linebacker Mo Lewis. It was a particularly brutal hit, but Bledsoe initially appeared to shake it off enough to reenter the game. It became clear he was not okay—Patriots coach Bill Belichick would say in the postgame press conference that Bledsoe was not acting like himself when he went back into the game on the Patriots' next drive; the coach regretted putting him back in the game at all.

The Patriots' medical team also suspected Bledsoe was suffering from more than a shoulder injury. The usually laid-back QB was "agitated" in the locker room and couldn't get comfortable. He was sent off in an ambulance to Massachusetts General Hospital, where doctors determined he'd suffered internal bleeding and a concussion when Lewis's shoulder crashed into his chest. The injury was serious; Bledsoe could have died had it gone undetected, if it had been dismissed as simply the player experiencing the aftershock of getting his bell rung by Lewis. At the least, it put his NFL season on hold.

For week three, the Patriots would have to start their backup quarterback, a sixth-round draft pick named Tom Brady, who would be making his NFL debut as a starter. Brady led the team to a 44–13 win against the Indianapolis Colts, at Foxboro, and more importantly in the bigger picture of Tom Brady and NFL history, Brady became the Patriots' permanent starting quarterback, launching a career that most will agree has seen him become the greatest quarterback in NFL history.

But in that first game after Bledsoe's injury, Brady was largely unknown to the wider NFL audience. He had been the 199th pick overall in the 2000 NFL draft. When he took over Bledsoe's job and gave the Patriots their first win of the season, then chalked up three wins in his first five starts, Brady, suddenly, was in the spotlight, and football fans wanted to know more about this new rising star.

That's when ESPN producer Ben Houser and reporter Greg Garber were tasked with creating a video profile package on Brady for the network's *Sunday NFL Countdown* pregame series. The assignment was wide open, and Houser decided a play on Brady's last name could be fun. The then-twenty-six-year-old was also a big fan of E!'s *True Hollywood Story* documentary series, and thus was born the *E!(SPN) True Hollywood Story* on Tom Brady, a deliciously clever spoof mash-up that involved E!, Brady, Bledsoe, and *Brady Bunch* stars Chris Knight, Barry Williams, and Mike Lookinland.

The concept for the video was that Tom Brady, now making good as a starting quarterback in the NFL, had a rather disastrous end to his childhood career as a television star. "Little Tommy Brady," the spoof revealed, was originally the fourth brother on *The Brady Bunch*. Weaving in some of the sitcom's best-loved moments—Houser was also a fan of the *Bunch*—the *E!(SPN) THS* revealed Tommy was kicked off the show when he tossed a football in the Brady family backyard and landed it right in the face of Marcia Brady. All these years, Peter Brady had been blamed for the spiral that ended Marcia's romance with BMOC Doug Simpson in "The Subject Was Noses," but it was actually Tom Brady! And he'd meant to throw it that hard!

"Tommy 'The Freak' Brady...he was always throwing stuff. He *really* threw it," Knight said in the video. "That was cruel. That went over the line. It was sort of downhill for him after that."

Knight, speaking as Peter, added that he was "kinda tired of taking the rap for it, because it wasn't me."

Part of the fun of the spoof was not only the deadpan delivery by the *Brady* cast (the *actual* series cast) and Tom Brady, but also the fact that the *Brady* actors seamlessly switched between speaking as themselves and speaking as their *Brady Bunch* alter egos. "The tabloids never got ahold of it, but he was there. He was our brother," Lookinland, speaking as both himself and Bobby Brady, said.

Williams, poking a little fun at the show and his memoir gossip about flirtations with co-star Maureen McCormick, said, "Even to this day, I have trouble forgiving him. Marcia was more than just a stepsister to me."

As for Brady, Houser said he was told the *THS* spoof had been the athlete's first sit-down national interview as a Patriot. Sporting a New England cap and looking young enough to pass as one of the sitcom's teens, Brady earnestly delivered his scripted lines. "I didn't want anyone, people, to find out my real identity," he said. "It's been hard enough growing up in a family with six other siblings…It's unfortunate that it comes out now, but I'm grown and I think I can handle it." About being fired after the fateful clocking of Marcia, Brady added, "I was disappointed. For them to weed me out like that, it was real frustrating, because I had grown up with them."

As fantastic as the final result was, the production of the *THS* spoof was just as impressive. Houser and Garber got the assignment on a Monday morning, and the video had to be ready to air by Sunday. In between, they had to write a script, get the Patriots to sign off on the concept and agree to make Brady and Bledsoe available for interviews at Foxboro, schedule and film the on-camera interviews with the *Brady Bunch* cast (who were scattered across New York, Los Angeles, and Utah), and secure rights from E! to use *THS* graphics. In an extra stroke of genius that really cemented the package as a beautifully produced and edited (and faithful) re-creation of a *True Hollywood Story* installment, the ESPN team also signed real *THS* narrator Phil Crowley to provide the voice-over for the spoof.

Houser and Garber also credit Bledsoe, the QB who was on the injured list and did not know at the time that he was in the middle of being permanently replaced as the Patriots' quarterback, with injecting a lot of humor into the clip.

Bledsoe explaining in the clip why he's not shocked to learn of his teammate's *Brady Bunch* shenanigans: "Tom, he's always been a coward like that. He's gotta let somebody else take the fall. He hits Marcia in the nose, he's gonna let somebody else take the fall. That's just the kind of guy he is in his personal life."

Bledsoe was actually a mentor to Brady. He liked him and wanted to help the shy media newbie out. "He's out of a job [later], but he's having fun because he was messing with the second-year quarterback," Garber said. "He thought [the idea] was hilarious. He actually made up some of those lines himself."

"I remember," Chris Knight recalled in the video, "the last thing [Tom] said after being fired and escorted off set was, 'I'm gonna make a name for myself.'" Tom "missed all the reunions, and the specials, and the variety show, which was too bad, because, oh, you should see him dance," Williams added. Football fan Lookinland/Bobby Brady forgave his TV brother for trying to steal his thunder when Joe Namath guest-starred on *The Brady Bunch*, then admitted he was proud Little Tommy was "keeping the Brady name alive." The *E!(SPN) True Hollywood Story* wrapped up happily, then, with the famous tic-tac-toe board of Bradys, as Tom took over Alice's middle square and looked all around at each of his blue-backgrounded faux family.

Getting footage for that sequence turned out to be the most stressful part of the whole *THS* mockumentary.

Houser and Garber were at Foxboro for the interviews with Brady and Bledsoe. Media interviews with players were usually scheduled during lunchtime at the stadium, and, because of the volume of requests for the players' time—especially given the situation with the injured QB and his thriving replacement—Houser worried he'd already gone past his allotment with Brady when he hit the twenty-minute mark. But in order to solidify his concept, he still needed to get Brady on camera, in front of a green screen, looking up, down, to the left, to the right, and to all four corners of an imaginary checkerboard.

"Greg Garber is now standing in the doorway," Houser said, "because the public relations guy says, 'Hey, Tom has to go.' I can hear Coach Belichick yelling from across this facility area, 'Hey, Tom needs to be in here for quarterback meetings!'"

Garber: "Houser is in the room with the door shut...We've overstayed our welcome. Belichick comes blowing through a door and he's like, 'Where's my fucking quarterback?' He was furious, because he was worried Brady's going to be late to practice. I went back a long way with Belichick, so I sort of hold him off at the door, because I knew that Houser needed to get that shot where he could put Brady in the box looking around."

Houser: "I'm panicking. I'm only twenty-six and Brady's like twenty-four. Brady, I remember, he looks at me and says, 'Hey, can I leave?' I said, 'No, you can't leave. I need you to sit here and do this, because I really need to make this pay off the whole *Brady Bunch* idea that you are a cast member.' He goes, 'Okay.' He sat there for another two, three minutes. We did what we needed him to do. We filmed him looking all around. Then he got up and shook my hand and quickly ran down the hall to the quarterback meeting.

"This is the most vivid memory I have of the shoot, because it would never happen today," Houser said. "Tom Brady would not just sit there and ask me if he could leave."

The Tom Brady *THS* spoof premiered in 2001, was replayed several times that season, and has been aired several more times since. And with every repeat, the urban legend starts again: Tom Brady was in the cast of *The Brady Bunch*!

Brady has said even some of his Patriots teammates have asked him about being in the classic TV show. The rumor is so persistent that Snopes.com, a website devoted to confirming or debunking urban legends, has a page devoted to Tom Brady as a *Brady Bunch* cast member. Aside from how convincing the crafty ESPN spoof is, the Snopes entry points out that viewers may also be willing to believe Brady played a fourth Brady brother because of Cousin Oliver, who was, sort of, another Brady sibling.

The rumor, and how many people are willing to believe it, also speaks to the show's popularity in syndication. Tom Brady's teammates and fans who believe the *Brady Bunch* story don't necessarily know that he is too young to have been a part of the series' original run. He was born in 1977, three years after the series finale. But many viewers only know the show from its post-1974 syndication airings.

One more bit of evidence that Tom Brady has absolutely no connection to *The Brady Bunch* came during the six-time Super Bowl champion's 2018 appearance on NPR's *Wait Wait...Don't Tell Me!* podcast. Host Peter Sagal asked him a set of *Brady Bunch* trivia questions, and he answered two out of three correctly, only with the assistance of the show's panelists. The (incorrect) answer he provided on his own: that J. Fred Muggs, the chimpanzee who co-hosted *The Today Show* from 1953 to 1957, was the first choice to play Mike Brady before Robert Reed signed on.

Tom Brady's knowledge of Bradydom is not strong.

* * *

This is how the squeaky-clean *Brady Bunch* inspired an X-rated spoof movie. Actually, five X-rated spoof movies.

It began with *Not the Bradys XXX* in 2007 and ended with *Not the Bradys XXX: Marcia Goes to College* in 2013. In between, adult film writer and director Will Ryder made three other movies in the *Brady* porn parody movie series, and started a wave of television-themed adult movies that briefly kept the whole industry, including small, local video stores, flourishing. The *Not the Bradys* series, which included Ron Jeremy playing Sam the butcher and James Deen as Peter Brady, is the best-selling porn parody series of all time.

But name a classic TV sitcom from the last fifty years, and there's almost certainly a porn parody version of it. *Friends, Seinfeld, I Love Lucy, Curb Your Enthusiasm, Happy Days*, and *M*A*S*H* have one. Animated series like *South Park* and *The Smurfs* do, too. Reality series aren't exempt; there are *Big Brother, Survivor, The Bachelor, Dancing with the Stars*, and *Jersey Shore* porn parodies. *Game of Thrones, Star Trek, The Six Million Dollar Man, The Bionic Woman*, and *Beverly Hills, 90210* have inspired porn parodies. So has *Jeopardy!* And Fox News. *Glee, The Golden Girls*, and *Supernatural*. And you can probably guess that the X-rated spoof of *Everybody Loves Raymond* is called *Everybody Does Raymond*.

The Brady Bunch was the first TV show Ryder decided to focus his porn parodies on after he created a successful series of Britney Spears spoof movies called *Britney Rears*. He had seen all the *Brady Bunch* episodes, and felt his knowledge of the show would allow him to create a legitimately funny script. He also had a certain amount of reverence for the series. As is true with so many other *Brady* fans, a big appeal of the show for Ryder had been the relatability of the cast. "I was Bobby and Cindy, I could identify with them because they were my age when the show first came on," he said. "Then a couple of years later, I felt more like Jan and Peter, and then Greg and Marcia. I went through all the cast; I could relate to everybody, including the parents when I was that age and older."

Affection for *The Brady Bunch* inspired purchases of *Not the Bradys XXX* by consumers who don't typically buy pornographic material. Sales figures (reliable ones, anyway) in the adult movie world are notoriously hard to come by, Ryder said. Sales of home video releases have plummeted in recent years because of the anonymity and instant gratification of buying streaming videos, not to mention the proliferation of free porn online. But the *Not the Bradys* series—which includes riffs on such *Brady* classics as Marcia's desperation to meet Davy Jones, Johnny Bravo, and Jan's jealousy of her big sister, as well as the *Brady/Partridge Family* crossover that never really happened—has sold around 350,000 copies, making it one of the best-selling DVD series ever, as per Ryder, in the modern porn business.

"We found in years and years of feedback from retailers that people would walk into the stores, and say, 'I heard about this *Brady Bunch* porn, do you have it for sale?' Or there were people coming in and buying gifts for people, jokes for people, Christmas gifts," Ryder said. "I can't even tell you how many people at video stores have told me that they used to get people walking in for that movie [who] they would never have expected to shop for porn videos."

Ryder's *Brady* knowledge and attention to details—not always paramount in adult films—added to the video series' success, too. Cast members wore retro clothing, and original sets were constructed for several of the movies. The producer, a professional musician who spent time in the studio with the Backstreet Boys and was the touring keyboard player for the Grammy-winning R&B group All-4-One when the band's 1994 song "I Swear" spent eleven weeks atop the *Billboard* Hot 100 chart, even wrote a theme song for *Not the Bradys XXX*. It is cleverly expository and infectious, and it plays during an opening sequence that, of course, features the tic-tac-toe board, a blue background, and Alice in the center square.

And the *Not the Bradys* stories, like the big-screen *Brady Bunch Movie*, took every opportunity to poke fun at certain *Brady* memes, like fan fantasies about the teen characters and the oft-repeated observations about hormones running amok between similarly aged kids of the opposite sex who were not biologically related and were separated by nothing more than a toiletless bathroom every night.

"I think it's just one of the shows that really touches something in people, and we never wanted to make a mockery of it," Ryder said. "That wasn't the point. We felt that the addition of sex into the storyline was enough to provide the parody element. That was the ironic point of our movies... You saw squeaky-clean Marcia, one minute going through the normal things that she went through on the TV show... and then seeing now she's completely naked. That really served to cater to fans that used to fantasize about what it would be like to date Marcia, or Jan, or the mom or Alice for that matter. It filled a need that nobody really knew was there."

The *Not the Bradys XXX* movies, unsurprisingly, were not authorized by anyone connected to Paramount or the Schwartz family. Ryder said the main reason his films, and the many other porn parodies based on television and movie properties, weren't the subject of lawsuits is because the resulting publicity would have drawn more attention, and sales, to the movies. *The Insider*, a now-defunct daily entertainment news series, did a story on *Not the Bradys XXX* in 2007, which Ryder said absolutely boosted his video's sales. And the segment was beneficial for Paramount, too. *The Insider* was distributed by CBS Television Distribution, a sister company of Paramount, which had recently released the complete series DVD box set of *The Brady Bunch*. The *Brady* collection was touted at the end of the story about *Not the Bradys XXX*.

Though Ryder didn't get sued, he did get direct feedback on his movies from Lloyd Schwartz.

In 2008, Schwartz, his sister Hope, and Hope's husband, Laurence Juber (a guitarist for Paul McCartney's band Wings), wrote *A Very Brady Musical*, a stage-show *Brady Bunch* story that featured some not X-rated but certainly PG-13-rated comedy of its own. Greg Brady, for instance, sang about having a woody in a tune about his new wood-paneled station wagon.

Ryder and a date (one of the *Not the Bradys XXX* actresses) attended a performance of *A Very Brady Musical* at Theatre West in Los Angeles. Afterward, when the cast and director Schwartz mingled with the audience, Ryder approached the *Brady Bunch* producer and told him how much he had enjoyed the show. Then Ryder asked if he was aware there was an adult film spoof of *The Brady Bunch*. Schwartz said he and his father were aware of the porn spoof, and he hoped none of the actresses had been forced into making it.

"I thought, 'My God, the general public thinks girls are forced to be in the porn business, drugged, forced, whatever happens to be pressured into doing these things,'" Ryder recalled. "When he said that, I looked at my date and I said, 'Were you forced?' She goes, 'Absolutely not.' Then he put two and two together, and he goes, 'Are you...?' I said, 'Yes, I'm the writer and director.' The conversation was over, and he was not pleased.

"I didn't want him to be mad at me...My goal was never to insult anybody, it wasn't to hurt anybody. If everybody that was working on *The Brady Bunch* had watched our version, I think they'd all be pretty damned impressed."

* * *

This is when *Family Guy* creator Seth MacFarlane and the show's writers revealed their irreverent reverence for *The Brady Bunch*: in the animated comedy's very first episode.

The first character who spoke in the 1999 *Family Guy* pilot, "Death Has a Shadow," was Jan Brady. The episode opened with the Griffin family gathered around the television, watching an episode of the *Bunch*. In the scene, Jan finked on brother Greg for having cigarettes in his pocket. Greg denied he was smoking, and as punishment for lying, Mike Brady sentenced his oldest son to four hours in a snake pit. Smug tattletale Jan didn't escape unscathed, either. She was punished with a day in the chamber of fire for snitching.

Never mind that Cindy was actually the Brady sis notorious for squealing on her siblings. The *Brady Bunch* references, and their prominence in *Family Guy*'s introduction, were just a hint of the many times MacFarlane and his writing staff would dip their pens in *Brady*-hued ink. For a show whose trademark is a deep, dizzyingly eclectic well of pop culture references, *Family Guy* has spent many moments on the Bradys. More than a dozen of them, in fact, including...

...In season two's "Road to Rhode Island," baby Stewie asked Brian to record an episode of *The Brady Bunch* for him, the one where Bobby saved Greg's life and Greg became Bobby's servant. That *Brady* installment is "My Brother's Keeper," though Bobby saved Peter, not Greg, from getting clobbered by a falling ladder.

...In "Holy Crap," from season two, Brian asked a band his owner Peter had hired to play "fluttery" musical cues like the ones that accompanied the Brady kids when they ran down the living room stairs. They did, and the magically summoned Brady kids ran down the Griffin staircase. Animated Cindy, voiced by *The Brady Bunch Movie*'s Cindy, Olivia Hack, "tattled" on the fact that Bobby was playing doctor. It was a cheeky nod to the Susan Olsen/Mike Lookinland puppy-love *Brady* set romance.

...In season three's "Emission Impossible," Stewie worried about his position in the family if Lois and Peter had another baby, as he insisted Bobby Brady had been replaced—forced to stay in the Brady garage by Mike—when Cousin Oliver moved in.

...In "PTV" from season four, the Griffins were once again watching *The Brady Bunch*. The scene found the entire Brady clan in the bathroom, and Cindy pointed out her use of the toilet, in a nod to the fact that viewers never saw a toilet in the Brady kids' bathroom. Olivia Hack and *The Brady Bunch Movie*'s Mike, Gary Cole, voiced their characters in the episode.

...It was a "Sunshine Day" for Pontius Pilate and Judas Iscariot as the duo skipped off arm in arm to the sounds of the Brady kids' signature bubblegum tune after bonding over their desire to crucify Jesus in the season-six *Family Guy* episode "Believe It or Not, Joe's Walking on Air."

..."Spies Reminiscent of Us," from season eight, featured the return of Gary Cole as Mike Brady, who murdered his first wife and got away with it, despite Alice witnessing the crime. "Alice, what did you see?" Mike asked. "Enough to know I'm getting a raise!" crafty Alice (voiced by *The Brady Bunch Movie*'s Alice, Henriette Mantel) responded.

...In season nine's "Excellence in Broadcasting," the family once again enjoyed an episode of *The Brady Bunch*, now broadcast in widescreen. Brian explained that meant for a scene of Mike and Carol (voiced by Gary Cole and his *Brady Bunch Movie* co-star Shelley Long) in bed, viewers would see more of what was off to the side: three men spooning behind Mike on one side of the bed, and another three spooning behind Carol on the other. After the couple said their good-nights, the screen dissolved into the *Brady* credits sequence, which now featured fifteen squares, to accommodate mom and dad's bedroom buddies.

..."*Family Guy* Through the Years," from season sixteen, imagined the series had been on the air for sixty years. In a clip from a 1969 episode, Mike Brady (Gary Cole) showed up to deliver his "tattletale" speech to Meg ("By tattling on someone, you're really just telling them, 'I'm a tattletale.' Is that the tale you want to tell?"), the one *Brady Bunch Movie* version of Mike dropped on Cindy when she gossiped about the Bradys' neighbors.

Family Guy writers continue to poke fun at the most memorable moments from *The Brady Bunch* and *The Brady Bunch Movie*. The *Family Guy* pilot referenced Greg's smoking scandal from the "Where There's Smoke" episode of *Brady*, which played out again in the season seventeen *Family Guy* story "Dead Dog Walking." Chris Griffin tried to convince his mom the vape pen she found was not his but a friend's, saying he "accidentally switched jackets, not unlike that episode of *The Brady Bunch*..."

Seth MacFarlane once explained the appeal of the series (aside from its abundance of spoofable fodder for his show). "*The Brady Bunch* asks nothing of you as a viewer," he said. "Sometimes it is just what the doctor ordered."

The Emmy winner and Oscar nominee has another, rather unique, pop culture connection to the Bradys. During his 2013 gig as host of the Oscars telecast, MacFarlane was compared to another celebrity on social media. Fans, including famous viewers like *Today* co-host Hoda Kotb and Olympic swimming gold medalist Dara Torres, commented on how the man who voices Stewie Griffin and the man who voiced a really bad impersonation of Humphrey Bogart—*Brady Bunch* star Christopher Knight—look exactly alike. Even MacFarlane admitted the resemblance is real. "I get a lot of, 'Hey, aren't you Peter Brady?'"

* * *

And this is another way *The Brady Bunch* lives on: Cousin Oliver Syndrome.

It is unfair, and untrue, to place blame for the demise of *The Brady Bunch* on Cousin Oliver, of course. For one, nearly everyone on the show—save Ann B. Davis—was sick of some*one* or some*thing* associated with the production, be it the Schwartzes vs. Robert Reed or the Brady kids vs. a desire for rock stardom, loads more money, and diverse storylines, three things that weren't likely to come to fruition. The ratings were falling, as the young viewers watching were starting to outgrow the characters and the storylines (and the idea of staying home on Friday nights). Adding a cutie like Robbie Rist's precocious tween was an attempt to counteract the downward slide, but it didn't work, and that is certainly not the fault of the character or the actor. Any *Brady Bunch* critic who charges the show with another TV trope, namely having jumped the shark, would certainly admit the slide happened before the final six episodes, the span of Cousin Oliver's stay at 4222 Clinton Way.

For a character who continues to take blame for the practice of adding a kiddie cast member to freshen up an aging TV series, it's important to note that Cousin Oliver himself would have been considered over the hill if Paramount and ABC had followed through on their original plan for the third season of *The Brady Bunch*.

During the summer and early fall of 1971—leading into the series' third and, ratings-wise, most successful season—ABC had floated a rumor among television reporters: A little bundle of joy would soon be added to *The Brady Bunch*. If six kids of varying ages attracted viewers to the screen every week, the thinking went, wouldn't it be an even bigger draw if those kids had a new baby brother or sister to ooo and ahh over? It would provide new story possibilities for everyone as they adjusted to the new "yours, mine, and ours" demographic of the family, and if critics thought the show was too fluffy, the Bradys' problems too easily and quickly resolved by the end of every episode, just imagine all the excitement a baby would bring!

And all the chaos.

Mike and Carol had already considered relocating to a bigger house during the first season ("To Move or Not to Move") with just eight Bradys (plus Alice!) crammed inside their current abode. And it was already a mystery how they fed and clothed and doled out cash for bicycles and allowances for six kids, plus paid a live-in housekeeper's salary and managed to take neato vacations to the Grand Canyon and Hawaii on Mike's salary as an architect... How were they possibly going to afford a baby? Where was it going to sleep? Who was going to have to share their square in the tic-tac-toe board to accommodate this?

Fortunately neither the fictional family nor real viewers had to endure such new dramas, and the Brady family kept on groovin' just as they were until the network convinced Sherwood Schwartz to recruit Cousin Oliver for season five.

And for all those Oliver detractors in the *Brady*verse, consider this: There's plenty of other junior nuisances at which to aim your Cousin Oliver Syndrome hatred, including Luke's surprise daughter April on *Gilmore Girls*, Mr. Drummond's stepson Sam on *Diff'rent Strokes*, and the Katsopolis twins, Nicky and Alex, on *Full House*. But Cousin Oliver Syndrome also helped launch the careers of Leonardo DiCaprio, who joined *Growing Pains'* final season as homeless teen Luke; Janet Jackson, who played Willona's adopted daughter on the final two seasons of *Good Times*; and Ralph Macchio, who was introduced as Abby's orphaned nephew Jeremy on the final season of *Eight Is Enough*.

CHAPTER TWELVE

Still Groovy After All These Years

Here's the story of an icon riding in an icon to visit another icon for the first time. Or, how Susan Olsen took her first trip to the real *Brady Bunch* house in the Oscar Mayer Wienermobile.

It was 2011, and Olsen's friend, Grammy-winning songwriter Allee Willis (who wrote one of TV's *other* biggest theme songs, *Friends'* "I'll Be There for You"), was given the opportunity to ride around Los Angeles for a day in the Wienermobile, the hot-dog-on-a-bun-shaped vehicle that is the official promo car of Oscar Mayer franks. Willis was allowed to invite a pair of friends to accompany her, and Olsen and author and pop culture historian Charles Phoenix were happy to keep her company. As the pals were being chauffeured around town—regular citizens cannot drive the Wienermobile; it can only be piloted by trained college interns, officially called Hotdoggers—Willis realized they were near 11222 Dilling Street in Studio City, a.k.a. the address of the house used for exterior shots of the

Brady Bunch home. Olsen had never been there, her friends were shocked to learn.

"Allee goes, 'Okay, that's it, we're going,'" Olsen said. "And that's how I wound up at the *Brady* house." In the Wienermobile.

The *Brady Bunch* star and Los Angeles resident had never made the trip to Dilling Street because of a disappointing experience she had as a child. She had wanted to be an architect (just like her TV dad) and noticed something seemed off about the house exterior. It was a one-story structure. The set at Paramount Stage 5 held a *Brady* home interior that was two stories. That house on the set would not fit into that house people were claiming was the real Brady house, Olsen pointed out to Sherwood Schwartz. "I'll have you know that if you walk into that house, it looks exactly like this set," the producer told the little girl. "Finally," Olsen said, "I told my mother that, and she goes, 'Honey, they're just trying to shut you up.' So I never went to the house. I refused to go."

Her visit via the Wienermobile was a brief one, documented with a few photos but limited to outside the house. Her second trip to Dilling Street would be a much more immersive experience.

After HGTV outbid all other wannabe Brady home owners in the summer of 2018 and became the landlords of the Dilling Street home, the cable network launched an ambitious project. *A Very Brady Renovation*—as the resulting TV series is known—chronicles the massive yearlong makeover of the property with the ultimate goal of making what Sherwood Schwartz insisted was true to Susan Olsen all those years ago become a reality. The inside of the house, which most definitely did not match the spacious, mid-century decorated interior so beloved to viewers of *The Brady Bunch*, was rebuilt by a cast of many, including HGTV personalities like *Property Brothers* duo Drew and Jonathan Scott, *Flea Market Flip* host Lara Spencer, and the full surviving *Brady Bunch* lineup.

In November 2018, Susan Olsen returned to the Dilling Street home, along with TV siblings Barry Williams, Maureen Mc-Cormick, Eve Plumb, Christopher Knight, and Mike Lookinland, to take more official photos, marking the beginning of their efforts to help turn the tourist attraction and ultimate *Brady Bunch* fan destination into the Brady home we, and they, have known for the last fifty years. Greg's groovy attic room, Mike's den, and one of the world's most famous staircases sprang to real life thanks to the demolition and renovation efforts of the HGTV crew and *Brady Bunch* stars, who were hands-on with everything from sledgehammering down walls to power-sawing wood to frame new ones. HGTV producer and showrunner Loren Ruch and his team doubled the square footage of the house and transformed it from a one-story structure into the two-story home it appeared to be in footage used in the series.

"Our goal was establishing a footprint and figuring out how to do it to scale and how to make [the house] feel like the viewer experience that we all had as kids," said Ruch, a lifelong *Brady* fan. "It's the most incredible thing you've ever seen. People were crying when they walked into the [finished] house. It was that true to our experience. It was like our childhood selves came to life when we walked inside that house."

With *A Very Brady Renovation*, the Dilling Street house has come full circle with the TV series that made it famous. But the home had an interesting history pre-*Brady*, too.

When Sherwood Schwartz and company were looking for a local house to serve as the exterior for the Brady homestead—he'd already decided nothing on the Paramount lot was suitable—his requirements were simple. "We didn't want it to be too affluent, we didn't want it to be too blue-collar," he said. He wanted it to be modern, with interesting details, though, as it needed to look like a house an architect would live in.

The Dilling Street house would do very nicely, except for one thing: It was a split-level building. The inside of the Brady home, already being built as per art director William Campbell's specifications on Stage 5 at Paramount, was a two-story domicile, the absolute minimum space a family with six kids and an Alice would need. Campbell, a trained architect himself, also modeled the Brady interior on his own home's look; he felt he and Mike Brady might share similar design aesthetics. Rather than continue the search for another house, *Brady* set designers decided to construct a faux window on the left side of the Dilling dwelling. It's a move that at least made the exterior look like a two-story structure, though it has always bothered *Brady Bunch* purists that the fake window's placement is on the wrong side. The staircase inside the house set makes it clear there is a second story on the right-hand side, which doesn't match the look of the exterior. But once the fake window was added to the house, it was filmed from various angles, and that footage was used for all five seasons of the show, frequently opening episodes.

Who was the homeowner who allowed such tinkering with the residence? Her name was Louise Weddington Carson, and she and her husband moved into the house in 1959. Luther Carson designed and built the home for his wife, but he died in 1969, before *The Brady Bunch* premiered. Mrs. Carson didn't get rich from the money she and her house earned from the show, but she did enjoy watching the sitcom, her son said, and didn't even mind that viewers had figured out the location of the home and would stop in the street in front to get an up-close peek.

That wasn't the experience for the house's next owners.

The widowed Carson decided the home on a large lot (more than 12,500 square feet) was simply more space than she needed. In 1973, she sold it for $61,000 to Violet and George McCallister, a former professional golf player and co-owner of a golf and tennis club in Studio City. The McCallisters' new residence would soon become the most recognized TV home in history.

The Brady Bunch was in the final seasons of its original run when the couple bought the house from Mrs. Carson, whose family owned the property that hosted George McCallister's sports club. But *Brady* syndication success was right around the corner, and the show's enduring, and rising, popularity meant more fans were making the trek to see the house, in cars, on foot, and in tour buses. By the time of the Bradys' pop culture peak in the 1990s, then-widowed Violet had a small brick-and-iron fence constructed in front of the home to dissuade the most intrusive fans from walking right up to her windows and trying to look inside.

Mrs. McCallister continued to live alone on Dilling Street well into her nineties—George died in 1990—and fans would come from across the country to see her house. Well, the Bradys' house. What they thought of as the Bradys' house. One time, a young woman knocked on the front door and asked if she'd finally arrived at the fictional family's home. When McCallister confirmed she had, the woman said she was from Arkansas and had been looking for the home all day. The kind homeowner allowed her to snap a photo of her TV mecca as a reward for her fruitful search.

But McCallister was later mugged in her own driveway, and in 2016, she was asleep in her bedroom when burglars broke into the home and ransacked it. She was shaken, but uninjured, and still remained in her home. Violet McCallister died in 2017, and it was her grandchildren who sold the house to HGTV in 2018. She told the *Los Angeles Times* in 1994 that she never regretted buying the home, nor its association with *The Brady Bunch*. "It was a good family show," she told *Times* reporter David Brady (yes, really, Brady). The McCallisters' granddaughter Kelsey is one of the many people who helped with the redo of the house for *A Very Brady Renovation*.

* * *

Like inspiring a "Weird Al" Yankovic parody song, being immortalized in vinyl as a Funko Pop! figure is an incontrovertible sign of a property's stature in pop culture. *The Brady Bunch* has been both Yankovic-ized and Funko-ized.

The Funko Brady figures, which debuted in 2018, are examples of the pop culture collectibles company at its very best. Little Cindy is sporting a half-zip shirt and braided pigtails. Marcia has perfectly straight blond locks and a miniskirt. Curly-haired Greg is strumming a guitar, not in his Johnny Bravo threads but in a red shirt and white pants that suggest he's singing about more romantic things, like those clowns that never laughed before, those beanstalks that never grew. Bobby's got a football in his hand—maybe he's got a playdate with the Joe Namath Pop! figure—and shaggy-haired Peter is wearing one of his most memorable shirts, a rainbow-striped pullover, just like the one he was wearing when he and his brothers were trapped in the tiki cave in Hawaii by Professor Hubert Whitehead (Vincent Price).

Alice, of course, is in her blue dress, white apron, white sneakers.

But someone's missing…who did Funko forget? Greg, Marcia, Peter, Cindy, Bobby…Jan! They forgot Jan! Except they didn't. A Jan figure followed several months after the rest of her siblings—temporarily fooling fans into thinking the beleaguered middle child was once again being treated like a Brady also-ran—as a limited-edition release in the Funko booth at New York Comic Con.

In one of the brand's cleverest launches ever, Jan was packaged in an extra-wide box with her boyfriend, George Glass. Sure, George Glass was Jan's fake boyfriend, which is why the two-pack package is half-empty, just Jan and a Funko-shaped hunk of molded plastic where her imaginary boyfriend stands beside her.

The idea for the Jan-and-George combination release was sprung from the mind of the company's creative director, Sean Wilkinson, who was tasked with doing something special for NYCC. "I just threw it out as a fan of the two-packs, where we can get away with doing something like this, and the fans wouldn't feel like they're missing a toy," Wilkinson said. "They immediately got the joke."

As for the spot-on appearance of the figures, the details for each licensed character have to be specific and memorable, since a trademark of all Pop! figures are the faces, with big, black, perfectly round eyes and no mouth. "It's about us coming together and figuring out the right outfit that seemed most distinctive to that character," Wilkinson said. "Everything is about their hair and their hairlines. The hairstyle is what makes the Pop! so distinctive in a lot of ways, just because they have these simple eyes and no mouth."

The Pop! line features thousands of figures, including professional athletes, movie and cartoon characters, rock stars, advertising icons for snacks like Twinkie the Kid and Franken Berry, and video game heroes. Wilkinson said the company has found retro TV series to be especially popular with collectors, which is why *The Jeffersons* and *Sanford and Son* are among the latest tube-inspired Pops!

As for the Bradys, yes, the company is aware they're still missing Carol and Mike, and the Brady 'rents may get their day in vinyl just to make the cast complete. But, as Sherwood Schwartz intended, *The Brady Bunch* is really all about the children.

* * *

As much as *A Very Brady Renovation* is a boon for fans who want their fantasies of seventies suburban TV real estate to come to fruition, the project also sparked that rarest of events in the *Brady*verse: a reunion of all six *Brady Bunch* kids.

The last time all six cast members worked together: the 2004 TV Land special *The Brady Bunch 35th Anniversary Reunion Special: Still Brady After All These Years*. What finally got them to reassemble for another *Brady*-related gig, when even 2014's first-ever *Brady Bunch* convention (Brady Con) couldn't do it?

"An open checkbook," Barry Williams told this author, about the HGTV project.

Williams, along with Susan Olsen, Chris Knight, and Mike Lookinland, had turned up at the Hilton Meadowlands in East Rutherford, New Jersey, one August weekend in 2014, where a thousand fans—from as far away as Australia and Hawaii—joined them to watch the cast on panels, have Williams lead them in a *Brady* sing-along and dance, and witness *Brady* superfan Michele Smolin get engaged, onstage, with Williams' assistance.

There were also celebrity photo ops and autograph signings aplenty; Lloyd Schwartz, Hope Schwartz Juber, Geri "Fake Jan" Reischl, Robbie Rist, and *The Brady Bunch Movie* cast members Jennifer Elise Cox, Olivia Hack, and Christopher Daniel Barnes were among the other *Brady* celebrities in attendance. Ann B. Davis, who died earlier that summer, was the subject of a special tribute at the convention, and *Brady* buffs like Matt Jisa, who flew in from Hawaii to get his groove on, and sixteen-year-old Alyssa Albarella, who has met *Brady* cast members on more than a dozen occasions, could buy sweet *Brady* merch, from character dolls and Fake Jan stickers to logo T-shirts and Candy Puppy Poop, the poo-shaped, chocolate-covered Marshmallow Fluff boxed candies that Susan Olsen made and sold to raise funds for an animal rescue organization.

And for the fan looking for the most unique, unofficial, and most definitely unauthorized of *Brady* products, there were "Have a Knight to Remember" condoms, adorned with a photo of a shirtless, teen-mag-pin-up-era Chris Knight. The actor was *not* associated with the selling of said prophylactics.

What was missing from the Brady Con fun was three lovely ladies.

Florence Henderson, Eve Plumb, and Maureen McCormick, according to a convention organizer, asked for more cash than was feasible to appear. The rest of the main *Brady* cast had, for the most part, worked under a "most-favored nations" type pact, where they would all get the same guaranteed amount of money to appear at the show, and the same travel and accommodations allowances. Henderson, Plumb, and McCormick wanted significantly more money, as much as $75,000 more than the others, the Con producer said, as well as perks like hair styling and makeup. Meeting their demands would have required more money than the entire convention cost, the producer joked. One of them also asked to be seated in a private room for her autograph sessions, away from the rest of the cast, who all appeared at tables in one main room.

As fans who follow *The Brady Bunch* and its cast even casually might guess, ongoing tensions between Plumb and McCormick complicated the negotiations, too. Rumors of a feud between the TV sisters have been as much a part of *Brady* lore as stories about Robert Reed's hatred of the series and the kid cast members' make-out sessions with each other, all of which predate even Williams' *Growing Up Brady* memoir. Various cast members have offered various explanations of why a Plumb/McCormick rivalry might exist, and some of it seems to revolve around the projection of Jan Brady's jealousy of Marcia Brady onto the actresses playing them. Sometimes it's reversed, and the story goes that it's McCormick who's jealous of Plumb. Plumb has a reputation, deserved or not, for not wanting to participate in *Brady*-related events.

When McCormick was preparing to release her 2009 memoir, *Here's the Story: Surviving Marcia Brady and Finding My True Voice*, a rumor spread across the entertainment media landscape that the book would reveal McCormick and Plumb had engaged in sexual flirtations with each other during their teen years (something that was not, and had never been, actually a part of the book).

When Christopher Knight hosted a syndicated *Trivial Pursuit* game show in 2008, the other Brady kids made appearances on the series…all but McCormick.

As recalled in chapter 9, friction among the castmates flared even as they gathered to pay tribute to their TV father, Robert Reed, whom they all have spoken about in nothing but affectionate terms.

In a 2016 *F.L.U.I.D.* podcast with Barry Williams and actress Jennifer Runyon (who played Cindy in *A Very Brady Christmas*), Susan Olsen discussed the details of a deal in which all six Brady sibling stars were set to make a handsome chunk of change for doing nothing more than signing their names to a piece of paper when Comcast wanted to use their recording of "It's a Sunshine Day" in an advertising campaign. It was an all-or-nothing deal, and according to Olsen, McCormick was the lone holdout. The deal was a "high stakes" situation for Olsen, Williams said, and Olsen said Mike Lookinland had personally called McCormick and asked her to sign on. With negotiations at a standstill, Olsen posted messages to a now-defunct Facebook account detailing the situation, in which she accused her *Brady* sister of not being willing to do what was best for the group. On *F.L.U.I.D.*, Olsen further alleged McCormick was holding out simply to make more money for herself.

Williams, as the reigning head of the *Brady* family since the deaths of Florence Henderson, Robert Reed, and Ann B. Davis, talked about trying to broker peace between his co-stars. But, as discussed in chapter 7, contract negotiations often led to a divergence of interests among the cast members (Runyon replaced Olsen as Cindy in the Christmas movie after contract negotiations failed for Olsen but worked out with more money for McCormick and Eve Plumb).

Clearly, as famously has been the case for the casts of series like *Friends* and *The Big Bang Theory*, sticking together in contract negotiations can often put more power, and ultimately more salary, in the hands of the actors. The *Brady Bunch* stars have not always taken that stance, however, throughout their long and complicated history.

About that history. Because of the longevity of the show's popularity and the enduring fame that accompanies it, the *Brady Bunch* kids have an experience like no one else: not other former child stars, not other stars of beloved classic TV shows, not the other surviving actors and producers of *The Brady Bunch*. For fifty years, more than 75 percent of their lives, the *Brady Bunch* actors have been famous for being Greg, Marcia, Peter, Jan, Bobby, and Cindy Brady. They have been inside people's homes for the last five decades.

"The one thing I never experienced was being a Brady," Lloyd Schwartz said. "So I imagine it can't always be easy being associated with a role you played so long ago."

Here is what it means to be a *Brady Bunch* kid. You are a beloved part of people's childhoods, maybe one of their happiest childhood memories. You were in their living rooms every week, sometimes every day. Sometimes more than once a day. The very sight or thought of you in your striped bell-bottoms and half-zip shirts will put a big smile on their faces. They didn't just love you and your family…they wanted to *be* you. They wanted to be a part of your family.

To be a *Brady* kid means all that work you did, so many years, decades, ago does not directly make you money anymore. Hasn't for a long time. Because of a contract law that changed in 1973, you stopped earning residuals for the series after the first ten cycles the series ran in repeats and syndication. That covered most of the seventies, meaning you stopped making money on the series around 1979. Each of the 117 episodes has aired more than 100,000 times, all around the world. People who had no direct input into those episodes make money from them, from your work as children.

Being a *Brady* kid means after the show ends, it becomes even more popular in syndication. You, your character, become even more popular. But new episodes aren't being made. You want to pursue other roles in other projects. You might get called in for auditions. Everyone wants to meet a Brady! But they don't necessarily want to *cast* a Brady in a non-*Brady* project. *The Brady Bunch*, in the 1970s, is popular. Kids love it. But it's not considered a hip show. Not by adults. Not even the ones who might call you in for an audition because they want to meet a Brady. They really want to be able to tell other people they met a Brady.

So others keep making money from that work you did for five years of your life. You might, too. If you join the variety show spin-off. Or the *Brady Brides* spin-off. Or celebrate Christmas with your TV family again. Or try to keep a straight face while starring in your old boss's attempt to do a dramatic version of your light-hearted comedy. You'll make *Brady* money again, but it means doing new work, more work.

Or you might move on to do something else. Musical theater. Movies. Be a country music star. Other TV series. Graphic design. Computer software. Still, you'll always be a Brady. People will always remember you as a Brady.

On the other hand, people will always remember you as a Brady. They will always want to see you in something. A game show. A reality TV series. A fan convention. They will always want to see you, meet you, shake your hand, tell you how much you mean to them, how much that show you worked on ten, twenty, forty-five years ago meant to them. They'll always want to take a photo of you, with you, and they're willing to give you cash for the privilege.

Sometimes you love this. Sometimes you hate it. Sometimes you wish you had never been a Brady. Sometimes you don't understand it. Sometimes you appreciate that you're an important part of an unforgettable slice of Americana, of television history. Sometimes you don't want to be called Greg or Marcia or Peter or Jan or Cindy or Bobby. You'd like people to understand, acknowledge that they understand, you're Barry, Maureen, Chris, Eve, Susan, Mike. You're happy that it makes them happy that you played Greg and Marcia and Peter and Jan and Cindy and Bobby on TV, but you are not Greg or Marcia or Peter or Jan or Cindy or Bobby in real life.

Being a Brady means you have a group, a family unit of people who've known you from childhood, through makeouts (sometimes with each other), breakups, weddings, births, reunions, spin-offs, and the sad loss of your real and TV parents (and Alice!). You love them, you like them, you keep in touch with them, you fight with them. Sometimes you disagree, separate yourselves from the pack, and follow your own path. You band together, present a united front, and make a formidable bunch. Sometimes, like all families, you don't.

Finally, after five, fifteen, twenty-five, fifty years of being a *Brady* kid, a *Brady* teen, a *Brady* adult, after decades of having complicated feelings about this relatively short time in your young life that has persisted in casting some shadows—and, okay, sure, you'll say it, lots of sunshine days, too—across your life, you're mostly all right with being a Brady. Lots of non-Bradys, lots of former TV stars, some on shows far more successful than yours, are no longer working, no longer alive, some traveling tragic paths after their TV fame.

You're still working. You continue to create new opportunities. Opportunities continue to present themselves to you. You're being paid—well paid—to help rebuild your fake childhood TV home!

Being a Brady is a job and a privilege. Being a member of *The Brady Bunch* is a good thing.

There's a moment in *The Bardy Bunch*, that wonderful play about the meeting of the Brady and Partridge families, where Mike Brady tells his offspring, "You can't make a career out of being a Brady kid."

Actually, sometimes you can. Sometimes they have. They've also been a graphic designer (Susan Olsen), the founder of a home furnishings brand (Chris Knight), a painter (Eve Plumb), the creator of a stage show celebrating the Bradys and seventies music (Barry Williams), a *New York Times* best-selling author (Maureen McCormick and Williams), and the craftsman of concrete kitchen countertops (Mike Lookinland).

They've also been a family on TV, and in real life, and they continue to be both. And they continue to vacillate between being a group that's stronger together—like with that open checkbook on *A Very Brady Renovation*—and one that still has its dysfunctional moments, just like the rest of us.

* * *

The Brady Bunch is a fixture on MeTV, a retro television hotspot with Barry Williams as its official spokesperson, and the network's quiz- and list-filled website. Hulu, CBS All Access, and Amazon Prime stream most episodes. And a 2019 *Brady Bunch TV & Movie Collection* DVD box set release has provided the most exhaustive *Brady* viewing opportunity yet, including all 117 episodes of the original series, the *Brady Kids* cartoon, *A Very Brady Christmas*, *The Brady Bunch in the White House*, and *Growing Up Brady* TV movies, both big-screen *Brady Bunch* movies, and, in their DVD debuts, the spin-off series *The Bradys* and *The Brady Brides*.

It's a set that would have made Sherwood Schwartz proud, with so many *Brady* memories in one package. The TV maker, one of the few non-performers to have a star on the Hollywood Walk of Fame, died on July 12, 2011, just a few months shy of his ninety-fifth birthday and his seventieth anniversary with wife Mildred. Schwartz had been looking forward to his hundredth birthday—his friend, Syracuse University professor and pop culture expert Robert Thompson, said Schwartz had already invited him to the centennial soiree he was planning. But when he became ill and it was evident he wouldn't make it to a hundred, Schwartz put pen to paper and wrote a farewell letter to fans. Released to the *Hollywood Reporter* after he died, the letter, headlined "A Conversation at the Gates," imagines a chat Schwartz would have at the pearly gates, where he recounts his happy, fulfilling life with Mildred, his four children, grandchildren and great-grandchildren, and a career that gave him wealth, accolades, and "plenty of hard knocks from critics." In an appropriately writerly twist at the end of the missive, Schwartz tells "The Voice" he was going to ask him if he was getting into Heaven or not. "Then I suddenly realized something when we talked," he wrote. "Heaven is where I've been since the day I was born."

Schwartz's TV legacy continues with new projects in development, though a Vince Vaughn–produced *Brady Bunch* reboot was a nonstarter at CBS in 2012. Lloyd Schwartz is happy about that. He wants his dad's most beloved creation to live on in new versions, but he didn't think the network had gotten it right in this instance, with a script he described as being like "*2 Broke Girls* with *The Brady Bunch*." He thought the humor went too far. CBS thought it didn't go far enough and passed on the script.

"We have a mission that's different than CBS's and anybody else's," he said. "I have to view these things and say, 'What would dad like?' I actually made a deathbed promise to him, when he was right at the end of his life, mostly about *Gilligan*, but I'm saying, 'Hey, we're going to be doing these things, and they're not going to be anything you wouldn't want.'"

Schwartz and his sister workshopped a new reading of their stage play, *A Very Brady Musical*, in New York at the beginning of 2019, and the siblings will launch a national tour of the show in September 2020.

An idea that will remain unexplored is one Lloyd had discussed with Florence Henderson before her unexpected death from heart failure in 2016. The actress, who was born on Valentine's Day and died on Thanksgiving (her life bookended by holidays synonymous with love and family), delighted in sharing her bawdy sense of humor, especially with those who expected Carol Brady when they met her.

Schwartz had seen her talking about dating much younger men—she preferred fellas in their fifties when she was in her eighties—and he approached her with the idea of a new *Brady* series that would have found her widowed Carol doing that very same thing. To put an extra twist on the blended-family and cougar-Carol concept, the new show would have revolved around Carol meeting and marrying a man the same age as her kids; he would have, in fact, been a friend of one of the Brady children. Schwartz said she loved the idea.

What might have been...

* * *

Christopher Knight remembers the exact moment he realized *The Brady Bunch* would be a part of his life forever. It's also the moment he realized that wasn't necessarily a bad thing.

It was 1992, and he was on a business trip to Australia—his first trip to the country—when he worked for a computer software company.

"I thought, 'This is great. I'm at least going to someplace where I'm not going to worry about getting recognized,'" Knight said. "I don't even get through customs, though, and I'm being recognized by the customs agents. I've never been to the other side of the world. The first time you do that...you imagine the world to be this huge place. We're on a plane for twenty hours. [Australia]

238

seems far, far away. I don't want to be recognized for something I did years ago, but this Australian in front of me is treating me like I'm a member of his family.

"That was a very powerful moment. Being far away from home, exciting as it was, it can also be a very lonely thing when you're away from everything you know. And now, while you're away from everything you know, you find out that all these people know you. All that lack of support you thought you would experience, you're not. I started realizing the reach of this *Brady* thing."

For Barry Williams, the realization of the permanent place the show would claim in his life happened more locally.

"I think it was 1986. I was in New York. I was walking down Third Avenue and a passenger bus stopped in the middle of the street. Just stopped," Williams said. "The driver put down his window, and he was pointing out to everyone that Greg Brady was walking down the sidewalk, and everybody in the back of this bus was looking out the window. They all moved to one side, and I was concerned about that. 'Wow, wow! I think this show has really, really had an impact across the board.'"

For the rest of the world, *Brady Bunch* fans in particular, the realization seems to have come years earlier that this little show that officially died in 1974 would, in fact, never really go away.

The very fact that we're still talking about and, most importantly, watching it and obsessing about it fifty years after its inauspicious debut—the fact that there is that much still to say about a show with a message that was simply about the power of people with differences and no inherent connection to forge a new family—promises that the story of *The Brady Bunch* will live on.

Fifty Years of
The Brady Bunch
in Pop Culture

A Timeline

Date	Project
1969–1974	*The Brady Bunch* aired for five seasons on ABC (September 26, 1969–March 8, 1974).
1970	The kid cast members released an album, *Merry Christmas from the Brady Bunch*.
1972–73	*The Brady Kids*, a Saturday morning cartoon spin-off series, aired on ABC.
1972	The kid cast members released *Meet the Brady Bunch*, an album that reached number 108 on the *Billboard* chart.
1974–75	The *Brady Bunch* kid cast members made multiple guest appearances on the syndicated competition series *Celebrity Bowling*.
1975	Syndication: The year after *The Brady Bunch* was canceled by ABC, all 117 episodes began airing in syndication.

Date	Project
1976–77	*The Brady Bunch Variety Hour* aired on ABC.
1977	In the *Good Times* episode "A Friend in Need," Jimmie Walker's J.J. promised family friend Willona he and his siblings would behave so well they'd look like "*The Brady Bunch* with tans."
1978	In the series premiere of the NBC family comedy *Diff'rent Strokes*, Gary Coleman's Arnold was so impressed with his new bedroom in the fancy apartment of his wealthy guardian Mr. Drummond that he exclaimed, "This is better than anything I ever saw on *The Brady Bunch!*"
1981	*The Brady Girls Get Married* TV reunion movie aired on NBC.
1981	*The Brady Brides* spin-off series aired on NBC.
1984	Parodist "Weird Al" Yankovic paid homage to *The Brady Bunch* in "The Brady Bunch."
1987–90	MTV aired the pop culture trivia game show *Remote Control*, which featured a "Brady Physics" category. Barry Williams, Eve Plumb, and Susan Olsen competed against each other for charity in a 1989 episode.
1987	In the *Love Boat* season-ten episode "Who Killed Maxwell Thorn?" Robert Reed and Florence Henderson guest-starred, playing Mike and Carol Brady.
1987	*A Very Brady Christmas* TV reunion movie aired on CBS, making *The Brady Bunch* the first series to air on ABC, CBS, and NBC.
1988–93	The *Teenage Gang Debs* zine became one of the first publications to usher in a Generation X–led revival of *Brady* fandom.
1989	The NBC sitcom *Day by Day* paid homage to *The Brady Bunch* in "A Very Brady Episode."

Date	Project
1990	The spin-off series *The Bradys* aired on CBS.
1991	*The Real Live Brady Bunch*, the stage show created by Jill and Faith Soloway, debuted in Chicago.
1992	*Partridge Family* star Susan Dey hosted *Saturday Night Live*, which included a skit pitting the *Brady Bunch* kids against the *Partridge* family.
1992	Barry Williams released his *Brady* memoir *Growing Up Brady: I Was a Teenage Greg*.
1992	Robert Reed died.
1993	MCA Records released *It's a Sunshine Day: The Best of The Brady Bunch*, a greatest hits collection featuring the *Brady* theme song, and memorable tunes like "It's a Sunshine Day," "Time to Change," and "Keep On."
1993	*Full House*, another blended-family sitcom, paid homage to *The Brady Bunch* in the episode "Grand Gift Auto," with the *Full House* characters interacting in the iconic tic-tac-toe board during the closing credits.
1993	Florence Henderson hosted the ABC tribute *Bradymania: A Very Brady Special*.
1993	The MTV Movie Awards featured Florence Henderson, Barry Williams, Christopher Knight, and Susan Olsen in risqué spoofs of award contenders *Basic Instinct*, *The Bodyguard*, and *A Few Good Men*.
1993	*2 Stupid Dogs*, a TBS animated series, had its lead characters—dogs—meet a very *Brady*-esque bunch of kids, who taught them valuable lessons throughout the episode "Family Values," with callbacks to half a dozen famous *Brady* episodes.

Date	Project
1994	Ann B. Davis, who confessed to being nowhere near as talented in the kitchen as her alter ego Alice, released *Alice's Brady Bunch Cookbook*.
1994	In the "Baby Doll" episode of Fox's *Batman: The Animated Series*, a family sitcom called *Love That Baby* added a character named Cousin Spunky for its final season. Robbie Rist provided voicework for another character in the story.
1995	*Brady Bunch* creator Sherwood Schwartz was diagnosed with a heart condition that made his heart beat more slowly than normal. The name of the condition: Bradycardia, a name given to the affliction in the late 1800s.
1995	Nick at Nite aired *Brady: An American Chronicle*, a mockumentary mash-up that tied *The Brady Bunch* to the Civil War via famed war photographer Mathew Brady.
1995	*The Brady Bunch Movie* premiered.
1995	*Sesame Street* spoofed *The Brady Bunch* with "The Braid-y Bunch."
1995	*Brady Bunch Home Movies* aired on CBS.
1995	In the season-seven episode "Home Sweet Homediddly-Dum-Doodily," *The Simpsons* paid homage to *The Brady Bunch* in its opening-sequence couch gag, re-creating *Brady's* tic-tac-toe-board opening.
1996	Florence Henderson was honored with a star on the Hollywood Walk of Fame.
1996	*A Very Brady Sequel* theatrical movie was released.
1997	In the *Simpsons* season-eight episode "The Simpsons Spin-Off Showcase," Homer and the family starred in their own variety show, a la *The Brady Bunch Variety Hour* (Lisa even opted out

Date	Project
	of the project in the storyline, just like original Jan actress Eve Plumb did for *The Brady Bunch Variety Hour*).
1999	*The Brady Bunch* was the subject of an *E! True Hollywood Story* episode.
1999	Eminem's music video for "My Name Is" featured "The Shady Bunch," with Eminem in *Brady Bunch*-ish tic-tac-toe squares.
1999	IKEA proved the company could modernize any house, even *The Brady Bunch*'s retro homestead, in a commercial that featured Alice in the kitchen, and callbacks to *Brady* details like Tiger the dog, Marcia's nose accident, and Cindy's Kitty Karry-All doll.
2000	NASA revealed that six radiators at the International Space Station were named Greg, Marcia, Peter, Jan, Bobby, and Cindy. The girls were there first.
2000	NBC aired *Growing Up Brady*, a made-for-TV movie based on Barry Williams' memoir.
2000	In *That '70s Show*'s season-three episode "Red Sees Red," the Forman family starred in an imaginary knockoff of *The Brady Bunch Variety Hour*, with a bonus reference to Brady rivals *The Partridge Family*, as *Partridge* mom Shirley Jones guest-starred.
2001	All six *Brady* kids actors, plus Florence Henderson and Robbie "Cousin Oliver" Rist reunited to compete for charity on the NBC game show *The Weakest Link*.
2001	*The Brady Bunch* was the subject of the million-dollar question on *Who Wants to Be a Millionaire*. Sadly, law student Steve Perry did not know the answer to "What is Carol Brady's maiden name?" He walked away with $500,000. (The answer is Tyler.)

Date	Project
2002	Fox aired *The Brady Bunch in the White House*, a made-for-TV movie sequel to *The Brady Bunch Movie* and *A Very Brady Sequel*, in which Mike Brady became the president of the United States.
2002	Old Navy employed Morgan Fairchild and the *Brady Bunch* house, theme song, and opening tic-tac-toe sequence to sell its rugby shirts in a series of TV commercials called "The Rugby Bunch."
2002	Vince Gilligan's *Brady Bunch*–themed episode of *The X-Files*, titled "Sunshine Days," aired on Fox.
2004	TV Land aired *The Brady Bunch 35th Anniversary Reunion Special: Still Brady After All These Years*, which reunited cast members on a set re-created to look like the *Brady Bunch* living room. The special was filmed before a live studio audience, who sang the theme song while the cast posed on the living room staircase.
2005–08	Christopher Knight starred in the VH1 reality series *My Fair Brady*, which chronicled his relationship and eventual marriage with *America's Next Top Model* winner Adrianne Curry, who he met while filming the fourth season of another VH1 celebrity reality series, *The Surreal Life*.
2006	At the TV Land Awards, Ann B. Davis earned Favorite Made-for-TV Maid honors, while Favorite TV Food honors went to Peter Brady's favorite meal, pork chops and applesauce.
2006	In *That '70s Show*'s season-eight episode "We Will Rock You," Barry Williams and Christopher Knight guest-starred as a gay couple who were the Forman family's new neighbors.
2007–13	The *Not the Bradys XXX* series of adult movie spoofs was released.
2007	Paramount Home Entertainment released *The Brady Bunch:*

Date	Project
	The Complete Series on DVD, in a super groovy box set that was covered with green shag carpeting.
2007	Maureen McCormick lost thirty-four pounds to become the winner of the fourth season of the VH1 reality competition series *Celebrity Fit Club*.
2008	Maureen McCormick competed to win the chance to record a country music record produced by music star John Rich on the CMT reality series *Gone Country*. Later in the year, McCormick, along with fellow contestants Bobby Brown and Carnie Wilson, starred in a spin-off series, *Outsider's Inn*, in which they operated a bed-and-breakfast in Tennessee.
2008	Sherwood Schwartz was honored with a star on the Hollywood Walk of Fame.
2008	Sherwood Schwartz was inducted into the Television Academy Hall of Fame.
2008	In an ESPN spoof of the *E! True Hollywood Story*, called *The E!(SPN) True Hollywood Story*, Barry Williams, Christopher Knight, and Mike Lookinland co-starred with NFL players Tom Brady and Drew Bledsoe and suggested Tom Brady had been a secret member of *The Brady Bunch*.
2008	Lloyd Schwartz and Hope and Laurence Juber wrote and produced the Los Angeles theater production *A Very Brady Musical*.
2008	In the *Big Bang Theory* episode "The Bat Jar Conjecture," Penny proved she was smarter than her genius IQ neighbors because she knew the names of the *Brady Bunch* girls, but Sheldon and Leonard didn't.
2008	Maureen McCormick released her memoir, *Here's the Story: Surviving Marcia Brady and Finding My True Voice*, a best seller that revealed shocking details about her addictions,

Date	Project
	trading sex for drugs, and ultimately winning battles with drugs and depression.
2008	Susan Olsen competed in the reality series *Gimme My Reality Show!* for a chance to become the star of her own reality show.
2009	In the *Scrubs* episode "My Soul on Fire: Part 1," a trip to the Bahamas prompted *Brady Bunch* fans J.D. and Turk to don tiki idol necklaces, similar to the tiki idol the Brady boys had during their island vacation in Hawaii. In J.D.'s fantasy, he imagined he bought the tikis from Greg Brady (played by guest star Barry Williams), who had a beaded-curtain door in his home.
2009	In the *Simpsons* season-twenty episode "Coming to Homer-ica," the opening couch gag included the family, dressed like the Bradys, standing on the Brady home staircase, where Lisa got hit in the nose with a football.
2009	Susan Olsen, Ted Nichelson, and Lisa Sutton released the book *Love to Love You Bradys: The Bizarre Story of The Brady Bunch Variety Hour.*
2009	In the *Family Guy* season-eight episode "Spies Reminiscent of Us," a fantasy sequence suggested Mike Brady murdered his first wife. The spoof was one of a dozen *Family Guy* episodes that have given a shout-out to *The Brady Bunch.*
2010	In the season-seven "Bottoms Up" episode of HBO comedy *Entourage*, Mike Tyson made a cameo appearance as a new client of agent Ari Gold. Tyson's dream project: He wanted Ari to help him sell a "black *Brady Bunch*" to help rehab his image. He would play Mike Brady, and he wanted Jessica Simpson to play Carol.
2010	Sherwood and Lloyd Schwartz released the book *Brady, Brady, Brady: The Complete Story of The Brady Bunch as Told by the Father/Son Team Who Really Know.*

Date	Project
2010	Florence Henderson competed on season eleven of *Dancing with the Stars*. She was the fifth contestant eliminated.
2011	In *Bridesmaids*, Annie Walker (Kristen Wiig) tries to make booty call Ted (Jon Hamm) jealous by mentioning she has another guy she can ask to be her date to her best friend's wedding: Jan Brady's virtual fella, George Glass.
2011	Sherwood Schwartz died.
2011	Florence Henderson released her autobiography, *Life Is Not a Stage: From Broadway Baby to a Lovely Lady and Beyond*, in which she offered her detailed version of her much-discussed date with co-star Barry Williams.
2011	*The Bardy Bunch: The War of the Families Partridge and Brady* premiered at the New York International Fringe Festival.
2012	CBS developed but ultimately passed on a *Brady Bunch* reboot that would have starred Vince Vaughn as the adult, divorced Bobby Brady, who headed a blended family of his own.
2014	Ann B. Davis died.
2014	*The Wil Wheaton Project* host Wil Wheaton mashed up *Game of Thrones* with *The Brady Bunch* tic-tac-toe opening sequence.
2014	The Ohio State University Marching Band paid homage to TV Land and classic TV series with a football halftime performance that included playing the *Brady Bunch* theme song and forming the tic-tac-toe opening board, complete with *Brady Bunch* cast lookalikes in each square.
2014	Barry Williams, Christopher Knight, Susan Olsen, Mike Lookinland, and various Brady universe movie stars and guest cast did a meet and greet with fans at the first-ever Brady Con fan convention, held in New Jersey.

Date	Project
2014	The University of Arizona College of Medicine Admissions paid homage to the *Brady Bunch* opening sequence for a recruiting video.
2015	Danny Trejo (as Marcia) and Steve Buscemi (as Jan) starred in a Clio Award–winning Super Bowl ad for Snickers that spoofed Jan's feelings about "Marcia, Marcia, Marcia!"
2015	Maureen McCormick finished in fourth place in the first season of the Australian reality TV series *I'm a Celebrity… Get Me Out of Here!*
2016	*Robot Chicken*, in its season-eight episode "Secret of the Flushed Footlong," offered yet another spoof theory on what happened to the Bradys' first spouses, this time suggesting a horrible accident led to Carol becoming a widow.
2016	In the "George! George Glass!" episode of the ABC family sitcom *The Goldbergs*, siblings Adam and Erica were inspired by Jan Brady to create fake dates (Lampie Tableman and the New Kids on the Block–inspired Jordan Wahlberg) to make their love interests jealous.
2016	Maureen McCormick competed on season twenty-three of *Dancing with the Stars*. She was the sixth contestant eliminated.
2016	Florence Henderson died.
2017	Hulu began streaming *The Brady Bunch*.
2018	Everi released *Brady Bunch*–themed casino slot machines, complete with *Brady* graphics, images, and the theme song.
2018	Yet another sinister theory about how Mike and Carol were freed to marry each other and form *The Brady Bunch*: In a tongue-in-cheek essay, Slate.com writer Craig Pittman posited the duo murdered each other's first spouses so they could be together.

Date	Project
2018	The *Avengers: Infinity War* cast paid homage to *The Brady Bunch* with a re-creation of the opening sequence and the theme song to tell the story of "The Marvel Bunch" on *The Tonight Show Starring Jimmy Fallon*.
2018	In the season-two "Cracker Casserole" episode of the over-the-top TNT drama *Claws*, various characters—who form their own kind of blended family of friends—shared their opinions on another character's abortion, and the opinions unfolded with the characters assembled in a *Brady Bunch*-ish tic-tac-toe board of talking heads.
2018	The Los Angeles–area home at 11222 Dilling Street, the house used for exterior shots of the Brady family home on *The Brady Bunch*, was put up for sale, setting off a bidding war that included celebrity would-be buyers Lance Bass, Miley Cyrus, and *Property Brothers* star Jonathan Scott.
2018	HGTV bought the Los Angeles home for $3.5 million and planned to launch a TV series that will chronicle the remodeling of the home to make the interior match the interior of the *Brady Bunch* TV show home.
2018	Funko released a set of its wildly popular Funko Pop! figurines depicting the Brady Bunch. Well, most of them...Greg, Marcia, Peter, Bobby, Cindy, and Alice figurines were released. Jan, with her imaginary boyfriend George Glass, was released separately, as an exclusive at New York Comic Con.
2018	In the season-three "The Brainy Bunch" episode of the NBC comedy *The Good Place*, the characters traveled together and commemorated the trip with "The Brainy Bunch" T-shirts, featuring their faces in the *Brady*-esque tic-tac-toe board.
2018	*The Brady Bunch* Party Game was released by Big G Creative.
2019	In the "Nine Birthdays" episode of the ABC family sitcom

Date	Project
	The Kids Are Alright, wannabe star Timmy told his brothers he'd been hanging out at the *Brady Bunch* house, hoping to be discovered, only to discover himself that the show didn't film there. "Showbiz is all lies...I can't wait to be a part of it!" he concluded, while his brother Joey fantasized about meeting Jan..."She's insecure. I could work with that."
2019	HGTV premiered *A Very Brady Renovation,* a reality series that documented the network's remodel of "*The Brady Bunch* house" in Los Angeles, complete with construction help from the *Brady Bunch* cast and stars of HGTV's series.
September 26, 2019	*The Brady Bunch* turned 50!

ACKNOWLEDGMENTS

Two things you immediately learn when writing a book: One, it's so much more work than you ever imagined it would be, and two, no one does it alone. My incredibly sweet and supportive husband, John Muraro, is not only my best editor, listener, encourager of TV obsessions, and sanity keeper ("It okay. Don't be cry") but he also has yet to complain that he now knows more about *The Brady Bunch* than anyone who isn't in the cast or hasn't written a book about *The Brady Bunch*.

Many thanks to the kind folks who were so generous with their time, encouragement, and sharing memories, including Christopher Knight, Susan Olsen, Barry Williams, Lloyd Schwartz, Hope Juber, Vince Gilligan, Al Yankovic, Betty Thomas, Jennifer Elise Cox, Bruce Vilanch, Steve Garvey, Robert Thompson, Geri Reischl, Will Ryder, Loren Ruch, Annie Phillips, Jodi Ritzen, Ben Houser, Alyssa Albarella, Erin Smith, Faith Soloway, Allie Dinan, Sean Wilkinson, Greg Garber, Jerry London, Marc Berman, Matt Jisa,

ACKNOWLEDGMENTS

Michelle Smolin, Nicholas Hammond, Stacey James, Tom Russell, Jessica Piha, Chelsey Riemann, Jay Levey, Tina Mahina Williams, Andy Hall, Josef Adalian, Jenn Carroll, Jeff Mullen, Alan Levenson, Jennette Fulda, Shaun Clancy, Brian Bahr, Courtney Sylvia, Nichole Calero, Amanda Spielman, Ahn Kim, Paige Albiniak, Lisa DiSante-Frank, and Olivia Dupuis. Special mention and appreciation to Jay Coughlin, whose *Brady Bunch Blog* is a lovingly curated collection of information on the show, and who shared many resources with me.

I am lucky to count as friends and creative sparks these talented people who also like to go deep nerd (shout-out to Adam Lance Garcia) on their pop culture passions: Jennifer Keishin Armstrong, John Ordaz, Mandi Bierly, Jeffrey Pattit, Ethan Alter (Jan and George were great mascots!), and Jen Jagers Mroczka (who can be persuaded to perform all the Silver Platters' routines). Another special thank-you to Pam McCarthy, who helped me and my high school classmates write our first book, and whose laughter at my "Humpty Dumpty Was Pushed" story made me think a girl from Fresno, Ohio, could make a living as a writer.

I am incredibly grateful to my agent, Laurie Abkemeier, who is not only a publishing industry guru but has the patience to share her knowledge, no matter how many emails that may entail.

And a big thank-you to my book editor, Suzanne O'Neill, whose calm guidance on structuring fifty years of Brady fun into this book was invaluable. Thanks to the entire Grand Central team, including Kamrun Nesa, Alana Spendley, Nidhi Pugalia, Rick Ball, Mari C. Okuda, Albert Tang, Lauren Peters-Collaer, Erica Scavelli, and John Pelosi, and to Chris Phillips for one of my all-time favorite illustrations.

SOURCE NOTES

INTERVIEWS CONDUCTED BY THE AUTHOR

- Alyssa Albarella
- Marc Berman
- Jennifer Elise Cox
- Allie Dinan
- Greg Garber
- Stephen Garvey
- Vince Gilligan
- Nicholas Hammond
- Ben Houser
- Stacey James
- Matt Jisa
- Hope Juber
- Christopher Knight
- Jerry London

- Susan Olsen
- Annie Phillips
- Geri Reischl
- Jodi Ritzen
- Loren Ruch
- Tom Russell
- Will Ryder
- Lloyd Schwartz
- Erin Smith
- Michelle Smolin
- Faith Soloway
- Betty Thomas
- Robert Thompson
- Bruce Vilanch
- Sean Wilkinson
- Barry Williams
- Al Yankovic

INTRODUCTION

Jennifer Drysdale. "Lance Bass Plans to Buy the Brady Bunch House," ETOnline.com, July 20, 2018.

Madison Roberts. "HGTV Shells Out $3.5 Million for Brady Bunch House—Which They Will 'Restore' to '1970s Glory,'" People.com, August 10, 2018.

Bill McKibben. *The Age of Missing Information* (Random House), 1992.

CHAPTER 1

Sherwood Schwartz and Lloyd J. Schwartz. *Brady, Brady, Brady: The Complete Story of The Brady Bunch as Told by the Father/Son Team Who Really Know* (Running Press), 2010.

Peter Desberg and Jeffrey Davis. *Show Me the Funny! At the Writers' Table with Hollywood's Top Comedy Writers* (Sterling), 2010.

Writers Guild Foundation. Interview with Sherwood Schwartz, Writers Guild Foundation YouTube channel, published 2013.

Television Academy Foundation. Interview with Sherwood Schwartz, The Interviews: An Oral History of Television website, 1997.

Sherwood Schwartz. *Inside Gilligan's Island: From Creation to Syndication* (McFarland), 1988.

L. Wayne Hicks. Sherwood Schwartz interview, TVParty.com, 2001.

CHAPTER 2

Sherwood Schwartz and Lloyd J. Schwartz. *Brady, Brady, Brady: The Complete Story of The Brady Bunch as Told by the Father/Son Team Who Really Know* (Running Press), 2010.

Erin and Don Smith. "Eve of Destruction," *Teenage Gang Debs*, Issue 4, January 1992.

The Brady Bunch Home Movies, CBS TV special, May 24, 1995.

Bob Rose. "'Rougher' Than a Gumdrop," *Democrat and Chronicle*, February 27, 1972.

Barry Williams with Chris Kreski. *Growing Up Brady: I Was a Teenage Greg* (Good Guy Entertainment), 1992.

Maureen McCormick. *Here's the Story: Surviving Marcia Brady and Finding My True Voice* (It Books), 2008.

Shirley Jones. *Shirley Jones: A Memoir* (Gallery), 2013.

Joyce Bulifant. *My Four Hollywood Husbands* (Tilton Bass), 2017.

Florence Henderson. *Life Is Not a Stage: From Broadway Baby to a Lovely Lady and Beyond* (Center Street), 2011.

Oprah Winfrey. *Oprah: Where Are They Now?* TV interview with Christopher Knight, OWN and OWN YouTube channel, 2013.

E! True Hollywood Story: The Brady Bunch, E!, 1999.

Jonathan H. Kantor. "15 Crazy Things Only True Iron Man Fans Know About Tony and Pepper's Relationship," Screenrant.com, April 16, 2018.

Dan Lewis. "Ann's Ready for Another Role," *Florida Today*, June 21, 1970.

Television Academy Foundation. Interview with Douglas Cramer, The Interviews: An Oral History of Television website, 2009.

Leslie Raddatz. "Attention Parents!" *TV Guide*, May 19, 1973.

CHAPTER 3

Lillian Kramer. "Doubling in Laughs," *Radio Life*, March 16, 1947.

Elaine Woo. "Studio Composer Frank DeVol Dies," *Los Angeles Times*, October 29, 1999.

Etan Vlessing. "Oscar-Winning Creator of 'The Brady Bunch Effect' Dies at 88," THR.com, October 27, 2015.

The Peppermint Trolley Company biography, DannyFaragher.com.

Television Academy Foundation. Interview with Sherwood Schwartz, The Interviews: An Oral History of Television website, 1997.

Sherwood Schwartz and Lloyd J. Schwartz. *Brady, Brady, Brady: The Complete Story of The Brady Bunch as Told by the Father/Son Team Who Really Know* (Running Press), 2010.

Television Academy Foundation. Interview with Howard Anderson Jr., The Interviews: An Oral History of Television website, 2005.

Ann B. Davis. *Alice's Brady Bunch Cookbook* (Rutledge Hill), 1994.

CHAPTER 4

"Fast Tempo Greets 'Brady Bunch' Star," *Fort Lauderdale News*, September 26, 1969.

Bill Martin. "Not Typical and Not Funny," *Los Angeles Herald Examiner*, September 30, 1969.

"The Brady Bunch: Friday," *TV Guide*, September 13, 1969.

Dick Kleiner. "Little Sorcery at the Track? Bewitched Star Plays the Ponies," *Racine Journal-Times Sunday Bulletin*, October 5, 1969.

Cleveland Amory. "Review: The Brady Bunch," *TV Guide*, February 7, 1970.

Donald Kirkley. "Look and Listen with Donald Kirkley," *Baltimore Sun*, October 27, 1969.

Irv Letofsky. "Do You Agree with the Critics?" *Minneapolis Star Tribune*, November 2, 1969.

TV Review Roundup, *Broadcasting*, October 6, 1969.

Television Academy Foundation. Interview with Douglas Cramer, The Interviews: An Oral History of Television website, 2009.

Florence Henderson interview, *The HuffPost Show*, May 8, 2015.

Sherry Woods. "If You're After Cuteness, 'Brady Bunch' Qualifies," *Palm Beach Post*, November 16, 1969.

Margot Reis El-Bara. "The Brady Bunch a Bit Too Sweet," *Florida Today*, October 20, 1969.

E! True Hollywood Story: The Brady Bunch, E!, 1999.

CHAPTER 5

Television Academy Foundation. Interview with John Rich, The Interviews: An Oral History of Television website, 1999.

"It's Legal Now; The Brady Bunch," *Daily Herald*, August 11, 1969.

Leslie Raddatz. "Attention Parents!" *TV Guide*, May 19, 1973.

Craig Tomashoff. "More Stories of a Bunch Called 'Brady.'" *Los Angeles Times*, May 16, 2000.

Gina Arnold. "No Empty-Nest Woes for Mrs. Brady," *San Francisco Examiner*, January 29, 1995.

"2 Formulas Merged in 'The Brady Bunch,'" *Philadelphia Inquirer*, September 26, 1969.

Raechal Leone Shewfelt. "'The Brady Bunch' Plays a Part in Tom

Hanks and Rita Wilson's Love Story," Yahoo.com, March 16, 2016.

Jane Lynch. *Happy Accidents* (Hachette), 2011.

Roger Ebert. "A Family Tree Grows in Spike Lee's 'Crooklyn,'" *Chicago Sun-Times*, August 5, 1994.

Barry Koltnow. "Rage in Brooklyn Comes 'Straight Out,'" *Orange County Register*, May 30, 1991.

Dana Sachs. "Straight Into Movies," *Mother Jones*, July–August 1991.

Peter Slevin. *Michelle Obama: A Life* (Knopf), 2015.

Jennifer Wishon. "Growing Up Bobby: Jindal's All-American Dream," CBN.com, September 8, 2014.

Maureen McCormick. *Here's the Story: Surviving Marcia Brady and Finding My True Voice* (It Books), 2008.

Florence Henderson. *Life Is Not a Stage: From Broadway Baby to a Lovely Lady and Beyond* (Center Street), 2011.

"Hooked on Needlecrafts," *Aunt Suzy's Needlecraft Journal*, December 1972.

"We Visit The Brady Bunch," *TV Star Parade*, April 1974.

"The Bradys—60 Sex-y Secrets," *16*, 1973.

Sherwood Schwartz and Lloyd J. Schwartz. *Brady, Brady, Brady: The Complete Story of The Brady Bunch as Told by the Father/Son Team Who Really Know* (Running Press), 2010.

Barry Williams with Chris Kreski. *Growing Up Brady: I Was a Teenage Greg* (Good Guy Entertainment), 1992.

Joshua Rich. "The Brady Bunch: The Complete First Season," *Entertainment Weekly*, March 4, 2005.

E! True Hollywood Story: The Brady Bunch, E!, 1999.

CHAPTER 6

Ann B. Davis. *Alice's Brady Bunch Cookbook* (Rutledge Hill), 1994.

Barry Williams with Chris Kreski. *Growing Up Brady: I Was a Teenage Greg* (Good Guy Entertainment), 1992.

Vernon Scott. "Schwartz A Big Man With Kids," *Beaver County Times*, March 15, 1972.

Biography: Robert Reed, A&E TV network, 2001.

Television Academy Foundation. Interview with Florence Henderson, The Interviews: An Oral History of Television website, 1999.

Lew Cedrone. "Robert Reed in Town," *Baltimore Evening Sun*, August 26, 1970.

Dan Lewis. "Bob, Alice: Double Exposure," *Hackensack Record*, September 13, 1970.

Leslie Raddatz. "Don't Tell His Pasadena Neighbors, But Robert Reed Is an Actor," *TV Guide*, April 4, 1970.

E! True Hollywood Story: The Brady Bunch, E!, 1999.

Elise T. Chisolm. "Versatility Could Be Middle Name," *Baltimore Evening Sun*, November 11, 1977.

Cecil Smith. "Robert Reed: A Little Mannix Cures the Blahs," *Los Angeles Times*, June 21, 1970.

Jane Mulkerrins. "Taking the Lead with Ellen Page," Net-a-Porter.com, February 22, 2019.

Andy Towle. "Matt Dallas: Execs Told Me to Stay in the Closet During 'Kyle XY' or My Career Would Tank," Towleroad.com, February 7, 2019.

Richard K. Shull. "Enters in a Suit, Exits in a Skirt," *Indianapolis News*, September 16, 1975.

"Reed Plays Transsexual," *Tampa Tribune*, September 7, 1975.

"Unusual Operation on Medical Center in Fall," *Hartford Courant*, July 13, 1975.

Charles Benbow. "'Medical Center' Opens with Tough Assignment," *St. Petersburg Times*, September 8, 1975.

The Brady Bunch Home Movies, CBS TV special, May 24, 1995.

Florence Henderson interview, "The Real Mike Brady," *Downtown*, ABC News TV, November 6, 2000.

Sherwood Schwartz and Lloyd J. Schwartz. *Brady, Brady, Brady: The Complete Story of The Brady Bunch as Told by the Father/Son Team Who Really Know* (Running Press), 2010.

CHAPTER 7

Barry Williams with Chris Kreski. *Growing Up Brady: I Was a Teenage Greg* (Good Guy Entertainment), 1992.

Sherwood Schwartz and Lloyd J. Schwartz. *Brady, Brady, Brady: The Complete Story of The Brady Bunch as Told by the Father/Son Team Who Really Know* (Running Press), 2010.

Craig Tomashoff. "More Stories of a Bunch Called 'Brady,'" *Los Angeles Times*, May 16, 2000.

"Boy 'Lives' TV Series," *Hammond Times*, January 8, 1976.

Lawrence C. Rubin. *Popular Culture in Counseling, Psychotherapy, and Play-Based Interventions* (Springer), 2008.

Barry Westgate. "Barry Westgate on Television," *Edmonton Journal*, November 6, 1976.

"Television Qs and As," *Mansfield News-Journal*, August 6, 1976.

Ted Nichelson, Susan Olsen, and Lisa Sutton. *Love to Love You Bradys* (ECW Press), 2009.

Charles Benbow. "The Plug Should Be Pulled on the Bradys," *St. Petersburg Times*, February 26, 1977.

Review: The Brady Bunch Hour, *Variety*, January 26, 1977.

"50 Worst Shows of All Time," *TV Guide*, July 20, 2002.

Jerry Buck. "'Brady Bunch' Show Recycled," *Desert Sun*, March 25, 1981.

David Bianculli. "Brady Bunch Comes Home for Christmas," *New York Daily News*, December 17, 1988.

Beverly Beckham. "Brady Christmas a Trivial Pursuit of Holiday Spirit," *Boston Herald*, December 23, 1988.

TV Insider: A Very Brady Christmas, *TV Guide*, September 17, 1988.

George Maksian. "CBS Ratings 'Bunch' Up," *New York Daily News*, December 21, 1988.

Alan Carter. "Here's the Story, of Cindy Brady," *New York Daily News*, February 13, 1989.

Richard Hack. "Review: The Bradys," *The Hollywood Reporter*, February 9, 1990.

Television Academy Foundation. Interview with Florence Henderson, The Interviews: An Oral History of Television website, 1999.

Norman Dresser. "'Brady Bunch' Ranked Toledo's No. 1 Show," *Toledo Blade*, December 22, 1975.

CHAPTER 8

David Cassidy. *C'mon, Get Happy: Fear and Loathing on the Partridge Family Bus* (Grand Central), 1994.

Robin Green. "David Cassidy: Naked Lunch Box," *Rolling Stone*, May 11, 1972.

"Let's Do Time Warp Again," *Tampa Bay Times*, January 23, 1997.

Elaine Viets. "Duking It Out: Brady Bunch vs. Partridge Family," *St. Louis Post-Dispatch*, April 28, 1994.

Rob Salem. "Former Partridge Brat Set to Stand and Deliver," *Toronto Star*, May 23, 1992.

Mary Houlihan. "Partridge Family, Brady Bunch Square Off in Shakespeare Parody," *Chicago Sun-Times*, September 11, 2016.

CHAPTER 9

Richard Cohen. "Here's a Story," *New Yorker*, September 16, 1991.

Scott Steele. "Bringing Up Brady," *Maclean's*, February 7, 1994.

Christopher Shea. "The Zine Scene," *Chronicle of Higher Education*, November 3, 1993.

Ryan Murphy. "Big-Screen Bradys: Have We Got Some Doozies for You," *Los Angeles Times*, September 20, 1992.

Amy E. Seham. *Whose Improv Is It Anyway?* (University Press of Mississippi), 2001.

Nicole Hollander. "'Here's a Story About a Bunch Called Brady...'" *New York Times*, April 21, 1991.

Bert Briller. "Will The Real Live Brady Bunch Stand Up?" *Television Quarterly*, Spring 1992.

Mark Goodman. "Lights, Camera—Bradys!" People.com, December 12, 1994.

Bruce Fretts. "Gary Cole on Veep, Will's Death on The Good Wife, and the Christopher Walken Rule," Vulture.com, April 7, 2014.

Lindsey Webber. "20 Years After Its Release, a Brady Bunch Movie Meme Emerges," Vulture.com, January 16, 2015.

Amy Amatangelo. "Growing Up in (But Not Outgrowing) 'The Brady Bunch,'" *Boston Herald*, May 20, 2000.

Barry Williams with Chris Kreski. *Growing Up Brady: I Was a Teenage Greg* (Good Guy Entertainment), 1992.

CHAPTER 10

Rob Owen. *Gen X TV: The Brady Bunch to Melrose Place* (Syracuse University Press), 1997.

Barry Williams with Chris Kreski. *Growing Up Brady: I Was a Teenage Greg* (Good Guy Entertainment), 1992.

"Hawaiian Adventure," *San Bernardino Sun*, September 3, 1972.

Sherwood Schwartz and Lloyd J. Schwartz. *Brady, Brady, Brady: The Complete Story of The Brady Bunch as Told by the Father/Son Team Who Really Know* (Running Press), 2010.

Mark Voger. *Groovy: When Flower Power Bloomed in Pop Culture* (TwoMorrows Publishing), 2017.

CHAPTER 11

Gael Fashingbauer Cooper. "Peter Brady, Is That You? Here's the Story of Oscar Host Resemblance," Today.com, February 25, 2013.

Patrick Carone. "A Chat With Oscar Host To-Be Seth MacFarlane," Maxim.com, October 2, 2012.

CHAPTER 12

David E. Brady. "Chateau Brady," *Los Angeles Times*, September 26, 1994.

"'Brady Bunch' House in Studio City Ransacked by Burglars," *Los Angeles Daily News*, August 18, 2016.

Sherwood Schwartz. "'Brady Bunch,' 'Gilligan's Island' Creator Sherwood Schwartz's Posthumous Farewell Letter to Family, Fans," THR.com, July 12, 2011.

ABOUT THE AUTHOR

Kimberly Potts has written about television and pop culture for *Entertainment Weekly*, the *Hollywood Reporter*, *Vulture*, *TV Guide*, Esquire.com, the *Los Angeles Times*, Yahoo, *Variety*, People.com, *US Weekly*, E! Online, Thrillist, AOL, Movies.com, and *The Wrap*. For several seasons, she covered the number one sitcom on TV *The Big Bang Theory* and the number one cable drama *The Walking Dead*. She's written oral histories of *Deadwood* and *Breaking Bad*, and think pieces defending the polarizing series finales of *Seinfeld* and *The Sopranos*, and co-hosts the weekly podcast *Pop Literacy*. She lives in New York City with her husband, John.

kimberlypotts.com
Twitter and Instagram: @tvscreener